The Theology of Griffith Jones and Religious Thought in Eighteenth Century Wales

The Theology of Griffith Jones and Religious Thought in Eighteenth Century Wales

John J. Harding

UNIVERSITY OF WALES PRESS
2024

© John J. Harding, 2024
Reprinted 2024

All rights reserved. No part of this book may be reproduced in any material form (including photocopying or storing it in any medium by electronic means and whether or not transiently or incidentally to some other use of this publication) without the written permission of the copyright owner except in accordance with the provisions of the Copyright, Designs and Patents Act 1988. Applications for the copyright owner's written permission to reproduce any part of this publication should be addressed to The University of Wales Press, University Registry, King Edward VII Avenue, Cardiff CF10 3NS.

www.uwp.co.uk

British Library Cataloguing-in-Publication Data
A catalogue record for this book is available from the British Library.

ISBN 978-1-83772-114-6
eISBN 978-1-83772-115-3

The right of John J. Harding to be identified as author of this work has been asserted in accordance with sections 77 and 79 of the Copyright, Designs and Patents Act 1988.

The University of Wales Press gratefully acknowledges the funding support of the Books Council of Wales in publication of this book.

Typeset by Richard Huw Pritchard
Printed by CPI Antony Rowe, Melksham, United Kingdom

With gratitude for the generous help and guidance of
Professor William Gibson,
and for
all the loving and patient encouragement of my family,
and in memory of a most loving wife and accomplished scholar,
Susan Howell (Harding) 1943–2006

CONTENTS

Editing of quotations		ix
Abbreviations		xi
Introduction		1
Chapter 1	Griffith Jones in his Setting	9
Chapter 2	Sir John Philipps, the SPCK and a New View of Mission	39
Chapter 3	Bishop George Bull as Griffith Jones's Mentor	63
Chapter 4	The Prayer Book Roots of Griffith Jones's Preaching	89
Chapter 5	The Theology of Griffith Jones's Preaching	119
Chapter 6	Griffith Jones's Moralism and Theology	151
Chapter 7	Catechizing, Baptism and the Trend Towards Evangelicalism	175
Chapter 8	Griffith Jones's Ministry and the Welsh Language	197
Chapter 9	Griffith Jones's Legacy to the Church of England in Wales	225
Bibliography		241
Index		253

EDITING OF QUOTATIONS

The book contains many quotations from manual transcriptions of Griffith Jones's sermons in Welsh. These are quoted with the original spelling, capitalization, punctuation, new lines, superscripts and underlinings. An English translation follows each separate quoted passage, within the text, bracketed, and without abbreviations. The numbering of points in sermons is retained, even in brief quotations which omit any preceding numbers. In quotations from Jones's pocket notebook, particularly, there are many abbreviations of the Welsh (e.g. 'Es.' for 'Isaiah', or 'Xp.' for 'Christ'). In the interest of clarity, these are given in full in the accompanying English translation. The context makes the sense of all the abbreviations clear, without the need to guess the meaning.

ABBREVIATIONS

BCP	Book of Common Prayer
CUL	Cambridge University Library
UCNWL	University College of North Wales (Bangor University) Library
NLW	National Library of Wales
ODNB	Oxford Dictionary of National Biography
OED	Oxford English Dictionary
SPCK	Society for Promoting Christian Knowledge

SHORT FORM OF CITATIONS

Short-form citations have the authors' surnames only, except for some Welsh surnames. These – such as 'Jones', of which there are ten – have the initial of a first name, or two in some cases, added to distinguish them.

INTRODUCTION

This book examines Griffith Jones's place within the Church of England in Wales, at a time of intellectual and religious unsettlement. It centres on a new examination of Jones's theology and practice, drawn principally from his own manuscripts, books and letters in print.[1] These give a fresh understanding of Jones's thinking and motives, being especially based on an analysis of the large corpus of sermon transcriptions in the National Library of Wales and Cardiff Central Library, and on a personal notebook of Jones, also in the NLW. Such an analysis appears never to have been attempted before. In the light of the documentary evidence, the book proposes that his outlook remained predominantly that of a High Church Anglican parson of the late seventeenth century till the end of his life. It is necessary to bear this in mind to understand his actions. Though his ministry evolved into displaying features which were taken up by full Evangelicalism, Jones is best understood as a developing High Churchman, rather than that, somewhat anachronistically, all the connotations of the phrase 'early Methodist' should be accredited to him. The cautious avoidance of consigning him to this category seems judicious, even though the epithet 'Methodist' became very current in his lifetime, and he endured the jibe of being a 'Methodist pope'. Surprisingly in the case of so influential a figure, no adequate theological analysis and comparison have been made in illustration of his place in Welsh theological thought.

Jones was a man whose work had a profound influence on the course of Welsh history, and yet is all but forgotten in the popular mind. Geraint Jenkins cites Aneirin Talfan Davies's surprise that: 'no-one had been moved to prepare a creative biography or novel based on the life and work of Griffith Jones'.[2] Among supporters of Welsh language and culture, however, he is recognized as a remarkably successful educationalist.[3] His name is also remembered, in some religious circles, as that of a forerunner of the eighteenth-century popular revival of Christianity, which resulted in Methodism, leading to a predominating Nonconformist influence upon Welsh life lasting until well into the last century.[4] This book is not the desired 'creative biography' of Griffith Jones, but seeks to fill a crucial gap in understanding him and his influential example. Even the best of the sparse literature on Griffith Jones has omitted to give a fully adequate analysis of the theological motives that shaped his work. This lack may be because a theological motive for his achievements – whenever touched upon – has been merely assumed, and not drawn analytically from manuscript evidence. It has been too easy for historians to class him summarily as an Evangelical, on account of his popular conversionistic preaching, and to avoid the need for an examination of his actual sermons. The book attempts to correct oversimplifications arising from neglect of the main evidence.

Moses Williams and David Jones gave valuable biographical colour and detail, but no theological analysis.[5] F. A. Cavenagh and Thomas Kelly were particularly concerned with his educational success.[6] Densil Morgan writing recently on Griffith Jones as a theologian, treated his standpoint as though it were so obviously 'Evangelical' that it needed no actual analysis of the documentary evidence: 'It is very obvious that Griffith Jones was a Reformed or Puritan theologian and in no way a High Church divine.'[7] Geraint Jenkins gave an excellent rounded view of him as an influential character and as contributing to Welsh literature. But he did not attempt to describe accurately Jones's theology, or even the functioning of his preaching ministry.[8] Earlier, R. T. Jenkins gave proper attention to Griffith Jones's social influence, but also lacked sympathetic interest in his theology, and therefore was disinclined to examine it.[9] Other modern historians merely mention Griffith Jones in passing. Perhaps the best book for a balanced narrative of Jones's ministry is Gwyn Davies's *Griffith Jones, Llanddowror: Athro Cenedl*.[10] Written to commemorate Jones's birth, it was for popular reading in 120 pages, but handles the topics well. Its size, of course, did not allow the more detailed theological analysis which this book attempts to supply.

This book seeks, therefore, principally to give a more accurate and detailed account of Jones's theology. This is identified basically as that of the Prayer Book, as held in the mixture of post-Restoration conservative Anglicanism, Continental Pietism and the growing introspective individualism of his time. His persistent commitment to realizing his ideal is examined as providing the direction of his successful preaching ministry. Almost from as far back as one can trace, Jones's plain and methodical practice of exposition had such wide, lasting – and to some unsympathetic observers, shocking – effect. These are traced through persons that influenced him, and especially, the lines of theological thought laid down from his early years.

The book dwells necessarily on the distinguishing elements of Jones's preaching that contributed to his influence on Welsh society and the Church. For example, the stress upon the doctrine of justification by God through faith was an important element in Jones's success in winning converts. It contrasts with the more reserved or qualified view of some other High Churchmen – but not of all. Griffith Jones's ministry, affecting large numbers of people to their becoming active Christians, was augmented by the parallel educational venture of the Circulating Schools which only began when he was nearly fifty years old. Jones's projects followed the lead of logical necessity, by steps to each successive innovation – although the original idea of each 'innovation' was always the fruit of other men's minds. Jones had the practical persistence to realize each proposal in turn: catechizing, simplified all-age Welsh literacy, training of teachers, providing schoolbooks, even adding training for aspirants to the ministry. Most scholarly writing has concentrated interest upon Griffith Jones's astonishing success in turning the Welsh peasantry into a literate people through his Circulating Schools.[11] This book does not examine the schools, nor add anything to the published analysis of their practice and success. It refers to how they sprang from his main evangelistic and pastoral purpose, and to the theology which inspired it. There is brief reference to his practical organizing methods for the schools, and to how far the results exceeded his original hopes and conceptions, coming at length to strengthen the use of the Welsh language and its attendant culture.

Under Griffith Jones's preaching, a renewed impulse, stemming from the SPCK's policy of instructing a new generation in Christian piety, led to wide circles of converts, religious societies and a new body of active evangelists, with an accompanying literature. Jones's part in winning large numbers to active faith is admired, in some quarters, as a point of departure for what was to become the distinct Methodist and Evangelical movements.[12] This book seeks to define the theological basis of his ministry, and to continue by tracing its line of development in his teaching. It discusses particularly the content of his evangelism within the congregations to which he ministered, and the way that this prominent movement set him on a path causing conflict, in some measure, with his own settled Anglican principles.

There is evidently a need for precision in historical writing, to show High Churchmanship as the lasting basis of Griffith Jones's work. Even reputable historians have created confusion by the loose use of nomenclature. Accuracy in categorizing can be exacting, because movements and their ideologies are fluid, changing and dividing as they are developed and transmitted. Some historical writers have called Griffith Jones 'Puritan', and others 'Methodist' or 'revivalist'.[13] The fault of a popular narrative of Jones's contribution to a movement leading to Evangelicalism has been, anachronistically, to assert that he himself was 'Evangelical'. This inaccuracy ignores the essential fact that he was a doctrinaire High Church Anglican parson to the end of his life. This book attempts to redress the casual inexactitude of terms in some writing, committed in the interest of simplification. One suspects that some writers have assumed, moreover, that precision is unnecessary in mentioning what seem groundless, long-dismissed religious vagaries. This book is not a thorough biography, and omits some important topics of research.[14] Because of the wealth of documentary sources, and the strong influence of Griffith Jones's basic ideals, the book is largely concerned with these.

Introduction

DOCUMENTARY EVIDENCE

This book is written from basic contention that Griffith Jones's theology derived from the formularies of the Church of England, drawing on his books and letters in print.[15] Particularly, an untapped source of information is found in six large volumes containing hundreds of sermons, four in Aberystwyth and two in Cardiff.[16] These appear never to have had precise theological analysis before. They are manual transcriptions made by Griffith Jones's curates, presumably intending eventual publication. These are written in the order in which the texts expounded are found in the Bible, not in the chronological order of their preaching. These carefully made transcripts contain all the theological points drawn from each chosen passage, with exposition and references to other relevant biblical texts. But they omit any extempore comments, allusions or references to other books that Griffith Jones may have made. Hence the attractive colour of his famously eloquent preaching is lost; but his theological outlook is thereby all the more recognizable. This massive resource gives ample evidence of Jones's theological range.

There is also a personal pocket notebook of Griffith Jones in the NLW, undated and without covers, containing, most usefully, a number of sermons in very abbreviated notes, forming skeleton outlines.[17] It too seems never previously to have had theological analysis. The notebook reveals further his approach to analysing biblical texts, and applying them in a robust, undeviating appeal for faith and repentance in his hearers.

This book traces the emergence of Griffith Jones's evangelistic preaching, in part, from the pattern of allusion to repentance, faith and forgiveness in the Prayer Book itself. It deals with George Bull, Jones's diocesan bishop, as an admired mentor at the time of his ordination. He had a great influence on Jones as a young cleric, and that influence remained a respected standard during his later ministry. The book compares Bull's published views with the evangelistic emphasis that grew in Jones's preaching. It examines a diverging trend which he took, whilst still holding to High Church ideals. It also notes Griffith Jones's thought as being in line with the reforming intention of the SPCK. Jones fully supported its ideals, including promoting charity-schools and foreign missions. The society was a forum for new ideas as well as supporting the position of Christianity in English society. The book touches particularly on the Continental pietistic influences on the society's theological outlook and projects, as relevant to Jones. Griffith Jones's ideas and activity are shown as in harmony especially with two gentry patrons, who gave protection and financial support. Sir John Philipps was a very important figure in the SPCK and other movements of the time, himself deserving historical research. He is seen in alliance with Jones from the early part of the century, till he died in 1737. Likewise, Madam Bridget Bevan was Jones's patron thereafter, till his death in 1761. She is mentioned as another figure very worthy of study, not least as one of the powerful women involved in the religious movements that emerged from the revived evangelism. She took over directing the Circulating Schools fully from Griffith Jones's death, eclipsing even his successes. Space does not allow for detailed examination of other important figures, such as the next generation of preachers (Howel Harris, 1714–73; Daniel Rowland, 1713–90; William Williams, 1717–91; or Peter Williams, 1723–96).

NOTES

1   Griffith Jones, *The Christian Covenant, or the Baptismal Vow, as stated in our Church Catechism* (London, 1761); *Letters of the Rev. Griffith Jones to Mrs Bevan*, ed. Edward Morgan (London, 1832); *The Platform of Christianity, being the General Head of the Protestant Religion, as Professed by the Church of England* (London, 1744); *The Welsh Piety* (London, 1740); *Welch Piety: or a Succinct Account of the Rise and Progress of the Circulating Welch Charity Schools* (London, 1761).

2   A. Talfan Davies, *Crwydro Sir Gâr* (Llandybïe, 1970), p. 251.

3   Cf. John Davies, *Hanes Cymru* (London, 1990); Meic Stephens, *Linguistic Minorities in Western Europe* (Llandysul, 1976), pp. 156–7.

4   D. Densil Morgan, *Theologia Cambrensis*, vol. 1 (Cardiff, 2018), pp. 288–9, 366–8.

5   W. Moses Williams, 'The Friends of Griffith Jones', *Y Cymmrodor*, XLVI (1939); David Jones, *Life and Times of Griffith Jones of Llanddowror* (London, 1902).

6   F. A. Cavenagh, *The Life and Work of Griffith Jones of Llanddowror* (Cardiff, 1930); Thomas Kelly, *Griffith Jones. Llanddowror, Pioneer in Adult Education* (Cardiff, 1950).

7   Morgan, *Theologia*, p. 288.

8   Geraint H. Jenkins, '"An Old and Much Honoured Soldier": Griffith Jones, Llanddowror', *Welsh History Review*, II (1983), 449–68.

Introduction

9 R. T. Jenkins, *Hanes Cymru yn y Ddeunawfed Ganrif* (Cardiff, 1931); and *Griffith Jones of Llanddowror* (Cardiff, 1930).

10 Gwyn Davies, *Griffith Jones, Llanddowror: Athro Cenedl* (Bridgend, 1984).

11 Morgan, *Theologia*, p. 305.

12 Morgan, *Theologia*.

13 Morgan, *Theologia*, p. 288.

14 Such as the gentry, an analysis of the teaching in the Circulating Schools, or the place of women in the movement.

15 Jones, *The Christian Covenant*; *Letters to Mrs Bevan*; *The Platform of Christianity*; *The Welsh Piety*; *Welch Piety*.

16 NLW, G. Jones, Transcripts of Sermons, *Trysor o Ddifinyddiaeth*, MS 24057B; MS4495A; CMA 8326; Cardiff Central Library, *Trysor o Ddifinyddiaeth*, MSS 2.162; 2.1103.

17 NLW, Pocket notebook, MS 5920 A.

Chapter 1

GRIFFITH JONES IN HIS SETTING

GRIFFITH JONES AS A PHENOMENON OF WELSH HISTORY

Griffith Jones is a phenomenon in the history of Wales and its Church that poses special problems of interpretation. Writing on his life has been marred by failures to identify the categories of public figure, theologian and churchman to which he belongs. It has been somewhat misleading to allot him loosely to conventional types: as Puritan or Evangelical. These categories can obscure the real man and his motives. It is necessary to clarify the sundry influences that made up his first formation as a conventional High Church cleric. A careful analysis of these can alone enable the understanding of his work and its lasting influence. Griffith Jones's career arose within the setting of the Church of England in rural west Wales. This remained the seat of the involvement with education, which became a field for the display of his special combination of gifts. It is important to understand how his already successful work as a preacher and parish parson was the platform upon which his Circulating Schools arose. In addition, Jones's links with the gentry, especially Sir John Philipps and his family, provided a secure base for his part in a period of exceptional growth – and complications – in Welsh religious life. In turn, they also help to account for the continuance into the present of Welsh as a medium of cultural expression.

One might not have expected the career of a man of such obscure rustic origins as Griffith Jones's to be so successful and of such lasting public influence in Wales. Geraint Jenkins wrote of this son of an obscure freehold farmer: 'there is a strong case for claiming that he was the greatest Welshman of the eighteenth century'.[1] Jones was born into a Carmarthenshire farming family of modest means, and baptized on 1 May 1684 at Cilrhedyn, Pembrokeshire.[2] Three other sons had been born before him to John ap Gruffydd and Elinor John of Pant-yr-efel.[3] His father died when Griffith was still a child.[4] His boyhood is mostly unrecorded, but he seems to have engaged in various rural activities including woodturning.[5] When young, he contracted smallpox, which left permanent marks on his face. Jones suffered from various other, lifelong ailments, including some existing mostly in his imagination.[6] Some were truly afflicting, like asthma and depression. He blended these recurring troubles with a fussy hypochondria and Christian convictions producing an inflexible moralism which, unsurprisingly, annoyed some fellow clerics when woundingly expressed.[7] Jones thus showed a somewhat unpromising temperament for a leading public figure and benefactor. His tireless clinging to purpose, complete want of any sense of humour, and measure of eccentric irritability could indeed make him a man difficult to relax with.[8] He always took life very earnestly, having 'a very serious Turn of Mind from his Youth up'.[9] Despite this, he succeeded well in negotiating and persuading, particularly in the interest of his Circulating Schools.[10] Griffith Jones had a subtle social intelligence and adaptability, which enabled him to pursue his aims whilst often keeping judiciously out of controversies. And he had a surprising gift for warm friendship which could never hold a grudge. His manner could be disarming; and his modest ambitions as the parson of a Welsh country parish blossomed into extraordinary success. Griffith Jones's unusual gift for persistent, selfless enterprise achieved lasting benefits for the Church in Wales, his poor 'underprivileged' countrymen, and their language.

Griffith Jones's commitment to High Churchmanship accorded with his temperament. His serious, moralistic view of his obligations to the Church, and to 'good works nourished by sacramental grace', put him far from Latitudinarianism. His ideals were 'High', in the sense of attributing to the Church and its ministry a divine foundation and mandate. The pre-Tractarian High Church's outlook was at one with the Reformed reliance on the Bible and Creeds, adding, as of essential value, the Prayer Book, Articles and Catechism. Also part of the same Reformed consensus was an exalted view of sacramental grace, but not necessarily as working *ex opere operato*. Hence, the High Church, in Peter Nockles's words, 'tended to uphold in some form the doctrine of apostolical succession as a manifestation of his strong attachment to the Church's catholicity and apostolicity as a branch of the universal church catholic'. This outlook entailed also holding a 'high view of kingship and monarchical authority'.[11] From the latter derived the duty of submissive obedience to government and the general established order in Church and state. The High Churchman saw this as fully in keeping with an approval of the Protestant Reformation's emancipation from the Papacy, whilst still defending as necessary the time-honoured forms of the western Church in episcopacy, and in a measure, traditional aspects of worship. In its conservatism, the High Church differed somewhat from the other Reformed churches, and was, furthermore, notably hostile to any dissenting call for more thorough ecclesiastical reform at home. Against the background of the Anglican ideal of moral reform shackled to a refusal of consistent Protestant polity, the controversies of Jones's time were played out.

Griffith Jones launched confidently into new projects – especially in connection with his schools – at a time of life when other clergymen would struggle to keep up their ordinary round of duties.[12] His character, despite its faults, stirred to admiration and loyalty such as Sir John Philipps, Madam Bridget Bevan, his generous English patrons, and some of the younger generation of evangelists, like Howel Harris, Daniel Rowland and William Williams.[13] In preaching, Griffith Jones used 'an agreeable Delivery, a musical voice, and a proper Action, to great effect'.[14] His facility for speaking pure, elegant Welsh was an effectual tool: moving, in his sermons, from an easy, even conversational, idiomatic delivery, into a rousing oratory.[15] He was able to preach without going over the heads of his unlettered hearers, or overriding the discipline of a judicious exposition of his biblical subject-matter. His hearers did not have to suffer wearisome repetition, for his searching exposition continually presented fresh views of biblical hortative doctrine. He seems, despite his humble origins, to have had a natural bent towards learning, and a gentlemanly social grace that eased his moving among the landowning, anglicized gentry of west Wales, and even fashionable circles in London or Bath. In these latter places, he cultivated his English benefactors, in the interest of supplying the ever-growing need of finance for his schools. Not least in his surprising cluster of talents, was the skill and stamina that he showed as an organizer, in the flexible, involved, shoestring maintenance of his Circulating Schools. He spent all of his career, from 1708 onwards, as an Anglican curate and schoolmaster, and then as rector, apparently remaining genuinely contented, though denied preferment, in two parishes in a small corner of his home county.[16]

Griffith Jones's widowed mother's straitened finances allowed his 'thirst for learning' only modest rudimentary lessons, when a boy, at an unidentified 'country school'.[17] After becoming convinced of some kind of inner divine call to the Christian ministry, Jones, then approaching manhood, was sent by his mother, not to Jesus College Oxford, like some other Welsh aspirants to Anglican orders, but to Carmarthen Grammar School.[18] Paul Langford called the ministry 'the one profession for which a degree was virtually obligatory'.[19] This is overstated, since education other than in a university, though it might fail to bring social connections and openings to a title, could provide an acceptable sufficiency of learning for a clerk in holy orders.[20] Jones appears to have been a pupil at Carmarthen from 1700, when aged seventeen, until he was ordained deacon by Bishop Bull in September 1708, aged twenty-five.[21] Education in the school was, of course, in English. Griffith Jones was under John Maddocks, headmaster from 1686 till 1714.[22] Maddocks, a graduate of Gonville and Caius College, Cambridge, was called 'an eminent Classic Scholar' in the *Sketch of the Life and Character of the Reverend and Pious Mr Griffith Jones*.[23] He was an efficient schoolmaster who produced some successful scholars, such as Moses Williams (1685–1742), who almost certainly was at school with Jones; and that opponent of Methodism, Theophilus Evans (1693–1767), who may have entered as a young pupil when the 24-year-old Jones was also there, probably acting as an usher.[24] The very hostile John Evans (1702–82), the minister of Eglwys Gymyn a neighbouring parish, wrote that: 'We have no means of knowing how long he stayed at Carmarthen Grammar School.'[25] The *Sketch* said of his education, however: 'Mr Jones made great Proficiency in the Latin and Greek Languages, and other Branches of Learning.'[26] This praise may perhaps be too generous, though Griffith Jones continued to improve his gifts by study after ordination, including seeking further tuition in Hebrew, about 1728.[27] His writings seem to give no hint of embarrassment out of a sense of deficiency of education. He showed a confidence in preaching, teaching and writing, although without any ostentatious display of his attainments. Moreover, his reputed allusion to the philistine waste of time by university students in 'smoaking and drinking' would not necessarily have been mere resentment of a withheld privilege, attributable to a sense of inferiority.[28] Cavenagh seems to have misunderstood Jones's reference to college students, when saying: 'it is plain that the grapes were sour'.[29] Jones had merely repeated conventional censoriousness. Jonathan Swift, for instance, wrote that he had heard: 'more than one or two persons of high rank declare that they could learn nothing more at Oxford and Cambridge than to drink ale and smoke tobacco'.[30]

GRIFFITH JONES'S BEGINNINGS

Griffith Jones was ordained deacon by George Bull (1634–1710), bishop of St Davids, at Abermarlais on 19 September 1708.[31] Shortly after this, he took up the curacy of the parish of Penbryn, Cardiganshire.[32] The next year, he became curate of Penrhydd, Pembrokeshire, where he continued to serve for less than a year.[33] On 25 September 1709, Bull ordained him priest. This short span of time included a train of confusingly rapid turns in Jones's career. Mary Clements related that, in 1708, a school was founded in Laugharne, along SPCK lines, by the vicar, the Revd Thomas Philipps (1682–1748).[34] Griffith Jones's name appears in the school records as schoolmaster.[35] Phillips was a consistent correspondent of the SPCK for forty years, from 1708 to the end of his life. A strong supporter of the society's educational aims, he founded a school also at Penboyr, when that parish was added to his charge in 1713.[36] It is not clear whether it was because of success in his studies at Carmarthen Grammar School, or for being known to have an aptitude and interest in teaching, that Griffith Jones was employed by Phillips as master at the new Laugharne school. Serving his week-day post in the school at Laugharne must have meant inconvenient journeys to minister as curate in Penbryn and Penrhydd churches. School-teaching seems somewhat of a first love; but he must have been a master for only a short while before being ordained. It is likely that his inclination to education remained inseparable from his sense of call to the Christian ministry. The exemplary teaching of Headmaster Maddocks may well have awakened in Griffith Jones a leaning towards pedagogy, as well as reinforcing the ideal of attaining scholarly skills for the work of the ministry. Scholarship and a love of teaching can go naturally together. Jones's personal appetite for learning continued. David Jones wrote:

> By means of these advantages, he qualified himself for the study of divinity, which became henceforth his favourite subject, and to which he devoted the remainder of his life. He became acquainted with the works of the most eminent divines, both English and foreign.[37]

It seems possible, therefore, that Griffith Jones discovered an aptitude for teaching, even before his appointment to Laugharne. The reference above to his reading of theology is consonant with the thorough analysis of biblical texts in his sermons. But the close attention to the detail of texts in his sermons is accompanied by no citations from the works of any 'eminent divines' in the numerous transcribed sermon outlines. Jones may have made literary allusions, especially when preaching in educated circles; but they, and the illustrative *obiter dicta* which helped to make his preaching so gripping to his hearers, are unrecorded in the transcriptions. The concern for education never left Griffith Jones. It was entirely in keeping with the ideals of the SPCK and others, to foster schooling, especially for basic literacy and learning the Church Catechism.[38] Schools were thought of as an ancillary arm, seconding the functions of the Church in its calling of the people to practical, Protestant godliness.[39] Bishop George Bull, in his proposals to his clergy, for instance, recommended charity-schools in parishes: 'wherein Children of the Poor may be taught to read and write, and to repeat our excellent Church-Catechism, and to understand the Principles of our Holy Religion'.[40] In 1709, Griffith Jones, already the schoolmaster at Laugharne, became curate there. He continued as schoolmaster until presented to the parish of Llandeilo Abercywyn in 1711.[41] When he was presented by Sir John Philipps to Llanddowror in 1716, this parish already possessed a school set up in 1707 by Sir John and David Lloyd, and which was thereafter supported financially by Sir John.[42] Jones's pastoral ministry was thereafter to remain fully linked to schooling.

Some suggest that Jones's strait Anglican orthodoxy, like that of some others, resulted from not having had the university education which would have opened his mind to then-current heterodox scholarship. However, the post-1660 growth of Rationalism and Deism was not confined to the universities, but their speculations were familiar elsewhere, as in some Dissenting academies. Griffith Jones, who may have been aware of the novelties, held to the Articles and Prayer Book with a firm conviction. His humble origins may perhaps have made him wary of straying from the ethos of his ministerial call. Influenced, it may be, by Jones's example, Daniel Rowland was another who later was to be noticeable for his aversion to any appearance of unorthodoxy.[43] Jones's driving purpose derived from the fact that the Prayer Book formulae held a persuasive authority for him, derived from their origin in the Bible itself: a conviction attested by his early sense of calling to the Indian mission.[44] He wrote to Bridget Bevan in January 1737, revealing something of his own motivation, but also probably, what occurred as a temptation for himself: 'three great things are first to be conquered, namely, the desire of preferments, the fear of man and the ambition of living in favour with the gentry and superior clergymen'.[45] Griffith Jones's successful promotion of conversion to self-conscious faith in the doctrines of the Church of England preceded the rise of English Methodism, and was therefore not derived from it. The persistent conventional assumption of Methodism's being an endeavour originated and popularized by John Wesley and the Oxford Holy Club grossly neglects the historical facts.[46] Ivor Bromham wrote: 'Welsh Methodism is frequently regarded as an offshoot of the

English Methodist movement. This is an error, for it is of native origin'.[47] The fresh quickening of faith did not derive from the invention of a new set of methods to influence men, nor from the dominance of one dynamic will. Griffith Jones's eventual wide influence in Wales was not the mere result of some concerted scheme for awakening religious concern. The phenomenon in Wales, England and elsewhere in the century was one of independent growth of serious religious interest in separate places. In the resulting religious renewal, those who were drawn into being leading preachers were themselves subjects, not the instigators.[48] Since the previous century, the religious societies and the steady dissemination of Christian literature by the Welsh Trust, and then the SPCK, seems to have laid a foundation and have fed a stirring appetite. During the ministry of Griffith Jones, religious renewal – 'revival' – consisted at first, not in novelties, but in an acceleration of the ordinary components of church life, centring especially on preaching. There was an efflorescence of normal Christian habits and experience: repentance, faith and increased commitment to worship and keeping the moral law of God. Jones urged a sober adherence to these as stated aims in the Prayer Book.[49] It must, however, be admitted that the popular movement, as in other ages, was marred at times by the 'enthusiastical and incredible fooleries' so deplored by Jones.[50] He was far from seeking irrational adventures in novelty: no bizarre feats of alleged prophecy or miracles, no communalist counter-culture, nor enthusiastical social triumphalism. His conformity to the proper duties of an Anglican clergyman was rather with a striving to avoid disturbing the established social order. Working within the constraints of Church practice, Jones aimed to rekindle an appetite for peace of conscience, and joy in conforming to biblical norms. In this sense it is highly misleading to call him a 'revivalist'.

THE EPISCOPATE AND THE WELSH CHURCH

In 1700, Wales was a part of the kingdom and Church of England. Yet it was something of a poor, discounted appendix. Apart from the thirty-five separatist congregations in 1715,[51] most of its people had been baptized

Griffith Jones in his Setting

as members of the established Church of England.[52] Henry VIII's so-called 'Acts of Union' of 1536 and 1542 had brought legislative and legal uniformity with England, claiming every Welshman for the single national Church. The Church nevertheless embraced Wales and districts of Shropshire and Herefordshire whose inhabitants did not speak English.[53] In 1700, a portion of western Cornwall likewise had its own language.[54] Wales, along with its Church, constituted a provincial 'nation within a nation' under English cultural domination. Welshmen served most of the many poorly paid cures; but some became bishops, and a few reached the highest offices, even beyond Wales. Among the latter was Archbishop John Williams of York (1582–1650).[55] Others were Bishop William Lloyd of Llandaff, and later Norwich (1636/7–1710) and Humphrey Humphreys (1648–1712), bishop of Bangor.[56] Humphreys was a fine preacher in Welsh, and an expert on its culture, but accepted translation to Hereford in 1701.[57] Other Welshmen also had to spend their talents where Welsh interests did not dominate.[58] The statistics of the Church of England from Elizabeth I to the beginning of George III's reign demonstrate frequent failure to appoint Welsh-speaking bishops.[59] Despite the numbers of Welsh speakers, the use of patronage as political rewards, or to safeguard political interests, sometimes overrode the spiritual needs of the people. Especially after 1714 perhaps, appointments of monoglot and transient bishops may have been politically useful for keeping watch over a lower clergy infected with Jacobitism. Edward Willes (1693–1773), a skilled cryptographer, for instance received the see of St Davids in 1743.[60] He was translated after eleven months.[61] Howbeit, there were conscientious bishops in Wales, both native and English, striving to improve spiritual life, despite poor remuneration or the shabby seclusion of Welsh cathedrals. George Bull showed pastoral solicitude for St Davids, though he lacked time to learn Welsh.[62] Some bishops needed to support themselves from the revenues of pluralism.[63] Absenteeism, in particular, presumably impeded some bishops from providing a prompt resolution as the crisis over Methodism arose.[64]

Notwithstanding the benefits of bishops, however worthy they were, it was the myriad of Welsh parishes which were the field of church life. It is usual, in any case, in all denominations, that the life of the people should be lived within the circle of local connections. Despite the existence or absence of good episcopal guidance, church life, for most people, would be limited to their own local parish. A bishop could mostly seem remote and of little interest, making rare appearances, for visitations or confirmations, though Welsh bishops were sometimes diligent in this.[65] By contrast, the parson or curate would be, by the nature of the office, personally close to the flock, and their link to the wider Church. Roger Brown aptly described the Church as:

> a collection of corporations sole, each parish forming such a body. Its incumbent was the vicar of a defined area, and had the legal right to various tithes and fees ... as well as the exclusive right of officiating at services and the occasional offices of baptism, marriage and burial in his parish ... These rights ... were jealously guarded.[66]

The life of the Church in its local settings had importance for more than one aspect of the rise of Methodism, as it had in other popular movements of Christian history, such as the *Devotio Moderna*.[67] In the Church of England, the local bond of parson and people was also a legal fact. Though under Queen Anne, there was official favour for the High Church theory of a divine authority for an 'apostolic', traditionalistic ministry with its mystique of sacramental grace, the Whig grip on power after 1714 encouraged looser opinion concerning this on the bench of bishops.[68] The careerism of some political appointees made their episcopal visits rare or even totally neglected. This could not but tend to increase the isolation of a rural, conservative clergy from its pragmatic, classically educated superiors. The Welsh language that seemed to some – mistakenly – to lack the refinement suitable to civilized culture was sometimes impatiently dismissed as an obstacle best to be abandoned.[69] Griffith Jones, especially by his Circulating Schools, helped to vindicate Welsh, in its lowly rural communities, as a language of civil and religious culture, and so encourage its preservation.[70]

Despite an appearance of ignorant disorder in religion, there were signs of a spiritual concern coming to be felt by scatterings of Welsh people, particularly in the south, in the first decade of the century. The sense of need appears to have been real, even if not fully articulated by people still groping for reassuring certainty. The remoteness of these ripples in rural communities would naturally pass unnoticed – at first – by elite circles; but the sequel was to be a wave of concentrated religious enquiry, conviction and emotion which the sophistication of polite opinion could not ignore, but was little disposed to comprehend.[71] Some few of the elite in England and Wales, however, would understand; and some, like Sir John Philipps and Bridget Bevan, felt more than mere sympathy. The often impoverished rural clergy struggled to acquit their calling, raising themselves with difficulty above the lowest level of poverty and inability to gain a modicum of literate culture. Institutional non-residence and pluralism further weakened the ministry.[72] A parson could seek office by the immemorial path of following his father and forefathers: like Daniel Rowland.[73] Some got into a living through favour amongst the gentry; but patronage was not always well judged. Necessitous country parsons tried to survive, tilling their glebes and often earning a little more in some rural craft, like wood-turning.[74] Even for the most sincere, poverty could not but be a distraction from the absorbing demands of daily preparation for preaching, visitation and catechizing. Pluralism offered the chance of a less penurious daily life, but tended to make a man's ministry thinner and more remote from his flock. This was not the first era, nor the last, when there was a serious crisis of need at the basic level of the Church: the local parish. The energetic, and often selfless, efforts of the reprobated evangelists – such as Howel Harris – however much these might show their human imperfections, were an attempt to satisfy a real human appetite. In 1713, Griffith Jones himself seriously considered going to the Madras mission, but felt compelled to remain in west Wales because of the needs of the numerous following of local people that had already become dependent on his ministry.[75]

Erasmus Saunders (1670–1724), vicar of Blockley,[76] was a protégé of Bishop William Lloyd, and friend of the antiquarian Edward Lhuyd.[77] He aided the SPCK with editions of the Welsh Bible.[78] In 1721, he published his *View of the State of Religion*, with the apparent purpose of pleading the need of finance for churches in the diocese.[79] The book emphasized the poverty of the clergy, but alleged a customary religiosity among the common people. Although the *View* and its statistics give a biased account of defects, the author, who knew the region well, includes much credible detail. Saunders aids the understanding of events in Wales leading to the 'Awakening'.[80] He touched on some of the same points of concern as those raised by others later, including the dire poverty of many parsons caused by alienation of tithes, and the dilapidation of the buildings.[81] Addressing his appeal to the prince of Wales – soon to become King George II – Saunders argued from the standpoint of a loyal contemporary Protestant. Any faithful adherent of the Church of England was expected to endorse the Protestant rejection of 'Popery'. Fear and suspicion of Papal pretensions and practices were imprinted on the English psyche – though, at that time, probably less so amongst the Welsh. The burnings of martyrs, including saintly reforming bishops, could not quickly be forgotten.[82] Robert Ferrar (born *c*.1500), once bishop of St Davids, a graduate of both Oxford and Cambridge, suffered this pitiless cruelty before a crowd of Welsh onlookers in Carmarthen in 1555, only 128 years before Jones's birth. The impression of the spectacle could not but remain fixed in the local folk-memory. Griffith Jones, cleaving to the common Anglican view, preached with 'a deep and abiding hatred of Catholicism'.[83] In 1721, despite the effect of the Laudian party's attempts to divert the Church from its Reformed theological foundations, there was not the present-day greater openness to Roman Catholicism.[84] Disappointed in his ambition for preferment, Saunders used the fact of the Reformers' complaints about former exactions as propaganda for better finance in his own time.[85] Saunders wrote:

> in times of Popery, the Clergy for their pious Frauds and Ignorance, were rewarded with a double Portion both of Wealth and Honour; but since the Reformation, for telling honest Truths, they are requited but with Contempt and Poverty[86]

Mixing history, legend and wishful thinking, he suggested a natural sympathy between the early Celtic Church and latter-day Protestantism. Esteem for pure 'primitive Christianity' was a significant note of the age, and especially circulated as part of the argument for authentic Catholic roots of the Church of England. Many clerics, including John Wesley, espoused the ambition for the recovery of the faith and manners of the early Church.[87] Saunders strengthened his appeal by alleging a peculiar natural piety among the Welsh. Though probably using hyperbole, the statement was true of some places, and was, in fact, to be spectacularly brought into prominence in the warmth of an artless popular Welsh response to Griffith Jones's preaching, especially after about 1711.[88] The mean state of the clergy, said Saunders, was degrading this remarkable Welsh religiosity:

> no part of the Nation more inclin'd to be Religious ... than the poor Inhabitants of these Mountains ... to travel three or four Miles, or more on foot to attend the Public Prayers, and sometimes as many more to hear a Sermon[89]

Saunders asserted also a particular Welsh inclination to literacy: 'common People ... take the Pains privately, by Reading and Discoursing to instruct one another ... and Servants and Shepherds, as they have an Opportunity'.[90] This overstated allusion to a popular Welsh literacy was published at the very time when Griffith Jones was beginning a work for schooling that was to realize the phenomenon in stupendous numbers after 1731.[91] Jones's actual, less optimistic view – of widespread ignorance – was, conversely, the spur to the educational revolution of his Circulating Schools. Saunders perceptively admitted that the peasantry lacked:

> the Catechising and Preaching of a regular Ministry; so that if we have not yet quite unlearn'd the Errours of our Popish Ancestors, it is because the Doctrines of the Reformation ... have not yet effectually reach'd us, nor is it indeed likely that they ever shou'd, without a fit and learned Clergy.[92]

This analysis touched on the very defects that the SPCK men – and Griffith Jones among them – were intent on correcting.[93] Saunders cited the Epistle to the Romans in support of the necessity of preaching.[94] His argument was firmly Protestant, and accorded with the central purpose of Griffith Jones's and the other evangelists' future efforts saying: 'how should we be taught, unless such as are duly qualify'd are sent to do it, and are encourag'd and maintain'd for to attend their Ministry'?[95]

Saunders's disapproval of 'the Errours of our Popish Ancestors' endorsed the common anti-Roman, Protestant opinion in the Church of England at the time. A century later, in 1820, in his review of Welsh Methodism, Robert Jones of Rhos Lan (1745–1829) also deplored the people's spiritual ignorance.[96] He wrote: 'yr oedd llawer iawn o weddill Pabyddiaeth yn aros yn y wlad' ('there was very much of the residue of Roman Catholicism remaining in the country').[97] This reflected the strong consensus concerning a need for didactic – even polemical – preaching, particularly in defence of Protestant soteriology. Griffith Jones was entirely 'conformist' in following this opinion. Saunders alluded to the clergy's need to be able to preach and teach in the language of the people. In this he hinted at an importance in the ancient British tongue.[98] English bishops in Wales ought, said he, to learn to speak Welsh, as some in fact did. Thus Saunders's patriotic love for the language, notwithstanding his loyalty to the Hanoverian establishment, paralleled that of Griffith Jones. Jones, moreover, demonstrated that love winningly in his eloquent popular preaching and in his Circulating Schools. In a constitutionally Protestant church, it was critical that ministers should, moreover, have the learning necessary for preaching soundly and informatively.

AN ENERGETIC MINISTRY AND THE PATRONAGE OF THE GENTRY

Despite being a pluralist, Saunders was apparently an active parish-minister. Exemplifying the mood of the times, in 1713, together with local gentry, he promoted the building at Blockley of a school on which he placed – intriguingly – an inscription in Welsh: *Aros a Llwydda* ('Stay and Succeed'). An SPCK supporter, Saunders bought fifty copies and paid much of the cost of its edition of the Bible in Welsh in the same year. More importantly, at the request of Griffith Jones, who was agonizing (from October 1712 to May 1713) over the question whether to go to Tranquebar, and leave the growing numbers of people attending his preaching, Saunders gave help by proofreading the edition.[99] Here, a revival of interest in Bible-reading amongst the people is indicated, well before a distinct Methodism coalesced.[100] Clamour for Bibles continued as an index of increasing religious interest, to be followed by the Circulating Schools' redoubling of the demand.[101] Saunders suggested that 4,000 or 5,000 copies would suffice, but when the edition was published, in 1718, five years later, 10,000 copies were not enough.[102] Griffith Jones continued agitating for the production of more Welsh Bibles by the SPCK. Saunders also published several sermons, one of which, on 'Household Government', was translated into Welsh by Samuel Williams. Thus, he too seems a good example of progressive clergymen who saw themselves, nevertheless, as Protestants, Anglicans and obedient subjects of the Hanoverian regime. He played a full and successful part within the whole establishment, moreover, but retained, like Griffith Jones, his connection and sympathy with his native land and its language, and without any suggestion that the use of Welsh could counteract the interests of Britain and its establishment.[103]

Sir John Philipps, fourth Baronet Philipps of Picton Castle, Pembrokeshire (*c.*1666–1737) was important in the events that affected the rise of Methodism. A wealthy and leading landowner and public person in west Wales, Sir John Philipps exemplified the motives and activities of other religiously minded members of the region's gentry, such as John Vaughan (1663–1722) of Derllys and John Philipps (1645–1730) of Carmarthen.[104] He was the son of the third baronet, Sir Erasmus Philipps (?–1697) and his second wife, Catherine Darcy (or d'Arcy) (1641–1713), daughter of Edward Darcy of Newhall, Derbyshire. Sir Erasmus's first wife had been Lady Cicely Finch, daughter of the earl of Winchilsea, marking the fact that the Philippses and others succeeded in preserving their Welsh links despite generations of lucrative cross-border alliances. Sir John had sisters: the younger, Elizabeth, married John Shorter and had a daughter, Catherine, who in 1700 married Sir Robert Walpole (1676–1745), the Whig grandee who was to be the first to have the title 'prime minister'. Very surprisingly from the standpoint of the later controversy over Methodism, and with a wide difference of rank, Sir John's elder sister was to marry Griffith Jones. Much of Philipps's time was spent in

London, as an MP engaged in national affairs.[105] But he was also often at home in Pembrokeshire, showing particular interest in schools, and in the churches of which he was the patron.[106] His life of practical piety and active encouragement of philanthropy is a link between the Church of England of 1701, the religious societies and the rise of the Methodism. One cannot exaggerate his importance for the Welsh Church and people in the eighteenth century. Thomas Shankland's opinion was that he:

> As a patriot, as a pre-eminent Christian philanthropist, as a religious and educational reformer, and as a great Welshman who accomplished a great work in the Principality ... certainly deserves to be counted among the greatest benefactors of the Welsh nation in the eighteenth century.[107]

Philipps's father had been a commissioner for the propagation of the Gospel under the commonwealth.[108] As a young man, Sir John began to follow his father's earnest faith, though with no apparent hint of repudiation of the monarchy. D. W. Hayton wrote of the Tory Sir John:

> Of puritan stock, and imbued with his family's sober piety, Philipps grew up a wholly devout Anglican, anxious above all for the survival and renewal of a church beset, as he saw it, by spreading laxity and licentiousness.[109]

This summary of Philipps's motives reinforces the understanding of Griffith Jones's views. Philipps was devoted to good causes, being the founder and patron of many charity-schools in west Wales, and an early and very active member of the SPCK almost from its beginning.[110] In Parliament, he was an avid supporter of measures for moral reformation.[111] It appears that he first took notice of the young Griffith Jones, probably hearing him, as early as 1708, preaching at Laugharne, where Jones was appointed as schoolmaster and curate in that year.[112] Philipps promoted Jones, and remained an 'intimate and constant friend', brother-in-law and collaborator in work in the Church and in education.[113] Griffith Jones's friendship with Sir John was founded on a remarkable unanimity of principles, and probably strengthened by a coincidental harmony of temperament, despite strong contemporary prejudices

Griffith Jones in his Setting

against overstepping the divisions of rank.[114] Griffith Jones's aims and achievements are to be understood throughout as closely agreeing with those of Sir John Philipps, until the latter's death in 1737.[115] The ideals and actions of each man illustrate those of the other: it seems, almost without exception. Griffith Jones's influential career in preaching and education was always co-ordinated with the work of his patron. Sir John Philipps's personal notebooks show the solid Anglican piety that he held along with Griffith Jones. Their faith was the foundation of their friendship, which included a principle of peaceable submission to temporal authority.[116] Honouring the king and praying for him according to the Prayer Book was an Anglican Christian's conventional duty, and a basic proof of constitutional loyalty. For Philipps, as a conscientious member of the established Church, disturbing the social order was unthinkable. An approving note made after hearing a sermon on 13 November 1724 perhaps sums up his peaceable approach in politics, as in life in general:

> To the Meekness of the Lamb must be added the Courage of the Lion. To the Innocence of the Dove the Wisdom of the Serpent. There's a persuasive Eloquence in Meekness and Softness yt carries all before It.[117]

Whatever sympathy Sir John may have had for a nostalgic, theoretical Jacobitism, his taking the required oaths and compliant service as a Member of Parliament from 1718, and his appointment of Griffith Jones to Llanddowror in 1716 suggest that he was not offending his own conscience by failing to be a non-juror. Equivocation was not part of his known character.

In 1701, means of travel were slowly improving, and allowing leaders of Welsh society more easily to play their part on the broader national stage.[118] As in every other part of the kingdom, Wales's day-to-day government was in the hands of local magnates, who as Justices of the Peace, administered the mass of duties laid upon them by many acts of Parliament. The privileged members of the leading families might also be individual JPs, sheriffs, *custodes rotulorum*, or lords-lieutenant, and they could also serve as MPs, being appointed at times without any rival candidate. As landowners and magistrates, they had much power over their tenants' lives, allowing

25

them to show patriarchal care or hostile intimidation. Whilst keeping close contact with their lands, tenants, local interests and duties, the Welsh gentry mostly followed the English path to social advancement, influence and acceptance. The gentry usually sought to fill their proper social niche, and rise by judicious marriages. The west Wales landowners indulged harmoniously, it appears, in intermarriage and social intercourse, when at home, amongst others of the neighbouring gentry and squirarchy, at minor centres of assembly such as Tenby or Aberystwyth.[119] Griffith Jones's marriage with Sir John's sister Margaret (1665–1755) in 1720 was very significant. The alliance is strong, even astonishing, evidence of the overruling unity of mind and sympathy effected by the two men's common religious outlook.[120] It seems clear that Jones was accepted into the Philipps family without any reserve, and thus elevated into the gentry with whom he mingled in Bristol, Bath and London. The strong contemporary prejudice against breach of social station, openly flouted by this marriage, would have been expected to degrade Margaret's social position.[121] It may be compared with the case of Benjamin Ingham (1712–77), a handsome Oxford graduate, and itinerating preacher entangled with the Moravians, who married an earl's sister on 12 November 1741. Lady Margaret Hastings (1700–68) was sister to Theophilus Hastings (1696–1746), ninth earl of Huntingdon, and so, sister-in-law to Selina (1707–91), his countess. Though Selina approved of the match, it was a shocking and perplexing transgression of an important prop of social stability for the mind of some of the nobility. Lady Mary Wortley Montagu (1689–1762) wrote from Rome: 'The news I have heard from London is Lady Hastings has disposed of herself to a poor wandering Methodist!'[122]

Griffith Jones's marriage seems an exceptional example of a congenial unanimity in Christian piety between widely separated social ranks. Jones and his patron both had a supreme motive in social benevolence by evangelism and the provision of Christian instruction; the latter, from the first in charity-schools. Sir John was devoted to these, founding and financing twenty-two such schools in Pembrokeshire, and some in Carmarthenshire.[123] Jones taught in them from, at the latest, 1708, and founded one in his own parish of Llanddowror.[124] Sir John acted as patron and supporter to Jones against attempts to remove him. For instance, during the episcopate of Adam Ottley (1655–1723), Jones was accused of: 'neglecting his own Cure, and intruding himself into the Churches of other ministers without their leave'.[125] Sir John affirmed the charge of intrusion was false at 'a Sort of Tryal', and Jones was exonerated by the bishop.[126] Griffith Jones was drawn into the gentry circle in which his Philipps relatives took a prominent part. As a regular visitor to Bath, he does not seem to have kept aloof, despite the loose behaviour of some of the gentry.[127] It was an age of societies; social clubs of many kinds served the leisure or peculiar interests of social improvers, politicians, aristocracy, literati, antiquarian mystics, or rising merchants and their hangers-on.[128] London fostered a varied cluster of like-minded gatherings, for Welshmen like Sir Watkin Williams-Wynn (1692–1749) who participated fully in contemporary English issues of debate. Whilst serving to state their Welsh connections within the ruling elite, they echoed live antiquarian interests, but with political overtones, as the Most Honourable and Loyal Society of Ancient Britons (1714), and the Honourable Society of Cymmrodorion (1751).[129] These societies were part of a 'background' to Jones's life as a Welsh cleric with strong gentry connections and a commitment to Welsh interests. But he kept clear of entanglements with anything which might compromise his work. The SPCK was pre-eminent as a society with a serious and respected purpose; and Jones became a correspondent on 18 June 1713, remaining very active thereafter throughout his career.[130]

SIR JOHN PHILIPPS, THE SEA-SERJEANTS AND WELSHNESS WITHIN THE NATION

Sir John Philipps belonged also to the Sea-Serjeants, begun in 1726: an ostensibly Jacobite, quasi-secret, quasi-masonic social club of local west Wales notables.[131] This hinted at questionable loyalty to the Hanoverians after 1714. Nicholas Rogers wrote: 'In Pembrokeshire it was said that the Philipps clan used "all the means that they could to make the common sorte of the people to turn to the Pretender's side".'[132] The fact that they advertised their meetings in the local newspapers evinced their actual commitment as that of harmless Tories, not plotters in secret. The club could scarcely be deemed a serious engine of sedition beyond, at most, toasting the Pretenders. Sir John Philipps, with Tory loyalty to the Church, was a leading member, but an upholder of dutiful submission to the established order. Indeed, his younger son, Sir John Philipps (1700–64), the sixth Baronet Philipps, provoked a more justified suspicion, and came to be eyed by Walpole, his cousin Catherine's husband, as a 'notorious Jacobite'.[133] However, Peter Thomas explained the Sea-Serjeants as merely 'An electoral organization, as well as a social club, in south-west Wales dedicated to securing the return of opposition MPs. It was not the Jacobite club of repute.'[134] Thomas added: 'It was the Sea Serjeants' control of Carmarthen that enabled [the younger Sir John] Philipps to enter the House of Commons in 1741.'[135] This elucidation of the club's aims explains the elder Sir John's equanimous membership. Like almost all theoretical Jacobites in England, he eschewed subversion and social upheaval, and was content to hold office under George I and George II.[136] Nicholas Rogers, although giving credence to the view of the Sea-Serjeants as in principle conspiratorial, pointed out that in any case:

> Despite the continuing unpopularity of the new regime, an English insurrection in favour of the Stuarts was never a serious possibility. Outside Catholic and non-juring circles, Jacobite militancy relapsed into nostalgia.[137]

The elder Sir John Philipps's office as an MP was part of a life of patriotic and eirenic commitment to common-sense order and public service. His general Christian philanthropy, like that of his protégé Griffith Jones, made violent revolt unthinkable. Sincere, religious Tories could hold in some measure to 'divine right' and the duty of 'passive obedience', and still hold office reliably under King William, Queen Anne and the Hanoverians. David L. Smith wrote:

> Many Tories came to accept the Hanoverian succession as a political and religious necessity, and virtually all of them supported the Act of Settlement ... many still clung to the principle of an indefeasible hereditary line of succession.[138]

Smith added: 'A minority of Tories (never as many as Whigs alleged) were Jacobites in that they supported a restoration of James and his descendants, although very few actively pursued such a goal.'[139]

In north Wales, the much more fiercely and openly Jacobite, Sir Watkin Williams-Wynn, was mover and host at Wynnstay of meetings of the oddly-named gentlemen's dining and drinking-club, the 'Cycle of the White Rose'.[140] Despite his being in correspondence with the pretender Charles Edward Stuart, even Sir Watkin made sure in 1745 that he was at Westminster, keeping well clear of any show of willingness to fight.[141] When the Continental Protestants' sufferings of persecution were vivid recent memories, there seemed good reason for supporting the Hanoverian status quo.[142] The conviction, held by many throughout Britain, was that the German Protestant dynasty was a necessary bulwark of English life, faith and liberties. Sir John Philipps gave no evidence of restless discontent with the regime after 1714; likewise, Griffith Jones taught Christian obedience, praying for the king, according to the Prayer Book and Homilies.[143]

In 1714, having a Welsh name and pedigree did not exclude provincials from the highest circles of society. The Welsh enjoyed entry to the universities, the law, army-commissions, and importantly, the Church, and acquiesced in the general English outlook and commitment to Protestantism.[144] Griffith Jones, as a loyal churchman joined in the fear of aggressive, 'alien' Roman Catholicism that was a factor in the sense of national unity. The English vogue of a Continental tour was increasingly a part of the education of young Welsh gentlemen who could afford it.[145] In 1718, the younger John Philipps (1700–64) travelled – not quite on the grand tour – through the north of England into the Scottish Borders, finding genteel welcome in sundry country houses.[146] He was accompanied, in the mode of a domestic tutor, by Griffith Jones, his father's protégé. Aspiring Welsh careers could not but be led through anglicizing channels, including the adoption of English as the language of genteel and educated conversation and letter-writing. Noticeably, even private correspondence and diaries of the leading Welsh evangelists were in English: according to Geraint Tudur, 'a hallmark of sophistication'.[147] The Welsh gentry's growing acceptance within high-born English society shifted the centre of their cultural balance, during the seventeenth and eighteenth centuries. Even when they were resident on their estates, their Welsh identity was ceasing to be seated among the *gwerin* (ordinary folk) in their native language, lore, dress and customs.[148] Because of this cultural disjointure, Griffith Jones had to use obsequious caution when defending his mother tongue in the *Welch Piety*.[149] The trend to assume the use of English as the unquestionable national standard was ominous of danger to the health and persistence of Welsh and its literature. Every culture needs an elite which may lead in setting standards by example and patronage; but the Welsh gentry was being deflected from its due function as a cultural model by marriage-alliances with prominent English families. Geraint Jenkins points out that:

> In terms of patronage by the gentry, the Welsh language had most certainly lost ground by the Restoration period and, even at this advanced stage, there were many who were still not persuaded that it was a suitable medium for theological controversy or politico-legal protest.[150]

Economic and political power, together with the prestige of family and rank, gave the gentry and minor nobility an important influence on their communities. In general governance, the gentry and nobility had power to be zealous patrons of good causes, but heavy-handed obstructors when they disapproved. As holders of the right of presentation to benefices, they could be earnestly pious, diligent guardians, like Sir John Philipps. After promotion by Sir John, Griffith Jones's work in charity-schooling, leading later to his Circulating Schools, was to begin the rescue of the language. The Welsh language and its culture were thus to be inspired and reinvigorated, from amongst the humbler sort, by a new religious impetus, particularly among Methodists, at a time when hereditary leadership was drastically faltering.[151] Griffith Jones's formative origins had promised to lead to nothing of outstanding fame or note. Despite his beginnings, a combination of fortuitous events, gave Jones the openings and means for the advance of his orthodox, but idiosyncratic, career. His staid, but venturesome, methods were to result in achievements that remained rural and provincial, but made his ministry lastingly significant of the new wave of individualistic spirituality, and a new door to confidence for ordinary Welsh speakers.

NOTES

1 G. Jenkins, 'Jones, Griffith [*known as* Griffith Jones Llanddowror]', *ODNB*.
2 Cilrhedyn, Pembrokeshire, 12 miles from Cardigan, and fifteen from Carmarthen.
3 F. A. Cavenagh, *The Life and Work of Griffith Jones of Llanddowror* (Cardiff, 1930), p. 5.
4 Gwyn Davies, *Golau Gwlad, Cristnogaeth yng Nghymru 200–2000* (Bridgend, 2000), p. 13.
5 Cavenagh, *The Life and Work*, p. 7.
6 G. Jenkins, '"An Old and Much Honoured": Griffith Jones, Llanddowror', *Welsh History Review*, II (1983), 450.
7 Cavenagh, *The Life and Work*, p. 8.
8 Cavenagh, *The Life and Work*, pp. 29–30.
9 Anonymous (Henry Phillips?), *A Sketch of the Life and Character of the Reverend and Pious Mr Griffith Jones, late Rector of Llanddowror in Carmarthenshire* (London, 1762), p. 4.
10 Cavenagh, *The Life and Work*, pp. 29–30.
11 Peter Nockles, *The Oxford Movement in Context, Anglican High Churchmanship, 1760–1957* (Cambridge, 1994), p. 26.
12 Jenkins, 'An Old and Much Honoured', 450.
13 Bridget Bevan (1698–1779), born Vaughan, of Derllys, wife of Arthur Bevan. Her husband not being a baronet or knight, she lacked the official title 'lady', but the vernacular courtesy title of 'Madam' was deemed necessary to mark her social eminence. Cf. Peter Coss, *The Lady in Medieval England 1000–1500* (Stroud 1998), p. 54.
14 Anon., *A Sketch*, p. 6.
15 Jenkins, 'An Old and Much Honoured', 456.
16 Jenkins, 'An Old and Much Honoured', 449.
17 Anon., *A Sketch*, p. 3.
18 D. Ambrose Jones, *Griffith Jones Llanddowror* (Wrexham, 1923), p. 43.
19 Paul Langford, *A Polite and Commercial People: England 1727–1783* (Oxford, 1989), p. 89.
20 Archbishop Thomas Secker (1693–1768) and Bishop Joseph Butler (1692–1752) were educated at Samuel Jones's Dissenting academy at Tewkesbury (these both received degrees later).
21 Martin Evans, *An Early History of Queen Elizabeth Grammar School Carmarthen 1576–1800* (Carmarthen, 1978), p. 74.
22 John Maddocks (1650–1714?), MA, Gonville and Caius Col. Cambridge, master of Carmarthen Grammar School 1686–1714. Cf. Evans, *An Early History*, pp. 73, 80.
23 Anon., *A Sketch*, p. 4.
24 Evans, *An Early History*, p. 80; Jones, *Griffith Jones*, p. 20.

The Theology of Griffith Jones and Religious Thought

25 John Evans, *Some Account of the Welch Charity-Schools, and the Rise and Progress of Methodism in Wales* (London, 1752).

26 Anon., *A Sketch*, p. 3.

27 Thomas Kelly, *Griffith Jones. Llanddowror, Pioneer in Adult Education* (Cardiff, 1950), p. 22.

28 Evans, *Some Account*.

29 Cavenagh, *The Life and Work*, p. 8.

30 Quoted in W. R. Sydney, *England and the English in the Eighteenth Century* (London, 1892), vol. 2, p. 97.

31 Cf. chapter 3.

32 Penbryn, on the Cardiganshire coast between Aberporth and Llangrannog, 26 miles north of Carmarthen.

33 Penrhydd near Boncath, Pembrokeshire, 5 miles from his birthplace at Cilrhedyn, and 18 miles as the crow flies north-west of Carmarthen. It no longer is a separate parish; and the church is closed.

34 Thomas Philipps, was vicar of Laugharne, and rector of Llansadwrn nearby, from 1707. Mary Clement, *Correspondence and Minutes of the SPCK Relating to Wales 1699–1740* (Cardiff, 1952), p. 24.

35 Mary Clement, *The SPCK and Wales 1699–1740* (London, 1954), p. 111. There his name has the puzzling appendage '(1705–16?)', suggesting that he began teaching whilst still a pupil at Carmarthen Grammar School.

36 Penboyr, Carmarthenshire, 22 miles north of Laugharne by road.

37 David Jones, *Life and Times of Griffith Jones of Llanddowror* (London, 1902), p. 35.

38 SPCK Original Plan, Second Part, 2. Cf. W. O. B. Allen and Edmund McClure, *History of the Society for Promoting Christian Knowledge 1698–1898* (London, 1898), p. 23.

39 Allen and McClure, *History of the Society*, p. 135.

40 Thomas Nelson, *The Life of Dr George Bull, Late Lord Bishop of St. David's* (London, 1713), p. 445.

41 Llandeilo Abercywyn, variously spelt, a tiny parish, no longer extant, was about six and a half miles by road south-east from Llanddowror, and about seven, south-west from Carmarthen. The church is a ruin.

42 Clement, *The SPCK and Wales*, p. 113.

43 Geraint H. Jenkins, 'The Established Church and Dissent in Eighteenth-century Cardiganshire', in Geraint H. Jenkins and Ieuan Gwynedd Jones (eds), *Cardiganshire County History: Volume 3* (Cardiff, 1998), p. 465.

44 CUL, SPCK, *Committee Minutes*, SPCK MS A33/1, Minute 3634, 29 August 1713.

45 G. Jones, Letter LX, 'Union of the Clergy in preaching weekly lectures', in *Letters of the Rev. Griffith Jones to Mrs Bevan*, ed. Edward Morgan (London, 1832), p. 197.

46 John Walsh, 'Origins of the Evangelical Revival', in G. V. Bennett and J. D. Walsh (eds), *Essays in Modern Church History* (London, 1966), pp. 132–8.

47 Howel Harris and Daniel Rowland felt spurred into evangelistic preaching in the summer of 1735, four years before any contact was made with the English Methodist leaders. Other leaders were William Williams, Peter Williams and Howell Davies, and from about 1739 George Whitefield joined them.

Griffith Jones in his Setting

48   Walsh, 'Origins of the Evangelical', p. 137.

49   Cf. *The Order for the Administration of the Lord's Supper, or Holy Communion*, Exhortation before Invitation to draw near, and general Confession.

50   Jenkins, 'An Old and Much Honoured', 452.

51   Nigel Yates, 'The Welsh Church and the Welsh Language', in Glanmor Williams et al. (eds), *The Welsh Church from Reformation to Disestablishment 1603–1920* (Cardiff, 2007), p. 266.

52   With an estimate of a mere 420,000. Cf. Davies, *Hanes Cymru* (London, 1990), p. 302.

53   Welsh districts added to English counties, Shropshire and Herefordshire under the 1536 Act. Cf. Davies, *Hanes Cymru*, pp. 222–3.

54   Cf. also complaints over a strange language by Cornishmen in the 1549 western Prayer Book Rising. John Guy, *Tudor England* (Oxford, 1988), p. 209. The Isle of Man, with Manx, the Channel Islands, with Norman French, and the Pale of Calais, with Picard, were adjuncts, but not part of the Kingdom of England.

55   John Williams, dean of Westminster in 1620, bishop of Lincoln 1621 and archbishop of York 1641 was a staunchly orthodox opponent of William Laud.

56   Not to be confused with William Lloyd (1627–1717), bishop of St Asaph, Litchfield and Coventry, and Worcester, grandson of David Lloyd of Anglesey.

57   Authors Edward Samuel (1674–1748), author and translator; Samuel Williams (*c.*1660–1722), poet and translator; and Ellis Wynne (1671–1734), author and translator (who dedicated to him Rheol Buchedd Sanctaidd in 1701). Cf. 'Humphreys, Humphrey', in Meic Stephens (ed.), *The Oxford Companion to the Literature of Wales* (Oxford, 1990).

58   Many occupations had to be carried on, wholly or in part, from London, including the law, administration and finance, from the Tudor period onwards. Cf. Emrys Jones (ed.), *The Welsh in London 1500–2000* (Cardiff, 2001), p. 28.

59   See F. M. Powicke and E. B. Fryde (eds), *Handbook of British Chronology* (London, 1961), pp. 274–80, which shows the greater provision of Welshmen appointed before 1714. There was no requirement that the chief pastors should be able to preach to their flocks in Welsh; after 1714, Englishmen predominated.

60   Willes, consec. January 1743, deciphered subversive letters between Francis Atterbury and Jacobite exiles.

61   To Bath and Wells December 1743, continuing until death in 1773.

62   Cf. George Bull (1634–1710), bishop of St Davids 1705–10.

63   Williams et al. (eds), *The Welsh Church*, pp. 83–4.

64   Cf. Bishop Ottley and Griffith Jones. Williams et al. (eds), *The Welsh Church*, pp. 92–3.

65   Williams et al. (eds), *The Welsh Church*, p. 90.

66   Roger L. Brown, *Reclaiming the Wilderness* (Welshpool, 2001), pp. 14–15.

67   Diarmaid MacCulloch, *Reformation, Europe's House Divided 1490–1700* (London, 2003), p. 23.

68   William Gibson, *The Church of England 1688–1832* (London, 2001), p. 233.

69   Cf. the adoption of the established literary forms in the Welsh translation of the Bible (1588): Eryn M. White, *The Welsh Bible* (Cardiff, 2007); Isaac Thomas, *Y Testament*

The Theology of Griffith Jones and Religious Thought

Newydd Cymraeg 1551–1620 (Cardiff, 1976), pp. 27–33, 238, 271–5. And the large – for a minority language – number of books printed between 1546 and 1660: Davies, *Hanes Cymru*, p. 229.

70 G. Jones, Letter, 11 October 1739, in W. Moses Williams (ed.), *Selections from the Welch Piety* (Cardiff, 1938), p. 50.

71 Paul Langford, *A Polite and Commercial People: England 1727–1783* (Oxford, 1989), pp. 277–8.

72 There had been longstanding complaints in the House of Commons about failures in church discipline. In 1556, William Strickland MP called for the enactment of the Edwardian *Reformatio*. A bill which sought to give statutory confirmation to the articles of religion was stopped in the Lords by the queen. Cf. David J. Crankshaw and Alexandra Gillespie, 'Parker, Matthew (1504–1575)', *ODNB*.

73 Eifion Evans, *Daniel Rowland and the Great Awakening in Wales* (Edinburgh, 1985), p. 27.

74 As alleged of the young Griffith Jones. Cavenagh, *The Life and Work*, p. 7.

75 Clement, *Correspondence*, p. 54.

76 Saunders was also prebendary of Brecon. He was of a landed family of Cilrhedyn. His mother was the daughter of Howel Philipps of Penboyr.

77 Bishop William Lloyd (1627–1717), bishop of St Asaph (1680–1692), Lichfield (1692–1699) and Worcester (1699–1717), one of the 'Seven Bishops'. Edward Lhuyd (1660–1709), linguist, botanist and antiquarian, director of the Ashmolean Museum, Oxford.

78 Clement, *The SPCK and Wales*, p. 35.

79 Erasmus D. D. Saunders, *A View of the State of Religion in the Diocese of St David's About the Beginning of the 18th Century* (London, 1721); facsimile edn (Cardiff, 1947). A report on affairs in the diocese, allegedly undertaken with the approval of Bishop George Bull, who died eleven years before its publication.

80 Revival, also called 'Awakening' (*Deffroad* in Welsh) is a term disliked by some scholars. Like 'the Reformation', it covers the confluence of a number of trends working for a renewal of Protestant faith – including the SPCK, and Griffith Jones's preaching and Circulating Schools – beginning in 1735. Distinguished by an increase in numbers and popular expression of 'conversion', resulting in a cultural change in Wales that would last well into the nineteenth century.

81 Saunders, *A View*, p. 4.

82 This is an important datum for understanding the English popular outlook, fostered by such books as John Foxe's *Actes and Monumentes* of 1563, until into the twentieth century.

83 Jenkins, 'An Old and Much Honoured', 454–5.

84 Laudians continued controversies against the claims of Romanism. Laud himself argued the Protestant case against the Jesuit, John Percy (*alias* Fisher), chaplain of George Villiers, first duke of Buckingham.

85 Cf. the strictures by the nineteenth-century Tractarians and Pugin also on the subject of run-down buildings. A. W. N. Pugin, *Contrasts: Or. A Parallel between the Noble Edifices of the Middle Ages, and Corresponding Buildings of the Present Day* (London, 1841).

Griffith Jones in his Setting

86 Saunders, *A View*, p. 8.

87 Saunders, *A View*, p. 32.

88 Jenkins, 'An Old and Much Honoured', 456.

89 Saunders, *A View*, pp. 31–2.

90 Saunders, *A View*.

91 M. G. Jones, *The Charity School Movement: A Study of Eighteenth Century Puritanism in Action* (Cambridge, 1938), pp. 296–313.

92 Saunders, *A View*, p. 37.

93 Saunders became a corresponding member of the SPCK in March 1709/10. Clement, *Correspondence*, p. 29.

94 Romans chapter 10, vv. 14–18: 'how shall they hear without a preacher?'

95 Saunders, *A View*, p. 37.

96 Robert Jones, *Drych yr Amseroedd* [Mirror of the Times], ed. G. M. Ashton (1820; Cardiff, 1958).

97 Jones, *Drych*, pp. 22–4.

98 Saunders, *A View*, Section III.

99 Clement, *Correspondence*, p. 60.

100 This steady early growth in appetite for the Bible, and for the preaching of Griffith Jones and others, disproves the common ascription of the origins of the 'Awakening' to the efforts of the later preachers. The latter were not instigators, but the beneficiaries of an earlier, less spectacular movement.

101 Clement, *The SPCK and Wales*, pp. 33, 78.

102 The 10,000 plus demand for bibles is huge, amounting to more than 1 in 50 of the Welsh population. Clement, *Correspondence*; Clement, *The SPCK and Wales*, pp. 32–3. Cf. Geraint H. Jenkins, *Literature, Religion and Society in Wales 1660–1730* (Cardiff, 1978), p. 38.

103 Saunders, *A View*, pp. 39–43.

104 Bridget Bevan, Griffith Jones's patroness, was the daughter of John Vaughan of Derllys, who was one of the most prominent Welsh supporters of the SPCK Cf. Clement, *The SPCK and Wales*, p. xv.

105 He was Member of Parliament for Pembroke boroughs from 1695 to 1702, and for Haverfordwest from 1718 to 1722. His London house was in Bartlett's Building, Holborn.

106 Jones, *The Charity School Movement*, pp. 289–91; Edward Tenison, 'Achives of the Archdeaconry of Carmarthen, 1710', *National Library of Wales Journal*, G. Milwyn Griffiths (ed.), summer XVIII/3 (1974); summer XIX/3 (1976).

107 Thomas Shankland, 'Sir John Philipps; the Society for Promoting Christian Knowledge; and the Charity-School Movement in Wales 1699–1737', *Transactions of the Honourable Society of Cymmrodorion* (London, 1906), p. 74.

108 Howell A. Lloyd, *The Gentry of South-West Wales 1540–1640* (Cardiff, 1968), p. 210.

109 D. W. Hayton, 'Philipps, John 1666–1737', *ODNB*.

110 Clement, *Correspondence*, p. 1.

111 Hayton, 'Philipps, John 1666–1737'.

112 Mention of Jones as schoolmaster at Laugharne, October 1708: Clement, *The SPCK and Wales*, p. 111; R. Jenkins, *Griffith Jones of Llanddowror* (Cardiff, 1930), p. 15.

113 Jones, *Life and Times*, p. 39.

114 Cf. John Wesley's view of 'genteel Methodism'; Langford, *A Polite and Commercial*, p. 254.

115 There appears no mention of a care by Sir John for the use of the Welsh language. He may not have been willing to go as far as Griffith Jones, who only began to publish *Welch Piety* after his death.

116 NLW, Philipps mss. notebook, MS 578.

117 NLW, Philipps.

118 Henry VIII's Acts of Union placed local government in the hands of the Welsh gentry.

119 By the 1780s added to the spas, Brighton led the trend, with other towns accepted as centres of fashionable gatherings by the popularity of sea-bathing. Cf. Langford, *A Polite and Commercial*, pp. 102–5.

120 As evidenced in Sir John's references to Griffith Jones in his letters to the SPCK committee. Cf. Clement, *Correspondence*, pp. 52, 55, 61, 71–2.

121 Langford, *A Polite and Commercial*, p. 113.

122 Lady Mary Wortley Montagu, Letter to Lady Pomfret, 15 February 1741. Quoted in Boyd Stanley Schlenther, *Queen of the Methodists: The Countess of Huntingdon and the Eighteenth-Century Crisis of Faith and Society* (Bishop Auckland, 1997), pp. 20–1.

123 Clement, *The SPCK and Wales*, p. 13; Jones, *The Charity School Movement*, p. 289.

124 Clement, *The SPCK and Wales*, p. 111.

125 Adam Ottley, bishop of St Davids 1713–23.

126 CUL, SPCK MS A33/1, 4163, *Committee Minutes*, 9 October 1714; Cavenagh, *The Life and Work*, pp. 11–12.

127 Kelly, *Griffith Jones Llanddowror*, p. 23.

128 Roy Porter, *Enlightenment, Britain and the Creation of the Modern World* (London, 2000), p. 22.

129 Langford, *A Polite and Commercial*, p. 324; Davies, *Hanes Cymru*, p. 292.

130 Clement, *Correspondence*, p. 52.

131 The club's quaint name seems not fully explained. It met annually from 1726 to 1763 in Tenby or elsewhere, and this caused the reference to the sea. Cf. Peter D. G. Thomas, *Politics in Eighteenth-Century Wales* (Cardiff, 1998), p. 95. The club's political interest may explain 'serjeants', in the sense of senior barristers, with a wry allusion perhaps to 'sea-lawyers' and their argumentativeness, or to the rebellious Dutch 'Sea Beggars'.

132 Nicholas Rogers, 'Riot and Popular Jacobitism in Early Hanoverian England', in Eveline Cruickshanks (ed.), *Ideology and Conspiracy: Aspects of Jacobitism, 1689–1759* (Edinburgh, 1982), p. 84.

133 Peter D. G. Thomas, 'Philipps, Sir John, sixth baronet (1700–1764)', *ODNB*.

134 Thomas, 'Philipps, Sir John'.

135 Thomas, 'Philipps, Sir John'.

136 Peter D. G. Thomas, 'Philipps Sir John, 4th Bt', vol. 1715–54, *History of Parliament*, *http://www.historyofparliamentonline.org/volume/1715-1754/member/philipps-sir-john-1666-1737* (accessed 12 June 2019).

137 Rogers, 'Riot and Popular Jacobitism', p. 82.

138 David L. Smith, *A History of the Modern British Isles 1608–1707* (Oxford, 1998), p. 318.

139 Smith, *A History*, p. 317.

140 Thomas, *Politics*, p. 138.

141 Thomas, *Politics*, p. 170.

142 Huguenot refugees after 1685, and those from the Palatinate in 1709. Julian Hoppitt, *A Land of Liberty? England 1689–1727* (Oxford, 2000), pp. 69, 215; E. N. Williams, *The Ancien Régime in Europe* (London, 1970), p. 392. After 1731, collections were made by 'Griffith Jones' for Salzburgers. Jones, *Life and Times*, p. 49.

143 Homily, 'An Exhortation concerning Good Order and Obedience to Rulers and Magistrates', in Thomas Cranmer (ed.), *First Book of Homilies* (London 1547), published in *The Two Books of Homilies, Appointed to be Read in Churches* (Oxford, 1859), pp. 105–17.

144 Langford, *A Polite and Commercial*, pp. 324, 700; Davies, *Hanes Cymru*, pp. 302–3.

145 Hoppitt, *A Land of Liberty*, pp. 183–4.

146 Before entering Pembroke College with his brother Erasmus in 1720.

147 Geraint Tudur, *Howell Harris, from Conversion to Separation 1735–1750* (Cardiff, 2000), p. 2.

148 Herbert M. Vaughan, *The South Wales Squires* (London, 1926), p. 234.

149 Jones, Letter III, in Williams (ed.), *Selections*, pp. 39, 44.

150 Jenkins, *Literature, Religion*, p. 37

151 Vaughan, *The South Wales*, pp. 233–4.

Chapter 2

SIR JOHN PHILIPPS, THE SPCK AND A NEW VIEW OF MISSION

GRIFFITH JONES, HIS PATRON, AND THE CHURCH

An understanding of the ideals and character of Sir John Philipps as an important SPCK member, and as his patron, is necessary for the study of Griffith Jones. Philipps's idiosyncrasies as a wealthy, Bible-reading, High Church magnate and politician formed an essential sympathetic, formative support of Jones's career until Philipps's death in 1737. His patronage, as also the personal admonitions of Bishop Bull, almost certainly helped to strengthen, or even form, the early development of Jones's convictions. This was an unequal but likeminded 'partnership', which overrode contemporary conventions of rank, even to the extraordinary extent of their becoming brothers-in-law. Philipps's personal notebooks, preserved in the NLW give clear evidence of the simple but consistent piety that drove his ideals and philanthropy.[1] His commitment to contemporary English Protestantism was shown in his involvement as patron of the parish of Llanddowror, his dislike of 'popery' and eccentric interest, along with William Lloyd and William Whiston, in deciphering 'prophecy'. Sir John Philipps, like other devout landowners, felt it his duty to use his influence for piety and reformation of manners. As a prominent gentleman, he was conscientious in his exercise of patronage, and generous with his time and money in supporting charity-schools.[2] Other members of the gentry, like John Vaughan of Derllys, John Laugharne and John Philipps of Carmarthen, showed similar zeal.[3] Sir John took care about appointments to livings, also remaining watchful over the continuance of the provision of services for their parishioners.[4] The report of the 1710 visitation of the archdeaconry of Carmarthen gives evidence of Sir John's beneficial influence. The archdeacon mentioned, for instance, neglect of the church and churchyard at Pendine, a chapel of ease to Llandawk. Here, as in many small parishes, there was evidently a lack of proper ministerial care. The visitor wrote: 'Mr John Evans Rector of Bridell in Pembrokeshire, distant about 20 Welsh miles, is Minister here, but never resides, and this at Llan dawk the Mother Church will appear to be very injurious to his Successors.'[5] Like other non-resident pluralists, Evans employed a curate for Pendine: George Thomas, who also had duties in another parish, Llanddowror.[6] The visitor pointed out the cluster of responsibilities: 'His Curate here & at Llan dawc is Mr George Thomas, who is likewise Curate of Llan ddowror where he resides.'[7] George Thomas was being accused of neglect of his duties in the care of Pendine and Llandawk. A reason was suggested for his omissions:

> The Parishioners complain that he dos not come to prayers at a constant hour. Prayers are read generally once a Sunday; but sometimes they are without Prayers, which is occasion'd by the Curate's having many Cures & living in another Parish, where Sr John Philips is Patron & insists upon having the Parish serv'd carefully. For the most there is a Sermon every other Sunday, unless very rainy weather or some other accident prevents the Minister's coming from Llanddowror.[8]

This reveals Sir John Philipps as an attentive patron. His monitoring of an overworked curate at Llanddowror included an insistence on what he saw as proper provision for that parish. But his interference there necessitated a failing to foresee its likely effects elsewhere. The 1710 archidiaconal report mentioned the good order of things in Llanddowror, which contrasted well with ill-served Pendine:

The Minister Mr John Jones is nonresident, & lives now at Oxford.[9] His Curate is Mr George Thomas, who is also Curate of Pendein & Llan Dawc. The Curate resides in the Parsonage house ... Prayers are read once a day on Sundays & Holydays. Here is a Sermon every Sunday. The Children are catechiz'd every Sunday during the Summer time.[10]

Sir John was obviously making sure that the proper round of 'reading prayers', sermon and catechizing should be kept up at Llanddowror.[11] Though commerce in benefices was a common preoccupation amongst patrons, as part of the patrician exercise of power and influence, Sir John Philipps sought pointedly to foster efficiency and diligence in the cure of souls. Roger Brown wrote: 'Some patrons insisted on their nominees being resident and zealously performing their duties, as did Sir John Philipps.'[12] The archdeacon made no mention at Llanddowror of any of the omissions that frequently appear elsewhere in the report. By contrast, at Pendine: 'The Proclamation against vice & profaneness & the Act against cursing & swearing are not read.'[13] No such irregular omission of statutory duties was raised concerning Llanddowror. If such had occurred it would surely have been mentioned. Philipps thus showed watchful concern for correct and punctilious order. His diligence also included advocating charity-schools, which he himself founded and supported with lavish generosity.[14] He even suggested to the SPCK the establishment of teacher-training 'almost a generation before Griffith Jones put it into practice', and the printing of Munro's *Just Methods of the Pious Institution of Youth*.[15] The archdeacon added a commendatory note on the parish:

A charity School since Nov. 1708 supported chiefly by the contribution of Sr John Philips who pays yearly 4 £ & the Incumbent pays 1 £. All the poor children of the Parish are intitul'd to come to this School to learn their Catechism, to read, write, & cast accounts. There are at present but 9 children at School. The Curate is School Mr.[16]

With exhaustive obligations at Llanddowror church and school, it is not surprising that time and energy were wanting for the competing calls upon George Thomas at Pendine and Llandawk.

Griffith Jones was admitted and instituted to the rectory of Llanddowror on 27 July 1716, six and a half years after the Revd John Jones's admittance. The circumstances of the vacancy illustrate the influence of Sir John Philipps on parish affairs, and the confidence that he had gained in his protégé Griffith Jones.[17] Sometime before July 1716 – presumably soon after the accession of George I in 1714 – John Jones had avoided swearing the required oaths: 'John Jones had refused accipere sacramenta per actum parliamenti in eo casu, limitata et appunctuata' ('to take the oaths according to act of Parliament on that occasion, fixed and defined').[18] This must refer to the Act of Parliament of 1714, which appointed for all holding a public post of more than £5 annual value an oath that 'George I was rightful and lawful King, and that the person pretending to be Prince of Wales had not any right or title whatsoever.'[19] Since the visitation record speaks not of *sacramentum*, but of the plural *sacramenta*, John Jones may have been held to be in default also under the Act of William III of 1701. This imposed an 'Abjuration Oath' which was made as a qualification for all office in church or state, abjuring 'the pretended Prince of Wales'.[20] Since John Jones had been admitted and instituted in January 1709/10, it may have gone unnoticed that he had not complied with the 1701 Act. The later oath came into force after George I's arrival and coronation.[21] This means that the usual period of grace following a refusal to take the oath must have run out, and that John Jones was legally deprived of office by the middle of 1715. By that time, Griffith Jones was already rising in the estimation of the patron of Llanddowror, Sir John Philipps, and was inducted there on 27 July 1716.[22] The foundation had been laid for what developed quickly into an unbroken partnership of Christian enterprise.[23] The powerful magnate and the minor rural cleric combined harmoniously in the promotion of High Church ideals, to continue, it seems, without any break in unanimity and mutual confidence. In 1721, the embittered Erasmus Saunders made strong complaints about impropriations, and the frequent misuse of temporalities.[24] Roger Brown wrote of the diocese of St Davids that it was: '"riddled" with these impropriatorships. D. W. Howell notes that in Pembrokeshire nearly all the major landowners possessed them:

Sir John Philipps, the SPCK and a New View of Mission

the Philippses of Picton Castle had nine'.[25] Presumably, impropriations had been inherited by Sir John Philipps. Leslie Baker-Jones wrote:

> while advowsons were an additional, although minor part of estate income ... their importance lay in the additional power given to the squire to provide for a younger son or relation, and to ward off a 'methodistical' or other 'enthusiastic' cleric from settling in the area ... might disturb the status quo and the quietude of rural parishes.[26]

Regardless of unease about the fomenting of 'enthusiasm', more than one landowner was willing to give his tenants the benefit of an evangelistically minded parson. Also, a clergyman might even be appointed as a resident tutor precisely because of his methodistical zeal. Griffith Jones complained of testimonials being signed for political reasons, rather than presenting men of true zeal.[27] An example of the contrary was given by Baker-Jones: 'The "Methodistical" leanings of the Bowens of Llwyngwair naturally led to the appointment of the Rev. David Griffiths, the enthusiastic evangelical cleric, as tutor.'[28] Roger Brown noted Bishop Bull's disappointed efforts to get impropriators to pay sufficient stipends to curates of parishes: 'according to the population of the parish and the value of their profits; but he had little success'.[29] Sir John Philipps, however, had notable success, wielding power as patron to monitor clergy in the interest of furthering High Church principles among his tenants.[30] His notebooks give evidence of an uncomplicated faith which warmed to the touching zeal of European Pietism, but remained relatively unaffected by the enticements of the rising rationalistic heterodoxy.[31] They express a sincere and stable Christian faith, producing a friendly kindness, but with only a slow grasp of ideas. His promotion of Griffith Jones stemmed especially from their common commitment to the Protestant faith of the Prayer Book and Christian morality.[32] His unflagging activism in private and public life appears to have stemmed from such a fundamental conviction. Philipps was temperamentally fitted to give sympathetic and loyal friendship to Griffith Jones which, until Philipps died, helped to sustain Jones's pastoral and educational ministry.[33]

The Theology of Griffith Jones and Religious Thought

THE PERSONAL NOTEBOOKS OF A BIBLE-READING PROTESTANT

Sir John Philipps remained a convinced High Churchman to the end of his life. His personal notebooks show not only that he attended church regularly, but that he took careful note of the sermons, which were the core of public worship.[34] Philipps noted the dates, preachers and the Bible texts which they expounded. He set down points that struck him particularly, sometimes with lengthy summaries of the preaching. His weekly routine in London was punctuated by sermons heard. On Sunday, 5 November 1724, he heard Dr William Lupton preach at St Dunstan's in the west, in Fleet Street, near his London house.[35] Philipps noted: 'He said inter al. that nothing was more diametrically opposite to the Spirit and Genius of the Gospel than Persecution.'[36] He followed this, as often, with other lengthy notes. On the following Wednesday, he was in church again, presumably at an afternoon 'lecture'. The practical expression of piety particularly struck him. He noted: 'We may please Man so far as is Consistent wth our reason and Conscience, but to humour 'em in all their Follies & Vices, is to expose our souls to very great Hazard.'[37] Again that same day, in the evening, Sir John was present for another sermon, in which the Revd John Banson spoke on not being ashamed of the Gospel.[38] Philipps approvingly noted, among other things, the mnemonic alliteration in the sermon headings: 'The Precepts of the Gospel are pure, pleasant and powerful.'[39] In the summer of 1725, the notebook lists the sabbath services in Picton Castle chapel, when he had returned home from London. He enjoyed the ministrations of invited preachers, who seem seldom to have come twice. These were mostly local parsons, but on 8 August, the newly consecrated Richard Smalbroke, bishop of St Davids preached once.[40] Sir John's earnestness was evident in that there were always two sermons on a Sunday, sometimes preached by different clergymen. Although Griffith Jones was high in Sir John's confidence, and by then his brother-in-law, he only ministered on one day in the castle chapel that summer, preaching morning and afternoon on 20 June. It is significant that, at the age of fifty-nine, Philipps's appetite for biblical instruction was undiminished. His novice-like interest and zeal were never jaded, unlike that of some pious gentry. Marmaduke Gwynne (1691–1769), supporter of Howel Harris, and father-in-law to Charles Wesley, decreased at length in keenness for evangelism; and his wife's nephew, Herbert Lloyd (1719–69) of Peterwell, after yielding to the preaching of Howel Harris, lapsed into a life of riot.[41]

Thoughtful study of the Bible can have capricious episodes. An undated entry in one of Sir John Philipps's pocket notebooks gives a revealing glimpse of his thinking:

> The Bp of Worcester (Dr Lloyd) Mr Whiston & I are of the opinion the Jews will be restored an 1716 and build their Temple at Jerusalem, after wch they will be converted to xianity.[42]

This startling prediction reveals an incongruous component of Sir John's thinking, but not of his alone. William Lloyd became bishop of Worcester in 1699, at the age of seventy-two, lived until 1717, by which time his mistake about 1716 would have been clear.[43] Like him, Phillips belonged to the Royal Society, and was on familiar terms with exponents of Newtonian physics. Probably the discussion and their agreement in this eccentric interpretation happened after Whiston gave his Boyle lectures of 1707, on *The Accomplishment of Scripture Prophecies*. Whiston's anti-trinitarian prejudice was detectable by some in his speculative handling of prophecy.[44] Despite the implications of his agreement with Lloyd and Whiston's erratic deductions, there is no evidence of any change in Philipps's approach to life after the failure of the expected events in the predicted year. The exegetical whimsy did not deflect Philipps from his public service and charities, since he served one term as MP after making the note (that is, from 1718 to 1722), and remained an active member of the SPCK in all its ventures.[45] He was appointed, on 2 December 1715, a commissioner for the erecting of fifty new churches, under the New Churches in London and Westminster Act of 1711. This involved a long process of planning and negotiation.[46] Such building for the future is hardly the service of anyone who believes that the present state of things is about to be completely overturned. Significantly, in the prognosticated year, 1716, Philipps showed enough trust in a stable future to present Griffith Jones to the rectory of Llanddowror. Jones himself was too intent on evangelism and edified morality to give any sign of being swayed by purported 'prophecy'. His unspeculative, practical theology dwelt upon immediate personal repentance and faith, with the hope that: 'the inviting things said to encourage sinners to come to Christ, will, by divine grace, lay hold upon some of them'.[47] Jones dared to protest in a letter of July 1715 to Bishop Adam Ottley that the 'the corrupt negligence of the ministers' was the cause of the pitiable condition of the common people.[48] The urgent need to preach and teach continued. His mind was as little inclined to speculation as to innovations. His efforts implied solid hope for growth in the Church in Wales, as also for future advances among the heathen, as in Tranquebar.[49] In the same notebook where the meeting with Lloyd and Whiston is mentioned, Sir John Philipps later left a few thoughts on the causes and remedies of errors of faith and manners:

> Perhaps, if magistrates were better Xians there wd be no Muggletonians or 5th Monarchy men, who are a sort of millenarias. So, if Pelagians, & Arminians, did not stand up to so much for free-will, there wd not be so many Antinomians, who hold that all is done by God & nothing the creature. So, if greater care were taken in the xian education of children, there wd not be so many Anabaptists. And if people were more moderate & decent in their Apparel, & more spiritual in their mind, there wd not be so many Quakers.[50]

His imprecise definitions and naive, simplistic suggestions of remedies help to explain Sir John Philipps's motives in his generous devotion to the works for social improvement. But he failed to notice the methodological likeness of the sects' fanatical pseudoprophecy to the weakly founded predictions of Lloyd and Whiston. Nicholas Clagett (1654–1727), rector of Little Thurlow, Suffolk, opposed the 'Newtonian' line of exegetical reasoning in his *Truth Defended, and Boldness in Error Rebuk'd* (1710).[51] Clagett maintained that Old Testament prophecies had meaning both for their time of utterance and later fulfilment at the appearance of Christ. Griffith Jones appears to have agreed, following what seemed to some, even then, a more reasonable and consistently biblical approach. Michael Mullett wrote that, by contrast, Lloyd's speculations: 'Seemed an old-fashioned intellectual pursuit which tended to be ridiculed as "but his dotages", and he as "Old Mysterio", a crazed and fanatical seer.'[52] Erratic speculation, detaching passages from their context, can be understandable, though not wholly excusable. The misapplying of scripture to grapple with critical choices can become influential, as with John Wesley's and Howel Harris's superstitious bibliomancy.[53] Dubious chronologies built up from biblical references were an intense interest of Lloyd's.[54] In stress and over-excitement, a further step can be from a daring millenarian interpretation of prophetic texts, to setting up as a prophet oneself.[55] Griffith Jones's sober exposition of scripture contrasted with Howel Harris's charismatic credulousness of Mrs Sidney Griffith's scandalous prophetism.[56]

THE ADDED INFLUENCE OF FOREIGN PROTESTANTS

The SPCK's members showed firm attachment to High Anglicanism, which tended to incline them correspondingly to hostility towards Dissent.[57] Though contention with Dissenters could be bitter, the society's links with some European Protestants were, contrastingly, especially cordial; and leading representatives of the latter were given membership without misgivings.[58] This lack of reserve is surprising towards European Protestants who included Lutherans and members of Reformed churches that functioned without bishops.[59] The society was stirred to admiration for Halle's avid piety and forwardness in foreign missions.[60] Sir John Philipps, for one, participated generously in the relief of French and German Protestant exiles, leaving a sum in his will for support of Salzburger refugees from persecution.[61] Griffith Jones, typically, also raised two large collections for their relief in 1733.[62] Speculation about prophecy was heightened by the news of the sufferings of Protestants, including those under bitter persecution in France, and Louis XIV's revocation of the Edict of Nantes in 1685 deeply shocked Britain.[63] Huguenot refugees in England were received with sympathy, and the public relation of their plight augmented the embedded national aversion to Roman Catholicism.[64] Huguenots, Moravians, Palatines and others were all treated accommodatingly by the Church of England.[65] Atrocities against Protestants in the Cévennes (1702–4) also excited in

England millenarian, 'end-time' interpretations of events. When some Camisards, including Mazel (1677–1710), a leader, fled to London in 1706, millenarian fanaticism attracted the attention of the wider public, and their numbers quickly grew, with British people joining, and becoming the majority in what continued to be known as the 'French Prophet' movement.[66] Their charismatic prophetism is said to have influenced the Mancunian visionary and ascetic Ann Lee (1736–84), instigator of the Shaker sect.[67] William Whiston (1667–1730) attempted to make a distinction between his own millenarian exegesis of biblical prophecy and the unbridled auguries of the 'French Prophets' and such 'enthusiastick impostors' as John Lacy (1664–1730).[68] The pervasive influence of European Pietism on members of the SPCK is illustrated by Sir John Philipps's friendly correspondence with August Hermann Franke (1633–1727) and others in Halle, and with Jean Frédéric Ostervald of Neuchâtel.[69] Philipps himself was a hub of communication with foreign correspondents. It was recorded of Sir John on 6 December 1712:

> That he is very glad to hear Mr Prof. FRANK at Hall is sending a Missionary Printer and an Assistant to India ... [and Sir John wished] if Mr FRANK and Mr. PLUTSCHO were desir'd to testify to their ffriends and Fellow Labourers in the work, the very grateful sence that is entertained here for the Encouragers of it.[70]

Sir John Philipps was an active member of the society, as shown by his many letters, and being often in Pembrokeshire, he was the main link in the negotiations with Griffith Jones.[71] From Picton Castle he sent a report on 13 December 1712, about a discussion with Jones: 'That Mr. JONES is inclin'd to imbrace the Society's proposal of going to Madras, but will not declare himself absolutely determin'd before he has been to London.'[72] Sir John added a mention of Jones's working on Spanish in preparation for learning Portuguese.[73] Philipps's notes reveal the stolid bent of his worthy, but pedestrian intelligence. He set store on striving to be a 'better Christian', and on supporting more, good 'xian education'.[74] He was not a nimble-minded luminary, but progressed with slow dependability in a life of philanthropy.[75] His notebooks confirm his solid, life-long commitment to orthodox Christianity, as he understood it. A self-admonitory note regarding taking Communion sums up his consistent purpose:

> An habitual good life is ye best preparati̲o̲ ... and not only come with our lamps burning, but make 'em burn brighter & wee sd not measure ourselves by ye tenderness of our Affections in prayer or any other holy duty, but rather by a fixt & steady resolution to persevere in well-doing.[76]

Sir John's patronage of Griffith Jones seems to stem from this heartfelt devotion to good works, and loyalty to High Church principles.[77] Near the end of his life, Philipps encouraged the men of the Holy Club in Oxford. The 21-year-old George Whitefield (1714–70) wrote:

> Unknown to me, some of them sent to that great and good man, the late Sir John Philips, who was a great encourager of the Oxford Methodists; and, though he had never seen, but only heard of me, yet he sent word he would allow me £30 a year, if I would continue at the University.[78]

In this attitude of mind, Philipps was fitted to work in harness particularly with Jones: a man of the same clear-cut principles and aims, whom he described as: 'really one of the most sincerest Christians I ever had the happiness to converse with'.[79] However simplistic and unyielding their ideals were, their joint endeavours were to produce lasting fruit in Wales.

Jones became rector of the tiny parish of Llandeilo Abercywyn in 1711, but continued as curate at Laugharne, where his preaching helped to effect 'a profound spiritual awakening in the parish'.[80] By 24 October 1712, Sir John had gained a very good impression of him.[81] The SPCK correspondence records a letter from Sir John Philipps of that date, with mention of Griffith Jones for the first time. He reported: 'That ther's a very worthy Clergyman in Carmarthensh whose name is JONES that has lately discover'd an inclination to goe to Tranquebar.' A month later, on 20 November 1712, a letter from Sir John expressed his approval of the society's active interest in the novelty of foreign missions, and so providing 'a Short Purpose Prayer composed to be constantly used at the society for the Protestant Missnrys. in India'.[82] He added:

> That he had communicated the Society's proposal to Mr. JONES for going as a Schoolmaster to the East Indies. That he was under some tyes by the affectns of the people where he is, however, that he would consider of it and by the latter end of this month make his answer.[83]

The SPCK, founded in 1699, had soon acquired a broadened vision of reaching the unevangelized heathen; but this came by way of an appeal for help, in 1709, from the Danish mission to India.[84] The society responded willingly, thus taking an early step towards the Evangelical ideal of foreign mission.[85] The Revd George Lewis acknowledged a lack hitherto among Protestants.[86] He said: 'The Missionary's at Tranquebar ought and must be encouraged. It is the first attempt the Protestants have made in that kind.'[87] But there had, in fact, been some previous Protestant missions.[88] The society's alert enterprise made it willing to second the foreign work, by sending useful Christian literature to trading posts in India, and by providing help through sending an Anglican clergyman as chaplain and schoolmaster.[89] The words 'mission' and 'missionary' became a familiar part of the SPCK minutes and communications.[90] Samuel Wesley (1662–1735), having formerly been a naval chaplain, became one of the society's correspondents early on; and so impressive was the report of Tranquebar, that he even thought of venturing himself to the mission, in 1705, seven years before Griffith Jones.[91] In 1712, Susanna Wesley also gave evidence of the widening effect of the stirring new ideal, having a 'deep emotional and spiritual experience' through reading reports of the Tranquebar missionaries.[92] There was a sympathy in the SPCK for Griffith Jones, and neither the committee nor Philipps pressed for a quick decision.[93] The 'judgement of divine Providence' was decisive on all sides; and plans developed after October 1712, with discussions coming down to provision for Griffith Jones's widowed mother.[94] Sir John acted as intermediary again a month later, reporting on 8 January 1712/13: 'That Mr JONES intirely acquiesces in the opinion of the Society as to the unpracticableness of going by the present fleet to the East Indies.'[95] It appears from this, that the society was first cautiously to suggest delaying Jones's departure: his final decision needed more time. In making up his mind, he was firm yet careful, as he was in all his projects, including the Circulating Schools.[96] It

Sir John Philipps, the SPCK and a New View of Mission

seems that all along the communication with Jones about his participation in the society's enterprises had been conducted in west Wales through Sir John Philipps, who thus gained a deeper acquaintance with him. The minute of 14 February 1713/14 showed that Philipps had formed a very high opinion of him: 'the Packett [consignment of books] ... I lodged in the hands of Mr JONES on Thursday last, who will be sure to make the most of them'.[97] Admiration, coupled with their remarkable oneness of outlook, fostered a lasting association between Jones and the Philipps family. Late in 1713, Griffith Jones was invited to Picton Castle. Sir John and his family were so impressed by Jones during his stay, that he wrote on 7 November to the society commending Jones's qualities:[98]

> That Mr. JONES of Laugharne lately made him a visit in which his family were much edified by his conversation and Sr John is more confirmed in his opinion of his abilitys and sincerity for a successful labourer in whatsoever harvest the Providence of God shall determine him to.[99]

The time of the visit was significant, because Jones had been agonizing over two different, but imperative, demands: the mission to India, and his growing Welsh 'flock'. By 22 November, he had decided to remain in Wales.[100] The fact that neither vocation promised ease or wealth made Jones's sincerity plain. The year before, he had discussed the Madras project with Sir John, whose mind was also favourable to furthering the venture of foreign mission.[101] But Philipps again equanimously ceded Griffith Jones's field of labour to the 'Providence of God'. For either the home field or the foreign, he seems to have been confident that there would be a beneficial result, a 'harvest' from the appropriate employment of Jones's 'abilitys and sincerity'.[102]

GRIFFITH JONES'S CHOICE OF MISSION: TRANQUEBAR OR TALACHARN

On 29 May 1713, there had been 'a letter wrote to him by the direction of the Malabar Committee'.[103] Jones's earnestness had impressed other members of the committee besides Sir John Philipps, and the correspondence contains a mention of Jones's approving the fact:

> That the great Love and Zeal the Society discovers to the Immense Glory of God and their Compassion for the good of souls, deserves to be acknowledged by all good men. That it is part of the Saints' Communion that they are all at work for one another ... throughout the whole earth.[104]

The SPCK minutes convey sympathy for Griffith Jones's dilemma and his need to come to London to discuss his uncertainties about going to India being:

> under many inconveniences and among others, that the little flock committed to his charge would be deprived of the Ministry of God's word during his absence ... That 'tis not the belief of his unmeetness and insufficiency only which hinders him from resolving upon the Mission to Malabar, but likewise the extreamly miserable blindness of his own country[105]

Thus, the spiritual state of his own people in Wales weighed heavily on his mind. Though they had to wait while Jones ruminated upon his choice, the expeditious committee were patient, apparently acceptant of his wish: 'to resign himself to the Will and Providence of God'.[106] His Welsh charge was remarkably undistinguished, in the small parish of Llandeilo Abercywyn. Three years before, the 1710 archidiaconal visitation contained a list of damage and neglect, reporting:

> No house, no glebe, no Minister resident. Minister Mr Thomas Thomas Rector of Merthyr. Salary 20 £ a year. Prayers are read once every Sunday, & here are two Sermons in a month. Bread & wine at Easter found at the charge of the Impropriator. Communicants at Easter 3 or 4. Families 12.[107]

Selfish ambition would hardly fasten on such an unremunerative backwater. He appears in correspondence as 'Mr Jones at Laugharne', despite his Llandeilo rectory, residing at Laugharne most notably as a preacher and schoolmaster there.[108] Shortly thereafter he paid his promised visit to the committee in London.[109] Despite the uncertainty about his future plans, on 18 June 1713, the committee showed confidence in Griffith Jones by electing him as a member of the SPCK.[110] On 13 July following, they interviewed him, and appointed him schoolmaster and missionary to Tranquebar, whilst still awaiting his confirming decision.[111] The close interest in this Indian mission familiarized members of the SPCK with a pattern of such enterprise, which they were ready to homologate, without finding anything to be discordant with the Church of England's principles:

> Evangelism: the mission was much more than the mere provision of chaplains. It undertook direct evangelism both amongst Tamil-speaking natives in the colony, and others who spoke Danish and Portuguese.[112]
> Language: the German Pietist leader of the mission, Bartholomäus Ziegenbalg (1682–1719), had himself begun by sitting with the pupils in a local native school to learn Tamil, and later preached to the villagers in the language.[113]
> Education: in a letter written in 1713, Ziegenbalg mentioned forty-seven pupils in the Tamil school, twenty in the Portuguese school and fifteen in the Danish.[114] Tuition, lodging and food were free in the Tamil and Portuguese schools. A Tamil-language 'seminary' was set up in 1716 for training native clergy.
> Literature: by the time of his death, Ziegenbalg had finished a translation into Tamil of the whole New Testament, and part of the Old Testament, and the first printing press in India had been set up at Tranquebar.[115]
> Philanthropy: Ziegenbalg set up the first school for girls in India in 1707, and worked for the abolition of the caste system.

There being such a broad unanimity amongst the members of the SPCK, it appears significant that all the parts of the Tranquebar scheme came to be replicated in Griffith Jones's work in Wales.[116]

The friendship of the Revd Anthony William Boehm (1673–1722) with SPCK members is evidence of a link to Halle Pietism.[117] A graduate of Halle like Ziegenbalg, Boehm came in 1701 to teach the children of German families in London.[118] In 1705, he became an assistant

Lutheran chaplain at St James's to Prince George of Denmark.[119] Residing in London, Boehm became an ally of Sir John Philipps, the SPCK committee including him regularly in their deliberations.[120] Griffith Jones also regularly corresponded with him.[121] By these connections, Boehm became an influential exemplar and conduit of Pietism into the Church of England. An example of this was his translating into English the *Pietas Hallensis*, August Francke's report on his schools and orphanage in Halle, and he also translated the letters from the Lutheran missionaries to India.[122] Boehm corresponded with many Welsh members of the SPCK, particularly with Sir John Philipps, George Lewis and Robert Powell, as well as Griffith Jones.[123] The Halle writings made a strong impression so that Griffith Jones even replicated ingenuously the *Pietas Hallensis* name in the title of his Circulating Schools' reports after 1738: the *Welch Piety*.[124] Boehm was thus a strong influence on the society's outlook, though other influences may also have been leading the members to absorb pietistic ideas. He was party to SPCK plans for literature, evangelism and education, not least in the case of Griffith Jones. Jones made a candid appeal to the committee in resolving his dilemma, asking whether:

> as no small favour ... each of them would be pleas'd to signifie their good advice and judgement particularly such as he has the happiness to be known to, viz:- Sir JOHN PHILIPPS, Mr NELSON, Mr HOARE, Mr CHAMBERLAYNE, Mr DOLINS, Dr BRAY, Mr BOEHM and Mr. COCKBURN.[125]

On 22 September 1713, Boehm wrote a considered answer to Griffith Jones's appeal for 'advice and judgement', giving an opinion on the proper, biblical choice between competing claims of duty.[126] Patrick Cockburn also sent Jones an opinion on the matter.[127] Boehm's detailed and reasoned reply contains the argument, drawn from scripture which seems to have enabled Griffith Jones to arrive at a conscientious decision against Tranquebar. On 22 November 1713, Jones's answer came to the committee, which recorded the anticlimactic news with mild equanimity:

> That as to ye invitation of going to the Indies as a Missionary, he thinks himself obliged to decline it, upon the prospect he had of doing more service in his Native Country than he can propose to do abroad.[128]

Douglas Shantz wrote: 'In Halle, mission remained one of many initiatives whose focus was primarily on German and European Christians; for the Moravians, mission was the central priority of their community.'[129] The work at Tranquebar does not fully validate this analysis, since its missionaries ventured beyond their christianized enclaves. It is, nevertheless, important as the first Protestant mission in India, and marked the change of attitude amongst English Protestants, to look beyond their national bounds and see foreign missions as a basic duty.[130] The SPCK's unquestioning eagerness to participate in sending literature, and even Griffith Jones, for this work, marked the arrival in England of a position much derived from Halle Pietism. It helped the preparation of British minds for a future worldwide extension of Christianity in a multitude of individual calls to conversion.[131] Furthermore, the foreign missionary movement could not but help also to cultivate the mentality which, reflexively, came to make evangelism at home an overriding preoccupation of the Church in Britain. On resolving not to go to India, Jones himself turned all the more decidedly to the work in Wales, a ministry which developed out of a burgeoning popular demand for personal spiritual conviction and confidence. His nervous temperament added to his impatience to answer the perceived need, and reach beyond his first parish and the curacy at Laugharne, and after 1716, at Llanddowror. F. A. Cavenagh pointed out the restless ambition of his preaching, which was to last till the end of his life:

> He suffered from asthma – often a neurotic disorder; he was moody – subject to fits of depression – felt best both in body and mind on Sundays, when it was essential for him to be vigorous.[132]

Already elected a corresponding member of the SPCK, in the same letter of refusal of 22 November 1713, he offered his services for work on an edition of the Welsh Bible.[133] Jones revealed his practicality and a recognition of the importance of using an appropriate language for the imperative urgency of evangelism. He later complained about serious harm in Wales being caused in parishes where English-speaking ministers did not learn to preach in Welsh.[134] Despite the success of his preaching at home, however, the work in India remained on Griffith Jones's mind. One duty could only transfer its compulsion to another; his developing 'forward' view of mission to Wales inevitably echoed that to Tranquebar. He grasped the calling to preach for conversions, augmenting this with the Welsh Bible, schools and their necessary literature.[135] Whilst Llanddowror was his parish, the 'miserable blindness', even of adjacent districts of Wales naturally seemed to cry out as a neglected 'field' that Jones could not ignore. They stood out as calling for mission, when even people of India were being converted.[136] Perhaps too, the airing of millennialism, entertained to some extent by men like Sir John Philipps, heightened the ambition to hasten the gathering in of the 'unchurched masses' at home, as well as the distant foreigners.[137]

NOTES

1 NLW, GB 0210PICTLE.
2 Mary Clement, *The SPCK and Wales 1699–1740* (London, 1954), p. 15.
3 Clement, *The SPCK and Wales*, p. 57.
4 G. Milwyn Griffiths (ed.), 'A Visitation of the Archdeaconry of Carmarthen, 1710', *National Library of Wales Journal*, summer XVIII/3 (1974), and summer XIX/3 (1976).
5 'Visitation' first section, 'PENDEIN'.
6 Pendine, Carmarthenshire, 5 miles south-west from Llanddowror.
7 George Thomas ordained priest 18 September 1708 with a title to the curacy of Llanddowror. NLW, MS SD/BR/4, p. 16.
8 'Visitation' first section, 'PENDEIN. A CHAPEL TO LLAN DAWC'.
9 John Jones BA, of Jesus College Oxford, ordained deacon 25 September 1709 and priest 17 January 1709/10, was admitted and instituted to the rectory of Llanddowror, 17 January 1709/10 on the presentation of Sir John Phillips, Bart. NLW, MS SD/BR/4, pp. 22, 24; SD/VC/7, p. 59.
10 'Visitation', second section, 'LLAN DDOWROR'.
11 Doubtless the admonitions to those whom he ordained regarding regular performance of these duties were known and approved by Sir John. Cf. Thomas Nelson, *The Life of Dr George Bull, Late Lord Bishop of St. David's* (London, 1713), pp. 419–21.
12 Roger Lee Brown, *A Social History of the Welsh Clergy circa 1662–1939* (Welshpool, 2017), part 1, vol. 1, p. 399.

13 'Visitation' first section, 'PENDEIN. A CHAPEL TO LLAN DAWC'.

14 Clement, *The SPCK*, p. 13.

15 CUL, SPCK, *Minutes*, 1462, 20 November 1708; Cf. W. Moses Williams, 'The Friends of Griffith Jones', *Y Cymmrodor*, XLVI (1939), 15.

16 'Visitation' first section, 'LLAN DDOWROR'.

17 Griffith Jones was now 32 years of age.

18 'Visitation'. NLW, SD/BR/4, p. 50; SD/VC/7, p. 120.

19 Act 1 Geo. I. st. 2, c. 13.

20 Act 13 Will. III. C. 6

21 Accession 1 August, coronation 20 October 1714.

22 Sir John was active in recommending Griffith Jones to the SPCK to go as schoolmaster to Tranquebar by 20 November 1712. Mary Clement, *Correspondence and Minutes of the SPCK Relating to Wales 1699–1740* (Cardiff, 1952), p. 53.

23 A close contact from about 1713 until Sir John's death on 5 January 1737.

24 Erasmus D. D. Saunders, *A View of the State of Religion in the Diocese of St David's About the Beginning of the 18th Century* (London, 1721); facsimile edn (Cardiff, 1947), pp. 63–73.

25 Roger Lee Brown, *A Social History of the Welsh Clergy circa 1662–1939* (Welshpool, 2017), part 1, vol. 1, p. 199.

26 Leslie Baker-Jones, *Princelings Privilege and Power, the Tivyside Gentry in their Community* (Llandysul, 1999), p. 94.

27 Brown, *A Social History*, part 1, vol. 1, p. 179.

28 Baker-Jones, *Princelings, Privilege*, p. 156. David Griffiths, Nevern (1756–1834) *c*.1774, was appointed private tutor to the Bowen family of Llwyn-gwair, Nevern, where he came to know some of the evangelistic leaders. He married the eldest daughter of his patron.

29 Brown, *A Social History*, part 1, vol. 1, pp. 210–11.

30 Brown, *A Social History*, part 1, vol. 2, p. 399.

31 D. Densil Morgan, *Theologia Cambrensis*, vol. 1 (Cardiff, 2018), pp. 259–60.

32 Morgan, *Theologia*, p. 260.

33 R. Jenkins, *Griffith Jones of Llanddowror* (Cardiff, 1930), p. 35.

34 NLW, Philipps mss. Notebook, 0210PICTLE MS578.

35 William Lupton (1676–1726), described as a 'violent artisan of the high church' (briefly curate to George Bull – later Griffith Jones's bishop – at Avening), rector of Richmond Yorks, 1705–6, lecturer at St Dunstan's 1706, in 1714 became preacher of Lincoln's Inn and afternoon preacher at the Temple. He preached strongly against Tillotson's liberalism. NLW, MS 578, Philipps notebook.

36 NLW, Philipps notebook.

37 NLW, Philipps notebook.

38 Rector of St Bartholomew the Less, Smithfield, London from 1708 till 1750.

39 NLW, Philipps notebook.

40 Bishop of St Davids from 1724 to 1731.

41 Derec Llwyd Morgan, *Y Diwygiad Mawr* (Llandysul, 1999), p. 57; Bethan Phillips, *Peterwell, The History of a Mansion and its Infamous Squire* (Llandysul, 1983), pp. 46–62.

The Theology of Griffith Jones and Religious Thought

42 NLW, Philipps notebook.
43 William Lloyd (1627–1717), bishop of St Asaph, 1680–92; of Lichfield, 1692–9; and of Worcester, 1699–1717.
44 Stephen D. Snobelen, 'Whiston, William (1667–1752)', *ODNB*.
45 Clement, *The SPCK and Wales*, pp. xiv–xv.
46 British History Online, *List of Commissioners and Officers of the Commission for Building Fifty New Churches*, https://www.british-history.ac.uk/london-record-soc/vol23/xxxiv-xxxvii (accessed 19 December 2018).
47 G. Jones, Letter XLVII 'Diligence and progress in religion', in *Letters of the Rev. Griffith Jones to Mrs Bevan*, ed. Edward Morgan (London, 1832), pp. 153–4.
48 Gwyn Davies, *Griffith Jones, Llanddowror: Athro Cenedl* (Bridgend, 1984), p. 27.
49 David Jones, *Life and Times of Griffith Jones of Llanddowror* (London, 1902), p. 36.
50 NLW, Philipps mss. Notebook, MS584.
51 Nicholas is not to be confused with Nicholas Clagett (1685/6–1746), bishop of St Davids and Exeter.
52 A. Tindal Hart, *William Lloyd 1627–1717 Bishop, Politician, Author and Prophet* (London, 1952.), p. 236.
53 *Sortes biblicae*. Frank Baker, *John Wesley and the Church of England* (London, 1970), pp. 30, 140; Geraint Tudur, *Howell Harris, from Conversion to Separation 1735–1750* (Cardiff, 2000), p. 25.
54 Hart, *William Lloyd*, p. 246.
55 James Naylor (1618–60), Ludowicke Muggleton (1609–98) or Christopher Feake (1611/12–82/3).
56 Tudur, *Howell Harris*, pp. 214–16.
57 Julian Hoppitt, *A Land of Liberty? England 1689–1727* (Oxford, 2000), p. 31; Paul Langford, *A Polite and Commercial People: England 1727–1783* (Oxford, 1989), pp. 129–30.
58 Cf. SPCK, *Minutes*, 16 November 1699: August Francke of Halle, a corresponding member, 'Mr Frank's letter read and approv'd of'. W. O. B. Allen and Edmund McClure, *History of the Society for Promoting Christian Knowledge 1698–1898* (London, 1898), p. 43.
59 The Swiss Reformed churches had no bishops.
60 Clement, *Correspondence*, pp. 54, 153, 154.
61 Peter D. G. Thomas, 'Philipps Sir John, 4th Bt', vol. 1715–54, *History of Parliament*, http://www.historyofparliamentonline.org/volume/1715-1754/member/philipps-sir-john-1666-1737 (accessed 12 June 2019)
62 SPCK, *Minutes*, 5 May 1733 (£69.3.9), 5 June 1733 (£8.2.6).
63 Robin Briggs, *Early Modern France 1560–1715* (Oxford, 1998), p. 148.
64 Roy Porter, *Enlightenment, Britain and the Creation of the Modern World* (London, 2000), p. 49.
65 Hoppitt, *A Land of Liberty*, pp. 69, 214–15.
66 'Abraham Mazel', https://museeprotestant.org/notice/abraham-mazel-1677-1710/ (accessed 4 February 2020).
67 'Abraham Mazel'.

68 Lacy practised 'speaking in tongues' and 'prophesying'. Timothy C. F. Stunt, 'Lacy, John (*bap.* 1664, *d.* 1730)', *ODNB*.

69 Clement, *Correspondence*, pp. 54, 153, 154, 207, 290.

70 Clement, *Correspondence*, p. 54.

71 Clement, *The SPCK and Wales*, p. xiv.

72 Clement, *Correspondence*, p. 54.

73 Clement, *Correspondence*.

74 NLW, MS 584 Philipps mss.

75 Morgan, *Theologia*, p. 259.

76 NLW, MS 584 Philipps mss.

77 Eifion Evans, *Daniel Rowland and the Great Awakening in Wales* (Edinburgh, 1985), p. 139.

78 George Whitefield, *Journals*, pub. separately 1738–41, unabridged edn (London, 1960), p. 67.

79 Clement, *Correspondence*, p. 55.

80 Jones, *Life and Times*, p. 36.

81 Clement, *Correspondence*, p. 52.

82 Clement, *Correspondence*, p. 53.

83 Clement, *Correspondence*.

84 Allen and McClure, *History of the Society*, pp. 260–1.

85 The SPG (founded in 1701) had been first approached, but refused. Allen and McClure, *History of the Society*, p. 260.

86 The Rev. George Lewis (d. 1729) Queen's College, Cambridge, oriental scholar, chaplain to Fort St George, Madras (1692–1714).

87 Clement, *Correspondence*, p. 58.

88 Cf. John Eliot (1604–90), the English 'Apostle to the Indians' in Massachusetts.

89 Clement, *Correspondence*, p. 53.

90 CUL, SPCK, *Committee Minutes*, MS A33/1.

91 Henry D. Rack, 'Wesley, Samuel', *ODNB*.

92 Frank Baker, *John Wesley and the Church of England* (London, 1970), p. 9.

93 Many letters from Boehm and Patrick Cockburn to Jones argued for his suitability for the Indian work. Cf. Clement, *Correspondence*, p. 60.

94 Clement, *Correspondence*, pp. 52–4.

95 Clement, *Correspondence*, p. 54.

96 The Circulating Schools were not promoted strongly until after Sir John's death in 1737.

97 Clement, *Correspondence*, p. 55.

98 Presumably Sir John's spinster sister Margaret would have been present.

99 Clement, *Correspondence*, p. 61.

100 Clement, *Correspondence*, p. 62.

101 Clement, *Correspondence*, p. 52.

102 The metaphor of the 'labourer' in a 'harvest' is an echo of a biblical parable (Matthew 9.37–8), and a trope significant of the standard of ideals accepted and understood in SPCK circles.

103 Clement, *Correspondence*, p. 57.

104 Clement, *Correspondence*.

105 Clement, *Correspondence*, p. 57.

106 Clement, *Correspondence*.

107 G. Milwyn Griffiths (ed.), 'A Visitation of the Archdeaconry of Carmarthen', *National Library of Wales Journal*, summer XVIII/3 (1974) and summer XIX/3 (1976).

108 Clement, *Correspondence*, pp. 57, 58, 60, 62.

109 Clement, *Correspondence*, p. 57.

110 Clement, *Correspondence*, p. 52.

111 Clement, *Correspondence*, p. 62.

112 The New Jerusalem Church building of 1718 is still in use; and the native Tamil denomination still exists under the bishop of Tranquebar as part of the Tamil Evangelical Lutheran Church.

113 Allen and McClure, *History of the Society*, p. 259.

114 Douglas H. Shantz, *An Introduction to German Pietism* (Baltimore, 2013), p. 243.

115 Allen and McClure, *History of the Society*, pp. 259–60.

116 Allen and McClure, *History of the Society*, pp. 260–1.

117 Anton Wilhelm Böhme in German.

118 Daniel L. Brunner, 'Boehm, Anthony William [formerly Anton Wilhelm Böhme] (1673–1722)', *ODNB*.

119 Boehm used the Book of Common Prayer in the chapel there. Cf. Council of Lutheran Churches website, *https://www.lutheran.org.uk/3406-2/detailed-history/* (accessed 4 February 2020).

120 Allen and McClure, *History of the Society*, p. 260.

121 Clement, *Correspondence*, p. 39 n.

122 Clement, *Correspondence*, p. 39.

123 George Lewis (d. 1729), chaplain at Fort St George, Madras 1692–1714, rector of Dolgelley 1715–23, orientalist. The Revd Robert Powell (1681–1731), headmaster of Cowbridge Grammar School.

124 *The Welsh Piety*. Published 1740, and yearly till 1760. W. Moses Williams (ed.), *Selections from the Welch Piety* (Cardiff, 1938), p. 9. In Ireland, Henry Maule (1676–1758), an SPCK correspondent, was also impressed by the pietistic works in Halle. In 1721, he published a pamphlet recording successes of charity schooling in Cork, under the title *Pietas Corcagiensis*. See Toby Barnard, 'Maule, Henry (1676–1758)', *ODNB*.

125 Clement, *Correspondence*, p. 60.

126 Clement, '"Special Letters Concerning Wales": Letter from William Boehm to Griffith Jones', in Clement, *Correspondence*, pp. 330–3.

127 Clement, *Correspondence*, p. 60. The Revd Patrick Cockburn (1688–1749), curate of St Dunstan in the West, Fleet Street, ejected as non-juror after 1714, but later took the oath.

128 Clement, *Correspondence*, p. 62.

129 Shantz, *An Introduction*, p. 238.

130 L. E. Elliott-Binns, *The Early Evangelicals, a Religious and Social Study* (London, 1953), pp. 452–3.

131 David Bebbington, *Evangelicalism in Modern Britain* (London, 1989), pp. 40–2.

132 Cavenagh, *The Life and Work*, p. 7.
133 Clement, *Correspondence*, p. 63.
134 Williams (ed.), *Selections*, p. 29.
135 G. Jenkins, 'An Old and Much Honoured'; 'Griffith Jones, Llanddowror', *Welsh History Review*, II (1983), 462–6.
136 Clement, *Correspondence*, p. 55.
137 NLW, 0210PICTLE notebook 936.

Chapter 3

BISHOP GEORGE BULL AS GRIFFITH JONES'S MENTOR

THE CONDITION OF THE DIOCESE OF ST DAVIDS

On 17 September 1708, Griffith Jones was ordained deacon by Bishop George Bull.[1] A year later, on 25 September, Bull ordained him priest.[2] Jones was entering the ministry at a time when it may have seemed to many in the diocese of St Davids that things were improving. Since 1687, when Griffith Jones was four years of age, the Church of England in west Wales had been the theatre of unseemly wrangling by Bishop Thomas Watson (1637–1717) to keep his position against accusations of simony and extortion, made by some of his own clergy.[3] Using a long series of litigious shifts, Watson had striven to cling to power, suffering suspension by Archbishop Tillotson in 1694, excommunication in 1702, and having his last appeal voted down in November 1704. Diocesan affairs had been conducted by commissioners until March 1705, after which George Bull was raised to the episcopate and instituted to St Davids. Bull's high ideals, zeal and famous orthodoxy gave, for those anxious about the state of the Church, promise of great improvements after years of decline. Amongst these men were leading landowners and grandees.[4] Mary Clement wrote that, during the vacancy, the see of St Davids:

had been cared for only by its few efficient clergy and occasional zealous laymen such as Sir John Philipps, John Vaughan of Derllys, John Laugharne and John Philipps of Carmarthen.[5]

She added that 'Their delight at the choice of so sincere and godly a man was unconcealed.'[6] The path of future improvements, including the successes of Griffith Jones's ministry, was thus founded on the unanimity of Bull and the godly gentry, particularly the most powerful of them, Sir John Philipps.[7] Writing of the promotion of SPCK ideals in west Wales, Clement pointed out that, Bull's appointment having been made shortly after the society's foundation, 'the efforts of its representatives in the diocese became far more effective when loyally supported by the bishop'.[8] Bishop Bull set goals and ideals; but perhaps the practicalities had been suggested by these 'representatives', including John Vaughan, who expressed particularly forceful opinions. The young Griffith Jones was to accept without demur Bull's advice about his ministry; but the 'network' of godly gentry was already in place to collaborate with him in its outworking. Sir John Philipps soon became Jones's committed patron and confidant; and John Vaughan of Derllys (1663–1722), Bridget Bevan's father, was to continue no less willingly his encourager.

Bull had been a sick man, even in April 1705. Already worn out with parochial labour and study, writing and publishing, he had only agreed to become a bishop reluctantly, out of a sense of duty, and that to a poor and remote Welsh diocese.[9] On 29 April 1705, when an old man of 71 years, he had been consecrated at Lambeth Palace as bishop of St Davids. After little more than four years of service, he was to be finally incapacitated, in the same month as his priesting of Griffith Jones, by the illnesses that would end his life five months later, on 17 February 1710. Mark Noble (1754–1827) wrote:

the only particular to be lamented in Dr. Bull's life, is, that he was not sooner a bishop, that he might have done more service to a church, of which he was a principal ornament.[10]

The ailing George Bull's arrival was an important turning point for the diocese. Bull, the respected patristic scholar and defender of trinitarian orthodoxy, was in patent contrast with the disputatious Watson. Though inclined to studious retirement, George Bull had been urged to accept advancement, much on the strength of his established literary and theological reputation. As a parson, George Bull had fulfilled ideals such as those he had been introduced to at Oxford, especially promoted by the episcopalian authors Richard Hooker (1554–1600), Henry Hammond (1606–60) and Jeremy Taylor (1613–67). Robert Cornwall wrote:

> As parish minister Bull applied himself diligently to the tasks of catechizing, performing baptisms, and celebrating the eucharist at least seven times a year. He also made it his custom to take a collection for the poor.[11]

He had been rector of Siddington, Gloucestershire from 1658. There he stayed for twenty-seven years devoted to pastoral work, and spending most evenings in the delights of study till late at night, robbing himself of sleep. This regime eventually damaged his health.[12] His tenure of Siddington was his most productive time: when most of his famous books were written. These included, notably, the *Defensio fidei Nicenae* (a defence of the Nicene Creed). Written in 1680, and published in 1685, by Bull to exonerate himself from an accusation of Socinianism, it gained Europe-wide fame. Jacques Bénigne Bossuet (1627–1704), bishop of Meaux, though harshly anti-Protestant, gave it his approval. Many amongst the English clergy came to use it as the standard work defending Nicene theology.[13] Gilbert Burnet (1643–1715) wrote of the *Defensio* that it was: 'the most learned treatise that this age has produced of the doctrine of the primitive church concerning the Trinity'.[14] Bull had left Oxford without a degree,[15] but his book earned him a nomination by Bishop Fell (1625–86) of Oxford for the degree of DD. [16] After induction to Avening in 1685, in 1686 he became archdeacon of Llandaff.

The Theology of Griffith Jones and Religious Thought

Having an established reputation in some circles as a leading champion of orthodoxy, and as a venerable exemplar of High Church piety, George Bull contrasted oddly with the obscure countryman Griffith Jones. Jones was impressed lastingly by Bull's 'advices' given at the times of his ordinations.[17] According to Bull's fixed practice, Jones must have been in conversation with the bishop at least twice for each ordination, in 1708 and 1709, and at that, alone in private.[18] Roger Lee Brown mentioned Bull's enlightened practice, to be compared with the preliminary examination of ordinands of many dioceses in the 1850s:

> Surprisingly, this had been the practice of Bishop Bull ... which gave him time to enquire into the candidates' papers and characters. He would ask questions about their faith, whether they were inwardly moved to offer themselves for ordination, while he emphasised the nature and dignity of the clerical calling, and advised them to spend time in prayer, fasting and in considering the vows they would be making.[19]

Any assessment of the formative influences upon Griffith Jones's career should assume weight, especially for its early years, in George Bull's punctilious example as a bishop, and in his helpful admonitions and encouragements given in person. Some suggest that Bull may have shown Jones special kindness out of sympathy for his being a fellow literate.[20] This seems doubtful, for many educated professionals also left university or inn of court, without graduating, and without any embarrassment by the fact.[21] More likely, the scholarly Bull may have warmed to the countryman who had made up for a slow start in education by long and successful classical study under the learned John Maddocks of Carmarthen Grammar School.[22] Griffith Jones's dedication to his calling, and perhaps also his state as an unusually studious literate, may have evoked Bull's sympathy, perhaps even a liking. Rather than seeing them both as academic underdogs, Bull perhaps had special words of approval for Jones's serious-minded approach to the ministerial calling. What would become Jones's lifelong learning proved to be somewhat as devoted as his own, though Jones's publications were not to be academic, but popular.[23] Jones, on his part, already knowing something of Bull's

66

reputation for orthodoxy and piety, may have felt some awe towards the bishop as an ordinand. Perhaps each felt a spark of sympathetic affinity for the other, as also was soon to happen between Griffith Jones and Sir John Philipps. The quirky, depressive and intense Jones had a surprising talent for winning friendships.[24]

From the very first, Griffith Jones was a serious exponent of Anglican orthodoxy. He was, from childhood, very serious, and humourless.[25] His thorough, schoolmasterly gifts tended to a didactic orderliness in his habits of mind. This extended to a willingness to state and defend his convictions, as derived from Scripture. His preaching of the Church's doctrine lacked any tinge of consciously provocative innovation. His stress was upon the authority of Scripture, rather than on tradition, but without showing any lack of respect for the latter. Jones asserted vehemently the allegiance of himself and others to the biblical teaching: 'in the Principles of our holy Faith, as Christians and Protestants, and as Members of the Church of England'.[26] One cannot believe that he was insincere in this. Jones's cordial exhortations to faith when preaching were made with the conviction that he spoke nothing 'but what the Holy Scriptures and the established Doctrine of our Church will support me in'.[27] His orthodoxy aligned him with George Bull and other High Church leaders, who evinced a similar integrity. Jones's expressions of respect for the bishop were probably sincere, but his convictions about one point of doctrine were to bring Jones into a certain divergence – even from Bull.[28] His disaccord in this instance was discretely *in pecto*, and unpolemical, without, it seems, any note of disagreement in writing. Bull's much-valued private 'advices and counsels' to Griffith Jones presumably dwelt upon his high ideals for the Christian ministry, and the need for sober commitment to them. If Bull was favourably impressed by the young ordinand, his first impression was perhaps similar to that of Sir John Philipps. Philipps probably met Jones shortly afterwards, and must have heard him preaching at Llandeilo Abercywyn or Laugharne.[29] He recommended Jones to the SPCK committee, on 24 October 1712, as 'a very worthy Clergyman in Carmarthensh'.[30] The good impression extended into his becoming Griffith Jones's lifelong friend, patron, colleague and brother-in-law.[31]

GEORGE BULL'S PASTORAL EXHORTATIONS TO HIS CLERGY

Despite his advanced age and burden of ill health, George Bull showed exemplary zeal and efficiency. Many were impressed by him. Erasmus Saunders (1670–1724) was one who recognized the qualities of: 'a Late most EXCELLENT Bishop of that Diocese ... so Great and Learned'.[32] Within three months of his consecration, Bull moved to Brecon, in July 1705, to reside in his diocese, and hastened diligently to put his principles into practice.[33] His episcopate in St Davids was brief, but its expedited reforms could hardly have failed to make an impression on the newly-ordained, 25-year-old Griffith Jones. In addition to holding private conversations with ordinands, Bull made known his ideals for the Christian ministry in an incomplete pastoral letter to his clergy, presumably written in 1709. Its preamble is revealing:

> Being desirous, according to my Duty, to promote the Salvation of those Souls which the Providence of God hath in a particular manner, committed to my Care; and being sensible that this great Work can be no otherwise effected, than by advancing the Interest and Power of Religion in the Hearts and Lives of Men: Give me leave to suggest to you, my Brethren, my Fellow-Labourers in the Lord, some few Methods, which I conceive may be of admirable Use to this Purpose; which, if we are so happy as to accomplish, will greatly tend to the Increase of Piety and Virtue in my Diocese, and enable us all to give up our Accounts at the last great Day, when we shall appear before the Tribunal of Christ, with Joy, and not with Grief.[34]

The tenor, and even something of the language, of this preamble strikingly match those of Griffith Jones's sermons. Jones spoke of his and others' ministry: 'Mai pregethiad Gair Duw yw'r modd i gyffroi a dihuno dynion, o gwsg a marweidd-dra pechod, i ofalu am eu heneidiau' ('That it is the preaching of the Word of God that is the way to rouse and awaken men from the sleep and deadness of sin to take care of their souls').[35] It is most likely that the instructions in his letter were equally part of what Bull felt it his duty to recommend in private. Jones, when being interviewed in September 1708 and September 1709, probably already had a sense of the seriousness of his calling as a clergyman. He later testified to the lasting impression made on him by the conversations with Bull. There seems to be nothing to rule out the possibility that the bishop's pointed recommendations crucially armed Jones's mind with some of the priorities of his pastoral duties. Possibly, it was Bull himself who clarified and fired Griffith Jones's still imprecise ideas of what ought to be the main goals of his ministry. Jones later acknowledged his indebtedness to Bull somewhat to that effect. The *Sketch* stated:

> He received Deacon's Orders from the Right Reverend and very Learned Bishop ... of whom Mr JONES always spoke with an Air of the highest Esteem; and from whom he received some Advices and Counsels that were always recent in his Mind.[36]

Whether Bull's admonitions in person to him were mild or compunctive, Griffith Jones can, nevertheless, be demonstrated to have pursued his bishop's policies to the end of his ministry, and almost to the letter. There was a detectible general agreement in ecclesiastical thought which included Bull, men of the SPCK and the rector of Llandeilo Abercywyn. Griffith Jones's ideals and achievements must be seen as born consistently from this current of opinion, and not from some intruding novelty. The vivid impression of Bull's early admonitions never – by his own admission – left his mind, but seem to have given impetus to his evangelistic assault upon ignorance and apathy. He thus followed Bull's object of 'advancing the Interest and Power of Religion in the Hearts and Lives of Men'.[37] Jones strove to follow Bull's aim: 'to promote the Salvation of those Souls', at Laugharne and Llandeilo Abercywyn. There he felt a moral duty of care, not from his own choice, but laid upon him by the 'Providence of God'. His difficulty was precisely over this when pondering whether Providence was opening a way, in September 1713, to lead him to the mission in Tranquebar, and desert his swelling congregations in Wales. Anthony Boehm, when consulted by Jones, revealed a sympathetic understanding of his sense of obligation to Providence:

> The difficulty you labour under to gain a sweet serenity of Mind about the
> Removal from a place where you see the Seed of the Gospell spring up to
> another that lyeth altogether barren and uncultivat'd as yet, is so far from
> being blamed ...[38]

They all needed more than a mere human impulse for the huge endeavour of seeking the 'Salvation of Souls' and 'advancing the Interest and Power of Religion in the Hearts and Lives of Men'. A trust in Providence was needed. As Boehm added: 'As it is God alone who must prepare us, so 'tis God alone who, by a Divine Impression, must convince us. I say by a Divine Impression.'[39] Dependence upon such divine guidance seemed an enthusiastical folly to men like John Evans, but Bull's mind was in accord with that of Griffith Jones and the SPCK. In 1705, because of illness, Bull had to appoint several clergy to conduct his diocesan visitation. In 1708, the year of Griffith Jones's ordination as deacon, he was too ill to conduct a triennial diocesan visitation, having to appoint his son-in-law Joseph Stevens to act for him. However, Bull gave evidence of his high sense of calling by driving himself, despite sickness, to fulfil his duties of confirmation at Brecon and elsewhere. He regularly held ordinations there, despite having also to travel to Westminster for Parliament.[40] He gave generously to the poor: the aged, orphans, prisoners, and indigent clergy and their widows. George Bull thus set an impressively high example of selfless ministry for his clergy, by his own actions. He also dedicated his literary skills and scholarship to defending Christian doctrine. His *Harmonia Apostolica* gained admiration as a most learned exposition. By his qualities, Bull seemed to many to fulfil the High Church ideal of a bishop. Some eminent churchmen, however, found that the book failed to be an adequate defence of orthodoxy.[41]

'INWARDLY MOVED ... FOR ORDINATION': GRIFFITH JONES AND GEORGE BULL'S VIEW OF A MINISTERIAL VOCATION

In 1705, Bishop Bull issued his first episcopal charge to his clergy.[42] He also sent instructions to his clergy for the triennial visitation of 1708.

His aim was, according to Robert Nelson, 'to set before his Clergy, the principal Parts and Branches of their pastoral Office, with Rules and Directions, for the most successful manner of performing them'.[43] Jones's admiration for Bull is unlikely to have been mere adulation for a famous man; rather, the conduct of his parish ministry paid Bull what seems to be the sincere compliment of imitation. His practice conformed closely with the bishop's High Church ideals, listed by Bull in his charge as the main duties of the ministry, in order.[44] Mention has been made of Bull's use of the Prayer Book from memory, during the Commonwealth, because of the risk of prejudice in some quarters against the liturgy, though many others learnt much of it by heart, in any case, through daily repetition.[45] Loyalty to the Prayer Book was a main distinguishing feature of High Churchmanship.[46] George Bull notably showed such allegiance by clear and earnest reading of the liturgy: 'a most excellent Talent in performing the whole Service ... His whole Deportment was grave and serious, and had withal an Air of that Authority.'[47] Reverence for the liturgy as a supreme product of the English Reformation was notably reproduced also in Griffith Jones's ministry. His careful and melodious reading of the Welsh version identified this allegiance. 'In reading divine Service ... a sacred Awe upon his Mind ... as he observed the Stops and Pauses with great Judgment, and pronounced his Words with a grave and pleasing Accent.'[48] George Bull emphasized this duty as conducive to a properly devout frame of mind in church:

> to read Divine Service *audibly*, that all who are present may join in it; *distinctly* and leisurely that they may not out-run the Attention and Devotion of the People; and with *great reverence* and devotion, so as to kindle pious Affections in the Congregation.[49]

His ideal of 'great reverence and devotion' excluded, therefore, any cold formality. Its intention was, oppositely, to stir up wholehearted desire for communion with God, a warm participation in all the Prayer Book rites, together with eager conformity with the moral law. Griffith Jones's public ministry entirely endorsed this aim: 'In reading divine Service he was devout without Affectation. – He did not hurry the Prayers over.'[50]

Preaching was regarded by all serious churchmen as an important means of teaching the faith and proper behaviour.[51] The cultivation of 'pious Affections' was at the very heart of Griffith Jones's ministry and the new evangelism. An appeal to the heart was nevertheless not a new departure; the same earnest intention was noted, for instance, in Lancelot Andrewes.[52] George Bull demanded an appeal to men's minds and consciences. But, for the same reason, he eschewed the rash, irresponsible enthusiasm of those who 'tell you they preach without the help of any precedent reading or study, by a mere and immediate dependence on the assistance of the Spirit'.[53] Robert Nelson wrote of Bull's wish for clergy capable as preachers:

> To qualifie them for Preaching, he pressed the Knowledge and Understanding of the holy Scriptures; ... some Skill in the learned Languages, with good Judgment and Discretion, and ... a tolerable Share of Elocution ... young Divines, not to trust at first to their own Compositions, but to furnish themselves with a provision of the best Sermons, which the learned Divines of our Church have published ... And where ... Ministers are incapable of discharging this Duty as they ought, he directed them to use the Homilies of the Church, and sometimes to read a Chapter to the People, out of that excellent Book, called, *The Whole Duty of Man.*[54]

Bull thus placed preaching in its proper position of importance, suitably in keeping with the Protestant elements in the constitution of the Church of England. Griffith Jones's commitment to preaching must be deemed to have been derived, in part at least, from his respect for tradition and accepted standards in the Church. His popular sermons were thus intended to fulfil what was enjoined by the most respected Anglican fathers, although their effect upon persuaded hearers could sometimes be an unsought-for disturbance by cries of distress for guilt, or joy for a lightened conscience.[55] Bull's own episcopal recommendations on preaching seem also to imply, however, a baffled compromise, in that he could not expect all candidates for the ministry to be able to acquit this demanding duty as well as men like Griffith Jones. 'Knowledge and understanding' of the Bible were essential, and a regular ministry of exposition committed a man to a life-long regime of study. L. E. Elliott-Binns mentioned the difference among clergy:

> One reason for the comparative inefficiency of the average cleric was that he had never received any special training for his job ... [inducing] the more conscientious clergy to spend much time in study in order to overcome their defects. Jones of Creaton 'fagged' so hard that it brought about a nervous disorder.[56]

George Bull had himself shown obsessive devotion to toilsome study.[57] Similar thorough preparatory work was evident in the biblicistic cross-referencing found in Griffith Jones's sermons.[58] It is a mistake, moreover, to attribute the attraction of Jones's preaching to mere oratory, though his eloquence did appeal to Welsh popular taste. John Dalton (1680–1724) of Clog-y-Frân, near St Clears, who lived near Llanddowror and heard his preaching, wrote in February 1713:[59]

> It is certain that Mr Jones is one of the greatest masters of the Welsh tongue that ever Wales was blessed with, both in respect of fluency of speech and eminence in Scriptural and Xian knowledge.[60]

Griffith Jones's mastery of the detail of the biblical text, accompanied by a skill for orderly construction and reasoning, singularly assisted his sermons' success.[61] Bishop Bull's recommendation of resorting to the Homilies and readings from *The Whole Duty of Man* amounted to an acknowledgement that he often could not be sure of obtaining properly educated or motivated candidates for ordination. It may be that he recognized an unusual gift of eloquence in the young ordinand Jones, or had a recommendation of him from John Maddocks, who must have known his intellectual gifts, and very probably heard him teaching.[62] Griffith Jones's drive seems always to have been for a fresh, first-hand exposition and application of biblical passages, never straying from the central call to faith, repentance and good works. His sermon transcriptions give evidence of careful analysis of the texts and, at least at times, flashes of originality. Geraint Jenkins alleged that his effect in preaching was brought about by working 'to drive points by sheer

The Theology of Griffith Jones and Religious Thought

repetition and insistence'.[63] 'Sheer repetition' seems, however, not an apt description. Though he held to his clear evangelistic aim, Jones's preaching had attractive force in its deftly chosen illustrations and arguments drawn from the Bible's rich diversity of theme, narrative and idiom. His sermons, whose topics were each based on a passage of biblical text, were structured as confident, impressively able and coherent expositions. He seems never to have been lamely dependent on mere repetition, or to have resorted to filling up his sermons by quoting passages from others' sermons.[64] Furthermore, Jones never appears to have felt a need to substitute, for proper sermons, readings from books like *The Whole Duty of Man*. He was clearly in his element when immersed in a fresh exploration of a passage of the Bible, and linking it to the whole, never being driven to reduce his addresses to a drab *crambe repetita*. His temperament fitted him for the never-slackening effort of preparing and preaching, with infectious delight, original expositions of the Bible. Though he suffered from asthma and depression, for Griffith Jones, Sunday, the preaching day, was especially when the qualities of his mind and temperament were raised to their best effect.[65]

Robert Nelson pointed out the care that George Bull recommended in the conduct of the Sacraments:

> He enjoined them to perform Baptism in publick, and chiefly on Sundays and Holy-days, when the Assemblies of Christians are fullest ... He exhorted to great Reverence and Solemnity in officiating at the Altar, and to the observation of every Punctilio, according to the Rubricks ... and especially to take care, not to administer the holy Sacrament of the Lord's Supper, to Persons known to be vicious and scandalous.[66]

Griffith Jones showed the same intention of treating the rites with due care. It is noticeable that Bull's recommendations failed to refer to frequency of celebration of the Holy Communion, although this was also recognized as a sign of earnest piety. L. E. Elliott-Binns wrote concerning early Georgian practice: 'George Herbert ... considered that there should be a minimum of five or six yearly ... In the towns there were more frequently... though the ideal of one a month was seldom attained.'[67] Here, there seems evidence of a gradual movement of renewal in the Church in Wales and beyond, which was already under way. It was marked in this respect by Archbishop Tillotson's sermon on *Frequent Communion*.[68] From the former custom of quarterly Communions, some ministers were moving to a monthly celebration of the sacrament.[69] Elliott-Binns mentioned numbers attending at such times:

> The attendance when they were available was sometimes very great, going into thousands at times, and the service might last for several hours ... There was no little anxiety lest unworthy communicating should bring not a blessing but a curse.[70]

Griffith Jones was notably zealous for frequent Communion, holding monthly celebrations at Llanddowror. In this incidentally, he excelled even the frequency of George Bull at Siddington, who 'brought it to seven times a year'.[71] Jones's Communion Sundays, with an enhanced air of occasion, attracted large numbers, including some making long journeys to be present. Even the hostile John Evans wrote that he had visited Laugharne to hear Jones preach, but had found it 'so full of strangers, that I could not come near the doors'.[72] Sir John Philipps mentioned numbers too great to be held in the church building: 'sometimes amounted to 3 or 4,000 people'.[73] The practice, offensive to some, of open-air gatherings must be seen as the practical expedient of coping with overflowing congregations, in Jones's case, not as a deliberate flouting of ecclesiastical custom.

The bishop's probing personal examination of Jones as an ordinand, and his exhortations may have compatibly reinforced the sense of calling that Jones had allegedly already received through some kind of spiritual experience during his youth. Geraint Jenkins wrote:

> in many ways, he epitomized the earnest, puritanical 'improver' in mid-eighteenth-century Wales. During his youth he received a 'heavenly call', a profound spiritual conversion which persuaded him that it was God's will that he should be of service to his people.[74]

In keeping with the High Churchmanship of his bishop, and others, Griffith Jones retained the sense of vocation which may have impressed George Bull during their ordination interviews. It was not a mere matter of professional dignity or bread-winning. In his preaching, he continually referred his hearers to the authority of Christ himself, lying behind the words of an ordained preacher. He spoke in general of what obviously could be applied to him personally: 'Ond wrth fod yn ddïofal ac esgeulus chwi ddylech gofio, Mai nid Gweinidogaeth dyn ydych yn dirmygu; ond amharchu yr ydych Weinidogaeth Crist ei hun' ('But being at your ease and neglectful you must remember, That it is not the Ministry of man that you are despising; but you are insulting the Ministry of Christ himself').[75] Jones's words lack any hint of the perfunctory performance of a prescribed office. In expounding his texts, Griffith Jones emphatically addressed his hearers.[76] For him, High Church principle, on scriptural authority, gave the preacher a right to claim attention for his teaching. But though holy orders – and his gentry marriage – gave him a certain provincial pre-eminence, Jones did not use them to claim mere social privileges. He did not exploit his secure income to give over his parochial work to curates in order to spend his time in conventional gentry pursuits.[77] He was convinced that a minister himself must have an inner divine calling before presuming to teach others. His own peculiar experience of conversion and call – whatever these were exactly – perhaps reinforced by the impression made by George Bull's teaching and example, seems to have fixed Griffith Jones in a lifelong sense of mission: 'Dylai Gweinidogion dderbyn galwad ac awdurdod oddi wrth Grist i waith y Weinidogaeth' ('Ministers must receive a calling and authority from Christ for the work of the Ministry').[78] Ivor Bromham related what was probably the folk tradition of his call to the ministry:

> One day, as he knelt to pray in the corner of a field, he fell into a trance and saw the Lord Jesus, Who said to him, 'My boy, I want you to be a witness for Me in the world'.[79]

Any suggestion of a personal divine call to an individual, above the ordinary general impressions of his own circumstances and the words of the Bible, was a sore irritant to anti-enthusiastical ears. Griffith Jones's language regarding some sense of personal vocation, and that by a dream or vision, may be accepted at very least as the way that his thoughts were led in his careful study of Scripture, not necessarily as delusional imbalance. At least in his choice of words, however, in mentioning his sense of having a divine call, and therefore of authority, he may have caused justifiable fears that he was straying towards Quakerish mysticism. F. A. Cavenagh speculated: 'And it may well be believed that he saw some hallucination. We have evidence of his neurotic nature.'[80] Some of Jones's expressions derive from his vivid metaphoricism, such as when speaking of temptation as having the Devil's personal attention, which might give the impression of an assertion of special revelation.[81] Deists would particularly reject the averment of supernatural communications in the present world as superstition.[82] Conversely, in a largely oral, inventive peasant culture, allusions to a divine calling were prone to a folklore transformation into melodramatic hagiography, with added *obiter dicta*, beclouding the understanding of events by later generations.[83] John Evans was able to build accusations of fanatical prophetism on what were probably merely incautious allusions to his God-given vocation. Evans wrote:

> first acquainting him by the Way, that it was one of the everlasting Decrees of the Almighty, whereby he had disposed of every thing, from the Foundation of the World, that Mr *Griffith Jones* was to be a *chosen Vessel to bear his Name*, a *peculiar Instrument* for *rescuing many Souls*[84]

Evans's attacks are bitter and exaggerated, but are founded here somewhat on facts. Griffith Jones, as a believer in divine sovereignty, would indeed have thought of the mere accidental details of his life as part of a timeless, higher plan. The biblical doctrine of Providence itself posits everything, including ordinary mundanities, as serving to work together to God's glory and man's good.[85] But Griffith Jones's personal commentary may have merged into self-congratulation; such can be irritating and verging on pride. In the controversial passions excited by evangelistic 'revival', exultant words were sometimes willingly misconstrued and thrown back woundingly as lasting proof of enthusiasm. For example, the immature George Whitefield's running commentary on his successes – in print moreover – provided polemical darts for his exasperated detractors.[86] In 1738, the headstrong Howell Harris aired to Griffith Jones his pondering on publishing extracts from his diary. Jones advised against it, and was wise enough to avoid such puerile self-advertisement himself.[87] Generally during the expansion of evangelism, individual converts could also assert that they had personal revelations and calls, beyond the ordinary effects of preaching. These could overlap later in heady enthusiasm, as in the case of the flamboyant 'prophecies' of Mrs Sidney Griffiths, incubated by Howell Harris's charismaticism.[88]

GEORGE BULL'S OTHER PROPOSALS

Robert Nelson mentioned an incomplete pastoral letter containing advice, drafted by George Bull in 1709, but never sent to his clergy. In it, Bull urged ministers to foster family prayers:

> *The* First *Thing* ... to apply your selves with great Diligence, to establish the Practice of Family Devotion, in all Families of your respective Parishes ... *nothing helpeth more to keep up a Sense of Religion in the Minds of Men, than a serious, reverent and constant Performance of this necessary Duty*[89]

Griffith Jones was completely at one with this proposal. He constantly urged the need for family prayers in the homes of his people. The ancient practice was an element of 'heart religion', along with private prayer. It brought the doctrine and worship taught in church into the home, and hence the daily life of the people. Thus it spurred on personal faith, and an 'upright walk', and bound households together as Christian units. Bull's own suggestion accorded with the wish of the SPCK to promote family prayer. Mary Clement commented on the promotion of the practice: 'from its earliest days the SPCK had laid particular stress on the importance of family devotion'.[90] She went so far as to suppose that Bull's exhortation to his clergy derived 'more probably (from) the continual pressure of John Vaughan's earnest request for attention to the matter'.[91] It seems doubtful that the bishop needed any strong persuading for this. Such pressure on him proves, however, the strength of a consensus among the pious gentry, in west Wales at least, but not any reluctance on the part of the exhausted and invalid bishop to recommend family prayers. John Vaughan's agitation with the SPCK committee for publishing Bull's letter is evidence of a strongly independent-minded initiative from the gentry in reforming efforts.[92] It seems most important therefore, for understanding the effect of Griffith Jones's ministry, to consider the solid framework of common principle and activity that was already at work in 1705. Jones's successes ought not to be explained by assuming either that he was a complete innovator or an atavistic Puritan implant. Family devotions needed the impetus of a new wave of religious life to make them an accepted common feature of Welsh communities.[93] They became indeed a distinguishing feature of rural Wales, with a new direction under the methodistical revival. The practice was not new, but an element of the system of worship proposed at the Reformation as well as later. The Church of Scotland, for instance, even enacted official guidelines for family worship.[94] Family prayers also gained renewed popularity, for instance, in middle-class English Evangelical families in the nineteenth century. Family devotions became a distinguishing feature of piety amongst those attending Griffith Jones's preaching. John Elias (1774–1841), for instance, later became an example of what had become an instilled compulsion to express faith in this way, in a basic domestic setting.[95]

George Bull was at one also with the reforming aim of the SPCK. He approved of the Societies for the Reformation of Manners and other reforming endeavours.[96] His name does not appear much in relation to schools, for his time in Wales was short, very busy and dogged by sickness. In 1705, however, Bull became patron of a school at 'Llangadock'.[97] That this and other schools were needed to repair the religious and moral integrity of the land was unquestioned. So it is significant that Bull placed schooling high in his list:

> *The* Second *Thing that I shall recommend and earnestly exhort you to, as very useful towards promoting Religion in a wicked and degenerate Age, is* to endeavour the erecting Charity-Schools in your several Parishes; *wherein Children of the Poor may be taught to read and write, and to repeat our excellent Church-Catechism, and to understand the Principles of our Holy Religion, which are so necessary to their Eternal Salvation*[98]

Griffith Jones continued an active interest in education from his first appointments as a curate.[99] It is probable that he showed an early aptitude and interest in teaching, which blended naturally with his teaching from the pulpit. But Jones was not a pioneer in this. Others had been very active in promoting charity-schools. When rector of Siddington, Gloucestershire, George Bull became tutor to the son of a neighbouring family, Robert Nelson (1656–1715). Nelson remained his old schoolmaster's close admirer until Bull's death, and wrote his biography.[100] Nelson was a very active SPCK correspondent and a lifelong donor to charity-schools and parochial libraries.[101] As such, Nelson was much in touch with other members of the society, particularly supporting charity-school work in York, Beverley, Oxford, London and elsewhere.[102] His zeal and courage, much approved by Sir John Philipps, was demonstrated in going to Bath to urge better behaviour amongst its wealthy frequenters.[103] Robert Nelson was doubtless aware of the SPCK activist circle amongst the west Wales gentry, who were already supporting schools. Bishop Bull's recommendations about such teaching merely confirmed their convictions and efforts already in hand. Among the circle, Sir John was pre-eminent in wealth and political influence, and perhaps also excelled others in constant zeal and piety. Of the 157 charity-schools founded in Wales between 1699 and 1740, Sir John Philipps was patron of twenty-one.[104] Of the other leading gentlemen of the district mentioned by Mary Clement, John Vaughan of Derllys was patron of one school; the Revd Thomas Philipps of Laugharne founded, but did not finance, two schools; the Revd Arthur Laugharne founded three.

Bishop Bull proposed a further extension of learning:

> *A Third Thing that I shall recommend and earnestly exhort you to, as of singular Use towards promoting Christian Knowledge, is...* all Parents that are of Ability ... to supply each of their Children, before they marry, or are otherwise settled in the World, with a small Library, containing Books of practical Divinity, to the Value of three, four, or five Pounds ... And ... to enjoyn their Children, at the same ... to read them often and seriously, and to keep them with care and safety during their Lives, and then to leave them in the same good Condition to their Posterity; by which means the Knowledge of Religion, may be propagated from Age to Age in all future Generations.[105]

The founding of family libraries was something of a visionary leap. John Vaughan of Derllys had made exactly the same suggestion to Sir John Philipps in a letter of 28 May 1709:

> that all Parents through the Kingdom and especially those of estate and abilitie be excited to bestow on each of their children a small library, consisting of good practical books, such as the Society should have to the value of 3, 4 or 5 pounds[106]

John Vaughan's suggestion is too noticeably similar in wording to Bull's for both men to have arrived at it quite separately. Regarding the book 'presses', Vaughan added a further detail: 'fixed in cases with locks and keys, like for the Carmarthen Librarie'.[107] Vaughan's persistent way of promoting his ideas appears in the SPCK records. On 27 June 1709, four weeks after his letter, he wrote again to the society, glad to know that they liked his project. He added revealingly: 'That he had lately waited on the Bp of St. Davids about his Circular Letter, which he had promised should soon be drawn up.'[108] Bishop Bull's pastoral letter was composed, according to Nelson, 'Some time before his last Sickness, after he removed from Brecknock to Abermarless.'[109] It emerges that Vaughan's visit was barely three months before the ailing Bull was taken seriously ill for the last time – to die on 17 February 1709/10. It seems likely that the bishop was presented with the idea about 20 June 1709 by John Vaughan, with his usual forceful importunity. One assumes that it was not just exhaustion which persuaded Bull to agree; but Vaughan persistently presented new ideas to the committee. For instance, in November 1721, he informed them: 'That he had wrote to the Revd. Mr. Lewis to hasten the Translation of the Bp. of Lincoln's (Edmund Gibson) Family Devotion into Welsh.'[110] John Vaughan did not rest till the translation was made and printed, but about other projects, after long agitation, he was still unable to persuade the committee.[111] The ideal of easy access to good books naturally followed from the policy of Bray's parish libraries. Individual family libraries seem a big step forward, however, because they envisaged seeing the benefits enjoyed by the clergy and gentry extended to many ordinary families, and being only limited to those 'of ability' to pay the cost. Many poor folk could not afford a small library in a little bookcase, of course; but the ideal was of further equalizing, as widely as possible, the liberating opportunities obtained by reading. Moreover, this educative proposal is for 'children' not 'sons', striking the note of advance as being to both sexes equally. Grammar schools remained reserved for boys; but this equal approach was precisely that of Griffith Jones also, in all his educational work, except for the training given at Llanddowror to men as candidates for the ministry.[112] The social implications seem radical: opening a range of knowledge for poorer people of both sexes, beyond the modicum of culture acquired from their parsons' instruction. This equality of treatment is paralleled also in that both sexes were teachers, mentioned as 'masters' and 'mistresses', in charity-schools supported by the SPCK, and in Jones's Circulating Schools.[113]

Vaughan's plan of miniature home libraries in specially made bookcases seems too impracticable for Wales in 1709. Nevertheless, it does show the liberal vision present in the Welsh reforming circle, implying a movement towards a magnanimous principle of equality – even between ruling families and the monoglot peasantry. Griffith Jones does not seem to have gone as far himself as to call for little bookcases, but would presumably have approved the idea of permanent home libraries of Christian books. He was an author himself. The intention of passing on a cultural heritage in this way from one generation to another suggests a link also with the important principle of a common religious inheritance within the visible Church.[114] Many rustic houses in Wales and elsewhere came to contain copies of much-read and pondered works, like *Pilgrim's Progress*, which passed into a vernacular culture, and were handed down, well thumbed, even till the twentieth century.[115] Bull's and Vaughan's plan did not propose that the libraries should be free gifts to families, but that they should be bought, by 'Parents that are of Ability', and at the lowest possible price. George Bull's inclusion of his fourth proposal could equally have been included because of pressure upon him by local gentry. It followed a preceding suggestion, with concern that Welsh-speaking people should be thoroughly integrated into church life and teaching:

> *The* Fourth *Thing that I shall recommend to you is,* to give notice to all your Parishioners, that the Common-prayer Book in *Welch* is lately printed in a small Volume ... *These Common-prayer Books are much wanted by the People of my Diocese, and I am informed, that they will be universally purchased, especially since they will be sold for about Eighteen pence apiece.*[116]

In a Protestant theory of worship, all in church should not merely be present, but understand and participate in the liturgy. This demanded involvement of mind and heart. George Bull, doubtless encouraged by Vaughan, Sir John Philipps and other pious gentry, seems at one with Griffith Jones in seeing the importance of books in Welsh, to supplement the spoken word. Many English SPCK supporters were not convinced of the value of the language for literature, being at most 'tolerant'.[117] Bull's broad-minded vision, especially as an English newcomer, was laudable. Not only Prayer Books, but Bibles continued to be in demand as the SPCK policy in Wales produced more evident results, and especially, greater numbers of people with a new thirst for Christian knowledge. The society understood the need for books in Welsh, giving much of its support to translation and printing. The result was one of literary improvement in Wales. Mary Clement wrote: 'much of the best religious literature in the Welsh language was produced in the first part of the eighteenth century by the Society's keenest Welsh supporters'.[118] An important fact is that, for Welsh speakers, there were many books suitable to fill the proposed home libraries. Geraint Jenkins listed 231 printed in Welsh between 1660 and 1730, most of them with a religious content.[119] Griffith Jones combined education and literature inextricably in his ministry. He encouraged the production of books in Welsh, being the author of two, the translator of another and the editor of yet another, besides three books in English. Moreover in this, as always, Jones was not the innovator, but the ingenious facilitator of a clutch of interrelated projects.

NOTES

1 NLW, *Register Diocese of St Davids*, 1705–58, fol. 15.

2 NLW, *Reg. Diocese*, fol. 22.

3 Stuart Handley, 'Watson, Thomas (1637–1717)', *ODNB*.

4 On 18 November 1701, Sir John Philipps organized a petition of notables to the Archbishop of Canterbury requesting that he issue a 'Circular Letter to the Clergy of the Diocese ... to promote the Erection of Charity Schools ... [promoting] The Catechising of Youth and Family Devotions'. Mary Clement, *Correspondence and Minutes of the SPCK relating to Wales 1699–1740* (Cardiff, 1952), p. 250.

5 Mary Clement, *The SPCK and Wales 1699–1740* (London, 1954), p. 57.

6 Clement, *The SPCK and Wales*.

7 Thomas Nelson, *The Life of Dr George Bull, Late Lord Bishop of St. David's* (London, 1713), p. 417.

8 Clement, *The SPCK and Wales*.

9 Nelson, *The Life*, p. 407.

10 Mark Noble, *A biographical history of England, from the revolution to the end of George III's reign*, 3 vols (London, 1806), vol. 2, p. 93.

11 Robert D. Cornwall, 'Bull, George (1634–1710)', *ODNB*.

12 Nelson, *The Life*, p. 86.

13 Jacques Bénigne Bossuet was a court tutor and orator, author of an attack on solifidianism and Protestantism generally in *Histoire des variations des Églises protestantes* (1688).

14 Gilbert Burnet was bishop of Salisbury 1689–1715; Gilbert Burnet, *The History of His Own Time* (1724; London, 1875), p. 767.

15 Because of the unsettled times of the English Civil War, not through poor abilities.

16 John Fell was bishop of Oxford 1676–86.

17 Nelson, *The Life*, p. 426.

18 Roger Lee Brown, *A Social History of the Welsh Clergy circa 1662–1939* (Welshpool, 2017), part 1, vol. 1, p. 123.

19 Brown, *A Social History*, part 1, vol. 1.

20 *OED*, compact edn (Oxford, 1971), A–O, p. 1604: 'Literate ... In the Anglican Church, a person admitted to holy orders without having obtained a university degree.'

21 Between the late sixteenth century and mid-nineteenth, gentlemen often left university without a degree, with no imputation of failure. Sir John Philipps did not graduate at King's College, Cambridge. But non-graduates might miss the avenues of college patronage. Cf. Hugh Kearney, *Scholars and Gentlemen, Universities and Society in Pre-Industrial Britain 1500–1700* (London, 1970), p. 168.

22 Martin Evans, *An Early History of Queen Elizabeth Grammar School Carmarthen 1576–1800* (Carmarthen, 1978), p. 73.

23 Nelson, *The Life*, pp. 76–7.

24 CUL, SPCK, *Committee Minutes*, MS A33/1, Abs. 3773.

25 Anon., *A Sketch of the Life and Character of the Reverend and Pious Mr Griffith Jones, late Rector of Llanddowror in Carmarthenshire* (London, 1762), p. 4.

26 Griffith Jones, *The Platform of Christianity, being the General Head of the Protestant Religion, as Professed by the Church of England* (London, 1744), p. lxxiii.

27 Jones, *The Platform*, p. lxxii.

28 I.e. the doctrine of justification by faith, dealt with elsewhere in this book.

29 Jones was appointed curate at Laugharne in 1708.

30 CUL, SPCK, *Committee Minutes*, MS A33/1, Abs. 3309.

31 They enjoyed a harmonious collaboration until Sir John Philipps's death, 5 January 1736/7. Griffith Jones married Margaret Philipps, 11 February 1719/20.

32 Erasmus D. D. Saunders, *A View of the State of Religion in the Diocese of St David's About the Beginning of the 18th Century* (London, 1721), p. iv.

33 Nelson, *The Life*, pp. 417–18.

34 Nelson, *The Life*, p. 442.

35 Cardiff Central Library, Griffith Jones, Transcripts of Sermons, *Trysor o Ddiwinyddiaeth*, MSS 2.1103, p. 28.

36 Anon., *A Sketch*, p. 4.

37 Nelson, *The Life*, p. 442.

38 Clement, *Correspondence*, p. 330.

39 Clement, *Correspondence*, p. 331.

40 As a member of the House of Lords, he was present for the passing of the Act of Union in 1707.

41 Nelson, *The Life*, p. 71.

42 Published in George Bull, *A companion for the candidates of holy orders, or, The great importance and principle duties of the priestly office* (London, 1714).

43 Nelson, *The Life*, p. 419.

44 [1] Reading of the Prayers of the Church; [2] Preaching; [3] Catechizing; [4] Administering the Sacraments; [5] Visiting the sick.

45 Nelson, *The Life*, p. 55.

46 Cf. Jeremy Taylor's defence of the liturgy; Leslie Baker-Jones, *Jeremy Taylor (1613–1667)* (Felindre Llandysul, 2016), p. 148.

47 Nelson, *The Life*, p. 54.

48 Anon., *A Sketch*, p. 6.

49 Nelson, *The Life*, p. 419.

50 Anon., *A Sketch*, p. 6.

The Theology of Griffith Jones and Religious Thought

51 William Gibson, 'The British Sermon 1689–1901', in Keith A. Francis and William Gibson (eds), *The Oxford Handbook of the British Sermon 1689–1901* (Oxford, 2012), p. 3.

52 Kenneth Hylson-Smith, *High Churchmanship in the Church of England: From the Sixteenth Century to the Late Twentieth Century* (Edinburgh, 1993), pp. 19, 22.

53 George Bull, *The English Theological Works of George Bull D.D.* (Oxford, 1844), p. 190.

54 Nelson, *The Life*, pp. 419–20.

55 Bob Tennant, "The Sermons of the Eighteenth-Century Evangelicals', in Francis and Gibson (eds), *The Oxford Handbook*, p. 119.

56 The Revd Thomas Jones (1752–1845) was an evangelical rector of Great Creaton, Northamptonshire. L. E. Elliott-Binns, *The Early Evangelicals, a Religious and Social Study* (London, 1953), p. 176.

57 Nelson, *The Life*, p. 49.

58 Anon., *A Sketch*, p. 6.

59 F. A. Cavenagh, *The Life and Work of Griffith Jones of Llanddowror* (Cardiff, 1930), p. 16.

60 Bodleian Lib. John Dalton, Letter to SPCK, 25 February 1713. *Rawlinson MSS.*, C.743, f. 25.

61 Anon., *A Sketch*, pp. 6–7.

62 Griffith Jones was a pupil at Carmarthen Grammar School, 1700–8, i.e. aged 17 to 25. Because of his age, when joining the school, Jones probably had the position of a senior student, and worked as an usher there. Cf. Evans, *An Early History*.

63 Geraint H. Jenkins, *Literature, Religion and Society in Wales 1660–1730* (Cardiff, 1978), p. 23.

64 His sermon notes and the volumes of sermons transcribed do not contain more than outlines. Mention made of other Bible texts, certainly to be quoted in full, but no references to theological authors.

65 Cavenagh, *The Life and Work*, p. 7.

66 Nelson, *The Life*, p. 420.

67 Elliott-Binns, *The Early Evangelicals*, p. 106.

68 John Tillotson, 'A Persuasive to Frequent Communion', Sermon on 1 Cor. 11. 26–7, in *Collected Works*, ed. J. Darby (London, 1728).

69 Elliot-Binns, *The Early Evangelicals*, p. 106.

70 Elliott-Binns, *The Early Evangelicals*, p. 106.

71 Nelson, *The Life*, p. 62.

72 D. Ambrose Jones, *Griffith Jones Llanddowror* (Wrexham, 1923), p. 45.

73 Clement, *Correspondence*, p. 72.

74 Geraint H. Jenkins, 'Jones, Griffith (*bap.* 1684, *d.* 1761)', *ODNB*.

75 NLW, Griffith Jones, *Transcriptions* (1760), NLW, MS 24057B, p. 94.

76 Anon., *A Sketch*, pp. 7–8.

77 Jones used his visits to Bath to liaise yearly with the English supporters of his Circulating Schools. Cf. W. Moses Williams, 'The Friends of Griffith Jones', *Y Cymmrodor*, XLVI (1939), 45.

78 NLW, G. Jones, Sermon no. 23. Mat: 10:15. *Transcriptions* (1760), NLW, MS 24057B, p. 287.

79 Revd Ivor J. Bromham, 'Welsh Revivalists of the Eighteenth Century', *The Churchman*, 72/1 (1958).

80 Cavenagh, *The Life and Work*, p. 7.

81 Cavenagh, *The Life and Work*, p. 14.

82 Gerald Robertson Cragg, *From Puritanism to the Age of Reason* (Cambridge, 1950), p. 58.

83 Scottish Highland oral history shows such wrapping of historical memory in flowery anecdote. Cf. Alexander Mackenzie and Elizabeth Sutherland, *The Prophecies of the Brahan Seer* (London, 1977), pp. 13–15.

84 John Evans, *Some Account of the Welch Charity-Schools, and the Rise and Progress of Methodism in Wales* (London, 1752), p. 6.

85 *Epistle to the Romans*, ch. 8, v. 28.

86 George Whitefield, *Journals*, pub. separately 1738–41, unabridged edn (London, 1960).

87 Geraint Tudur, *Howell Harris, from Conversion to Separation 1735–1750* (Cardiff, 2000), p. 8.

88 Derec Llwyd Morgan, *Y Diwygiad Mawr* (Llandysul, 1999), pp. 58–9; Tudur, *Howell Harris*, pp. 225–8.

89 Nelson, *The Life*, pp. 442–3.

90 Clement, *The SPCK and Wales*, p. 57.

91 Clement, *The SPCK and Wales*, p. 57.

92 CUL, SPCK, *Committee Abstracts of Correspondence*, 2473, 2874.

93 'Dyletswydd deuluol', 'family duty', in colloquial Welsh.

94 *The Directory for Family-Worship*. Issued by the General Assembly of the Church of Scotland in 1647. Published together with *Westminster Confession of Faith* (London, 1646; Glasgow, 1994), pp. 417–22. J. H. S. Burleigh, *A Church History of Scotland* (London, 1960), p. 166.

95 Edward Morgan, *John Elias, Life and Letters* (Edinburgh, 1973), p. 11.

96 Clement, *The SPCK and Wales*, p. 51.

97 Presumably Llangadog, Carmarthenshire. Clement, *The SPCK and Wales*, p. 116.

98 Nelson, *The Life*, p. 445.

99 Griffith Jones was appointed curate and schoolmaster at Laugharne in 1708.

100 Alan Cook, 'Nelson, Robert (1656–1715)', *ODNB*.

101 Clement, *Correspondence*, p. 19 n.

102 M. G. Jones, *The Charity School Movement: A Study of Eighteenth Century Puritanism in Action* (Cambridge, 1938), p. 9.

103 Clement, *The SPCK and Wales*, pp. 51–2.

104 Clement, *The SPCK and Wales*, pp. 101–46.

105 Nelson, *The Life*, p. 448.

106 CUL, SPCK, *Committee Minutes*, MS A33/1, Abs. 1650; Clement, *Correspondence*, p. 21.

107 Clement, *Correspondence*.

108 Clement, *Correspondence*, p. 22. Abs. 1656.

109 Nelson, *The Life*, p. 441.

110 Clement, *Correspondence*, p. 113. Abs. 6840.

111 E.g. his project to publish Bull's circular letter posthumously.

112 Nelson, *The Life*, p. 441.

113 CUL, SPCK, *Committee Minutes*, MS A33/1, 11 June 1713.

114 P. A. Lillback, 'Covenant', in Sinclair B. Ferguson and David F. Wright (eds), *New Dictionary of Theology* (Leicester, 1988), p. 174.

115 David Bebbington, *Evangelicalism in Modern Britain* (London, 1989), p. 35.

116 Nelson, *The Life*, p. 449.

117 Clement, *The SPCK and Wales*, p. xvi.

118 Clement, *The SPCK and Wales*, p. xiv.

119 Jenkins, *Literature*, pp. 312–17.

Chapter 4

THE PRAYER BOOK ROOTS OF GRIFFITH JONES'S PREACHING

A DAMAGED POCKETBOOK AND THE TRADITION OF PREACHING[1]

The tendency in Griffith Jones's ministry towards seeking conversions as a priority is illustrated in an early document. A very damaged notebook, without its covers, kept in the National Library of Wales, contains notes apparently in Griffith Jones's own hand.[2] Undated, it presumably comes from the earlier part of his ministry, before the dated transcription of sermons was made. At the top of the first page, he wrote, in English, what seems to be a preamble or summary of the content of his preaching, and of the Welsh sermon, outlined in its main points thereafter:

Is. 55.7. Let ye wicked forsake his way, & ye unrighteous Man his Thoughts: & let him return unto ye L^d who'll 've Mercy upon him, & our God, for he'll abundantly pardon –[3]

The quotation from Isaiah is written in English, and not in Welsh like the sermon sketches that follow. This addition seems likely to have been placed there as self-admonition by Jones, of the necessary tenor of his biblical expositions that follow. In the biblical text, Isaiah had given a call to his contemporaries that Jones felt obliged to repeat to people in the same needy state.[4] The prophet addressed them as 'wicked' and 'unrighteous'. Such upbraiding seemed to Griffith Jones appropriate for many in his own world who came to hear him, including the rich.[5]

Griffith Jones gave the greatest part of his ministry to preaching.[6] The Prayer Book mentions no sermon in the Morning or Evening Prayer, and only after the Creed in that of Communion.[7] Despite the lack of mention, preaching had a central importance for leading clerics, and in the popular concept of public worship. The ideal had not quitted the Church of England in 1662, along with those banished for nonconformity. Francis Sheppard commented of Samuel Pepys's diary: 'he never mentions having received Holy Communion ... [typically alluding to] "A good sermon, a fine church, and a great company of handsome women."'[8] Edmund Gibson (1669–1748) recommended thorough preaching in his Primary Visitation of 1717:

> This was the Foundation of that standing Rule among our Ancestors, to proceed upon every Head, expressly, by way of *Doctrine* and *Use*; ... the Things [i.e. this practice] never must [be discontinued] if we resolve to preach to the true Edification of our Hearers.[9]

By preaching, a Protestant stamp remained explicitly upon Anglicanism. Lowther Clarke wrote: 'The sermon was the climax of the service in spite of the manuals of devotion ... [having preaching with] a new clarity and simplicity of style.'[10] The Church of England as known to Griffith Jones would seem stark and unfamiliar, at worship, to many churchgoers today. The trend of his flourishing ministry, and more so of those who followed his example, was towards change. There was a change from a simple 'reading of prayers', with little or no music, having usually, one sermon a week – but with additional 'lectures' sometimes, mostly in bigger towns. The Church was moving from Communion perhaps four times a year, towards the norm of weekly – or daily – Communion, and to prayer-meetings, and more singing, using the new hymnody. The evangelizing movement and 'Awakening' cultivated all these. Roger Lee Brown sets out the changes at length.[11] The bishops, and all thoughtful clerics, wished the laity to be informed concerning essential doctrine and stirred up to active piety, whilst it had become a settled social habit for people to expect to sit under preaching accepted as the core of public worship.[12] To wish to hear good sermons, and read many in print, had become the disposition of the English, and continued long after 1660. John Brewer wrote of reading habits in Griffith Jones's time and later:

> Members of all classes who were active Christians – which meant the overwhelming majority of the people – read the Bible, collections of sermons and pious tracts with a care and assiduity that they did not often give to novels.[13]

As an essential engine of spiritual life and worship, the sermon when preached, had even come to seem for some so to predominate as, in William Gibson's words, 'to blot out the rest of church services'.[14] Griffith Jones's commitment to intense exegetical instruction was an exercise of a practice widely considered a prime duty.[15]

Griffith Jones added in his notebook, below his opening biblical manifesto, in English, the words '2 Things in y^c Text'. This presumably refers to the two salient headings drawn from the text, in the expository sermon that follows. Thereafter the brief sermon outline in sub-headings follows in Welsh, to be delivered entirely in that language. Jones's approach was evidently to appeal to consciences.[16] The skeleton notes in Welsh begin with a rhetorical question and answer. They warn of the need to return to God, and avoid a mere pretence of faith and obedience:

> 1.   Pwy sy'n cael eu galw a'u rhybuddio i adel eu ffordd, a dychwelyd?
> Y Drygionus, sef y rhai sy'n myned ymlaen yn ddigywiledd mewn Pechod
> Tyngwyr Godinebwyr &c
> Yr Anwireddus, sy'n ymddangos yn afoesol; ond etto yn esgeuluso Dyleds.
> Cref. neu ynte yn rhagrithiol yn eu proffes. Inst. Ananias & Saphira.
>
> [1.   Who are being called and warned to leave their way, and return?

The Wicked, that is, those who carry on unashamedly in Sin Swearers Adulterers &c.

The Untruthful, who show themselves to be immoral; and yet more neglect Religious Duties or even are hypocritical in their profession of faith. Inst. Ananias & Sapphira].[17]

Griffith Jones could not take a light view of his parishioners' loose behaviour, and he was not alone in deploring a decline in public morals.[18] The SPCK, the parochial religious societies and the Societies for the Reformation of Manners were leaders in the response to what many observers saw as a widespread decline into ignorance of, and departure from, Christianity. Sir John Philipps reported: 'the State of Religion in some parts of Wales is very melancholy'.[19] Many were alarmed by the wave of defiance of Christian standards in public and private life, and ignorance of the faith in a Christian country.[20] Jones's sense of calling was unequivocal: he attempted to combat these things, calling back an erring people to true faith and godliness. His drastic terms express this endeavour.[21] The 'Drygionus' (wicked) or 'Annuwiol' (godless) occupy one side of Jones's paradigm of the biblical message of salvation. In his thinking, these run on heedless of their guilt, and of their need of repentance and new obedience. He never ceased from warning his flock with a strident moralism. The answer to the predicament was at the opposite pole: 'dychwelyd' (to turn back, return or be converted). The word became central in the vocabulary of those responding to the preaching of the new evangelists, 'dychweledigion', meaning those converted to a lively faith, and joining with the 'seiadau'.[22]

A MOTIVATION IN THE BOOK OF COMMON PRAYER

Above the quotation on this first page, Griffith Jones had also written 'Ez. 18.27'.[23] This verse is used as the first of the introductory sentences in the Prayer Book services of Morning and Evening Prayer. The rubric directed: 'At the beginning of Morning Prayer the Minister shall read with a loud voice one or more of these Sentences' (Evening Prayer, the same).[24] The theme of this verse recurs in all the other introductory sentences, and through the daily services. By its constant repetition, it would have been familiar and, presumably, have carried a familiar reminder for Jones and his congregations. It is the clue to understanding his sense of purpose. Twin axioms appear in Prayer Book teaching, and laid down Jones's spiritual map: of the need to turn away from sin; and of the certain access to new life, in reconciliation to God – life expressed in godly behaviour by those who obey the call. He continued untiringly to issue this twin exhortation, the divine promise taken as applying to whoever heard it.

The terms making up Griffith Jones's thought are important. 'Repentance' for sins of transgression and omission was, for him, inseparably part of a Christian's living faith. At Morning and Evening Prayer his parishioners were led repeatedly to acknowledge their sin and pray for grace to amend.[25] The liturgical rationale is clear in the sequence, after the opening sentences:

First: Exhortation to honest confession ('Dearly beloved brethren ... we should not dissemble nor cloke them ...'), followed by;

Second: General confession ('We have erred and strayed from thy ways like lost sheep'), with prayer for strength to amend ('And grant ... That we may hereafter live a godly, righteous and sober life'), and a reassurance of mercy;

Third: Absolution or remission of sins ('Almighty God ... who desireth not the death of a sinner ... he may turn from his wickedness and live'). The Welsh version of the latter reads: 'eithr yn hytrach ymchwelyd o hono oddi wrth ei anwiredd a byw'. The verb 'ymchwelyd' is somewhat archaic. Griffith Jones used its more modern form 'dychwelyd' (to return, come back, turn back or retreat). The idea is of return to one's proper state or, as of the Prodigal Son, coming back to a welcoming home: St Luke 15:18–19.[26] This 'coming back' could only consist in actual turning from sin. It is seen as inseparable from trust in the promise of mercy.

Another text noted at the top of the same page of Griffith Jones's pocketbook, next to the reference to Ezekiel 18:27, is 'Galar. 3.40' (for 'Galarnad', 'Lamentation'). The verse in the English Bible is: 'Let us search and try our ways, and turn again to the Lord'.[27] From the lighter tone of the ink, and its being Welsh, not English, this seems an added afterthought, reinforcing his view of his message. One suspects that his introspective mind would value the biblical dictum as a reassurance of his heavenly commission. He took up something of the prophetic impulse. The theme of self-examination, testing faith – including his own – recurred in Jones's sermons. Each of his three admonitory texts uses the same verb 'dychwelyd' in the Welsh Bible.[28] An insistent call to repentance from unbelief and besetting sins, with its warning of judgement, filled Jones's sermons. The compunctive warning of guilt was balanced by a consoling promise: of the sinner's faith being met by God's ample 'pardon'. He seems never to have tired of expounding the Bible in the light of this Gospel of warning and promise: 'Heb i'r drygionus adel ei ffordd ni's gall byth Hedd. â D. Es.5.7. ult Rhuf. 8.7:8' (Unless the wicked leave his way he can never have peace with God).[29] The two texts noted thereafter are Isaiah 5:7 and following, and Romans 8:7–8. These, presumably, would have been quoted in full to reinforce his exhortation, addressed to those present needing to be stirred up.[30] Without leaving his present course of careless formality and lax morals, a lukewarm church attender was warned: 'ni's gall byth gael hawl yn xt Eph. 2. 12. Eich bod y pryd hyny heb xt. 2 Cor. 5. 17' (never to be able to have a claim in Christ. Ephesians. 2.12. That you are then without Christ. 2nd Corinthians. 5.17).[31]

The hortatory preaching that Griffith Jones adopted was his crucial point of development from the High Church agenda. Emphasis on what was necessarily an 'individual' response to preaching became the core and engine of a new movement. But also crucially, the 'revival' in the Church was never intended to be a 'reformation'. The efforts of Griffith Jones and others were not a rebellion against the High Church ethos. Peter Robinson commented on the tradition into which Jones came: 'the Caroline Divines established a new, High-Church Protestant orthodoxy which remained dominant for over a century'.[32] The High Church was generally not reformist, but new conditions brought new choices and a gradual modification of ideas.[33] The High Church strove especially to maintain its own settled principles into the Hanoverian age, avoiding the peculiarly Puritan ideal at the root of Dissent. The High Churchmanship represented by Sir John Philipps and Griffith Jones had a clear social aim:

the redeeming of a lost generation through the religious societies and charity-schools. Griffith Jones and subsequent evangelizers set the Church, unwittingly at first, on a debatable new course.[34] Being moralistic, rather than reformist, both sides of the conventional-versus-evangelistic divide could not avoid the path of gradual self-transformation. Born of the High Church, the methodistical movement and its 'revival' experience followed a development in doctrine, worship and organization which rejected the goals of the Reformation.[35] Predominating 'conversionism', with its waves of new converts, set the course of the emerging Evangelicalism. Even Griffith Jones's sincere efforts contributed towards a dismantling of contemporary English Protestantism.[36]

Griffith Jones's preaching, practised within the Church of England, was delivered in its consecrated buildings (at least at first), to congregations assembled in due form for canonical worship. It sprang from his commitment to the principles and ethos of a national establishment: including its Erastian episcopalianism. His sermons addressed worshippers who were legally already considered as belonging within the body. The concept of such 'membership' for Griffith Jones was not that of post-Enlightenment voluntarism.[37] For him, therefore, the Church was not a gathering of autonomous individuals, within a fluid, agnostic commonwealth. He saw his congregations' participation in the Church's rites as equally a statutory and a spiritual obligation. Worshippers were deemed to have their place through incorporation into the one 'visible', 'Catholick' Church, as present among English subjects legally constituted for worship. Richard Hooker wrote:

> There is not any man of the Church of England, but the same man is a member of the commonwealth, nor a member of the commonwealth which is not also a member of the Church of England.[38]

This is a view of 'membership', compatible with the Prayer Book, and accepted by Jones. Thus Jones eschewed the individualism implied in some sectaries' belief in separatist, 'gathered churches' consisting only of members purportedly identified as true believers.[39] Of the spirit of

The Theology of Griffith Jones and Religious Thought

independent opinion and worship, prominent after 1644, J. R. Tanner wrote:

> Its principle ... deriving from the earlier Brownists and Barrowists, was the autonomy of each separate congregation, and its independence of bishops, or presbyteries, or any other external authority.[40]

The tendency to gathered independency was yet to be a common component of what became Evangelicalism. Unavoidably, the calling out, and nurturing, by the evangelistic preachers – prominent among them Griffith Jones – of a distinct class of believers would contribute to the trend.[41]

The place of children in the scheme of 'membership' especially made plain Griffith Jones's conservative, Prayer Book approach. Infants were to be baptized 'into the number of Christ's Church',[42] thus being made 'members' in this sense, professing 'my Baptism, wherein I was made a member of Christ'.[43] This concept of inclusion in a national corporation was expressed through biblical texts which compare the whole Church to a body, with each worshipper as a component organ, or 'member'.[44] The *Form of Prayers* of the English congregation in Geneva contains a reference to this membership: 'And for that we be all members of the mystical body of Christ Jesus, we make our requests unto thee, O heavenly Father.'[45] Belonging to the Church as 'members' contrasted for Griffith Jones with another, dire membership. A sermon heading refers to being 'Yn aelodau o Deyrnas y Tywyllwch, ac yn Eiddo Satan: yn awr mae ganddt. gymundeb a holl Sts. D' (Members of the Kingdom of Darkness, and Property of Satan: now they have fellowship with all the Saints of God).[46] Jones showed a general agreement with the ecclesiology of the Reformed churches, apparently with no reserve about the constitution of Anglicanism. The English Reformation had given statutory force to all subjects' constituting a Christian Establishment, within a Christian commonwealth.[47] However, for the body of opinion represented by the SPCK, this legal state did not end the question. To Griffith Jones's mind, bare acquiescence in doctrine, or respectability in attending worship, by those considered part of the Church by baptism, were not sufficient.

His trenchant policy was evangelism within the 'visible' body.[48] For him and others,[49] despite automatic 'membership' in a national Church, there remained room for affirming an emphatic biblical call for a 'religion of the heart', a piety to be expressed in moral rectitude.[50] In the event, however, the calling together of a body of converts to a renewed zeal was unavoidably to put a strain upon the sense of harmonious solidarity of worshippers in the Church. Archbishop John Tillotson (1630–94) expressed caution regarding the call for such committed religiosity. He mistrusted the quest for introspective certainty of peace with God, calling for: 'the ancient virtue of the nation ... that solid and substantial ... plain and unaffected piety (free from the extremes both of superstition and enthusiasm), which flourished in the age of our immediate forefathers'.[51] Wholehearted zeal seemed dangerous to him, but Griffith Jones was fervent about obtaining spiritual insight. He recommended 'true godliness', which necessarily implied a will to augment its beginnings with the whole gamut of attendance on catechizing and worship, daily self-examination, family prayers and reiterated faith evidenced by purified living.[52] For Jones, consistency in his ministry entailed impressing on all a duty to search their own consciences and to respond to the divine revelation. The demand for such scrutiny had also in view a resulting confidence through personal assurance of divine forgiveness.[53] In his private memorandum book, Sir John Philipps commented to the same effect:

> Regenerate persons, when about to receive [Holy Communion] should examine themselves touching their degrees of hope and love in believing, and of ye degrees of their joy in ye holy ghost, rather than of their bare faith wch is to be sopos'd they have.[54]

ADHERENCE TO THE PRAYER BOOK

Griffith Jones persistently adhered to Prayer Book forms, but he was aware of a lulling repetitiousness often attending its use. He wrote in a letter of 16 August 1739: 'we have so many mere formalists, acquiescing in the use of some religious forms and ordinances only, without pressing forward to religion itself'.[55] He directed his ministrations, rather, as an engine against spiritual inertia. The liturgy was for him, not a disincentive to self-examining piety, but a means for cultivating the same stirring experience popularized in some Puritan teaching. At variance with the misgivings of some Dissenters over the Prayer Book, Griffith Jones believed that it was, with ancillary catechesis, an aid to firm faith, as well as a remedy against schismatical vagaries:

> From hence also it comes to pass, that some unhappily launch out into strange opinions, and querulous notions, contrary to the essentials of the Christian faith, or at least destructive of Christian and brotherly love and union[56]

Jones's wish seems to have been for consolidation, rather than radical reform. The text of Isaiah 55:7 quoted in full, in English, in Griffith Jones's private notebook seems clearly to bear witness to an uncomplicated loyalty to the Prayer Book doctrine and form of worship. His very work of evangelism was bedded in the Anglican liturgy. One detects no hint of his wishing to depart from the Church's settled forms. His work was not intended to be one of 'reformation', in the Puritan sense of removing, according to New Testament patterns, a residue of accumulated practices.[57] His was the ideal of spiritual and moral renewal expressed by Josiah Woodward, writing of the religious societies, 'that the general odium, and the threatening dangers of informing against Vice and Profaneness are almost extinguished, and the Blessed Work of Reformation set into such an excellent and successful method'.[58] For Jones, 'reformation' meant moral restoration in line with the Bible and the Prayer Book. This fact seems to contradict the opinion: 'Griffith Jones was a Reformed and Puritan theologian and in no way a High Church divine'.[59] There is no need to posit some putative external influence affecting Griffith Jones's High Church outlook. He could, of course, scarcely fail to be aware of intellectual developments in England and Wales and beyond, though these are not needed as an explanation of his practice. In 1710, he was a 27-year-old curate and schoolmaster at Laugharne, soon to be inducted as rector of Llandeilo Abercywyn. The Sacheverell controversy, related in pamphlets, his trial and mob riots could not have been unnoticed by Jones. Serious riots took place in Wrexham, bringing Wales into the orbit of the polemic. Griffith Jones held steadily to strengthening the Church: a 'High Flier' who avoided inflammatory language or mob rule.[60] His convictions about the best way forward for the Church and society were not original or unique; rather they were held by many other serious churchmen, notably supporters of the SPCK. Letters to the society had long recorded many evidences of the same zeal, for example: 'Mr. Arnold Bowen of Pembrokeshire, Nov. 29 '99 ... Saith the Clergy are zealous to promote Reformation and intend to unite very speedily'.[61] Jones was fervent, and undeviating in his Prayer Book outlook to the end of his life. Geraint Jenkins wrote:

> Griffith Jones never wearied of affirming his love and devotion for the Church of England and he used his best endeavours to try to persuade the young evangelists to submit to the organization and discipline of the established Church.[62]

In a letter dated 30 March 1738, on the subject of his schools and catechizing, he wrote of adults keenly joining the children in his Catechism classes, on Saturdays before a Communion Sunday, 'particularly such as desired to partake of that blessed Ordinance'.[63] Such reverential language used of the Sacraments ought not to surprise one in Griffith Jones. The 'High' respect for the ordinances, and especially for the monthly Communion days, was not at variance with the popular appeal in his preaching. He continued, in the same letter, by adding that in the accompanying catechesis he inculcated a 'system of divinity ... and discoursed ... in an easy, familiar, and very serious way ... explaining it clearly to their understanding, and strongly applying to their consciences'.[64] Here one recognizes in Griffith Jones the adept schoolmaster combined seamlessly with the clergyman.

The salient doctrine of the Prayer Book, in its liturgical setting, and with its biblical, admonitory ethos and magisterial finality in presenting the Catholic faith, itself can account for the provenance of his principles. D. E. W. Harrison alleged a lack of theological consistency in the Prayer Book: 'The Prayer Book, then, is neither Lutheran not Calvinist ... the Prayer Book and the Articles do not precisely fit.'[65] Harrison's analysis, however, is partly misleading. The tenor of the appointed services, especially the daily prayers, has general consistency. The Prayer Book's limited doctrinal range is out of harmony with neither the earlier nor the latter stages of Reformation thought. The dominating tone of the prefatory sentences is, moreover, carried into the General Confession and Absolution.[66] It is also expressed in the Prayer for Clergy and People, the penultimate prayer after the Litany, and several of the Sunday Collects. Griffith Jones's thinking seems fully in keeping with the Prayer Book view of renewal to repentance. His notes contain: 'Q. Pa lûn y mae'r rhai drygionus yn cael dychweliad o'u ffordd ddrwg? ... 2. Trwy fod goleuni ysb.l yn llewyrchu yn eu cal. tywyll' (Q. In what manner are the wicked brought back from their wicked way? ... 2. By spiritual light illuminating their dark hearts).[67] The same note of urgent penitence occurs in the Collect for Ash-Wednesday:

> [God who] ... dost forgive the sins of all them that are penitent; Create and make in us new and contrite hearts, that we worthily lamenting our sins, and acknowledging our wretchedness, may obtain of thee, the God of all mercy, perfect remission and forgiveness[68]

The teaching of radical spiritual renewal was reiterated in Jones's preaching, alluding to prevailing 'wretchedness':

> 3 – yn aelodau o Deyrnas y Tywyllwch, ac yn eiddo Satan; ond yn awr mae gandd.t gymundeb a holl sts.(?) D. Act. 26.18.
> 4 – blant Dig.t ond yn awr yn blant i D. ac mewn heddwch ag ef. Gal. 4.4,5,7[69]

> [3 – members of the Kingdom of Darkness, and belonging to Satan; but now they have fellowship with all the saints of God. Acts 26.18
> 4 – children of wrath but now children of God and at peace with him. Galatians 4.4,5,7]

The same idea of transition was repeated in another Collect: 'ministers ... turning the hearts of the disobedient to the wisdom of the just ... at thy second coming to judge the world we may be found an acceptable people in thy sight'.[70] The Prayer Book's appointed Venite, Magnificat, Cantate Domino and Deus Misereatur also particularly include an amplification of the same twin themes of penitent return to God and gracious forgiveness evinced by new obedience (also with the accompanying stress on the reverence due to God), for instance:

> Today if ye will hear his voice, harden not your hearts: as in the day of provocation, and as in the day of temptation in the wilderness... It is a people that do err in their hearts, for they have not known my ways.[71]

This call to responsive faith is followed by the prospect of mercy. Griffith Jones sought to lead his hearers to an appreciation of the Gospel as a personal offer: one issuing from God, and confirmed in a personal attachment by faith in Him. He wrote of the means of bringing this about:

> Trwy fod Athr. Efeng. xt yn eu hargyhoeddu o'u pechod.
> Mae ysb. D. a'i Ras. yn gweithio yndd.t Ddymuniad hiraethlon a'rol xt ac am gael hawl yn y Cyf.d Gras. Jer. 50.4,5.[72]

> [By the doctrine of the Gospel of Christ convicting them of their sin.
> The spirit of God and his grace works in them a longing desire after Christ and to obtain a right in the Covenant of Grace.]

The Cantate Domino presents the same gateway to a hope of mercy from God: 'The Lord declared his salvation ... He hath remembered his mercy and truth ... and all the ends of the world have seen the salvation of our God.'[73] And 'God be merciful unto us, and bless us: and shew us the light of his countenance, and be merciful unto us'.[74] Griffith Jones preached from a piety cultivated by these themes, always with a surprising freshness and vigour, with intense seriousness, but, it seems, no sense of humour. It has been recognized that he and younger clergy that followed his example, especially William Williams Pantycelyn and Daniel Rowland, laboured in the spiritual interest of the Church of England. John Morgan-Guy wrote:

'Their fundamental desire was to breathe new life into old traditions and an existing institution.'[75]

A LIMITED SCOPE OF PREACHING

Griffith Jones's scope in preaching was 'limited', in the sense of avoiding topics that he considered distracting, unprofitable, divisive or too abstruse. But that is not to say that his matter was simplistic, nor did it avoid leading even his rustic hearers into theological loci demanding intellectual effort. He kept close to what he deemed to be matters of life and death, wisely dismissing finer, debatable points which might breed controversy: 'Empty speculations, high and lofty or quaint phrases, scholastical or controversial divinity above the reach of ordinary capacities that they can't be the better nor the wiser for it.'[76] In this Jones was not out of keeping with the approach taken by other preachers. Even Henry Stebbing (1687–1763), who defended, with abrasive tenacity, High Church Anglican orthodoxy against Nonconformity, Methodism, Deism and 'freethinking', stated his motive in choosing from his sermons those fit for printing: 'the Author has chosen those Sermons only which point out and enforce the duties of a Christian. Contested and abstruse points of divinity [were to be omitted]'.[77] The Prayer Book's aim in worship appears to be consonant with the impulse of Griffith Jones's preaching, which was always delivered with the 'issues of life', in mind. The famines and epidemics during his early ministry could not but weigh upon his mind for this added reason. Bad harvests wore down the people in 1708 to 1711, and 1727 and 1728.[78] Malnutrition fostered various diseases, and shortened lives. Smallpox flared up from time to time; and Griffith Jones commented on the suddenness of a kind of fever striking down many of the poor with little warning.[79] He spoke pointedly in the pulpit: 'Mae'n Ams. ini a phawb ddeffroi, pan fo'nt mor agos at Iecht.th neu Ddamnedig. th ag ŷm ni oll heddyw' (It is time for us and all to awake, when they should be so near to Salvation or Damnation as we all are today).[80] Here, his sense of urgency is such that he includes himself: 'ini', 'for us'. Jones's apprehension of the shortness of the present life and its opportunities was heightened perhaps by his hypochondria. His absolutist presentation of the call to faith also strikingly attunes with the disputatious posture of the Quicunque Vult:

> Whosoever will be saved: before all things it is necessary that he hold the Catholick Faith. Which faith except every one do keep whole and undefiled: without doubt he shall perish everlastingly.[81]

Griffith Jones appears thus to have been able to exercise his evangelistic ministry in happy conformity with the structure and tenor of the Prayer Book. He was a dedicated conformist, recoiling from any apparent deviation from the appointed path. Upon the authority derived from Scripture and the Prayer Book, Jones developed his undeviating policy of evangelism. Notwithstanding this, the minds of other Anglicans were not led in the same direction, though nurtured by the same liturgy. He was unlike some leading churchmen who demurred especially at the dogmatic radicalism of the Athanasian Creed. Archbishop John Tillotson, writing to Gilbert Burnet, was frankly disparaging of this signal adjunct of Anglican orthodoxy: 'I wish we were well rid of it'.[82]

It was in these terms, preaching to the 'mixed multitudes' attending the services, that Griffith Jones sought to call worshippers to heart-committed faith. In a letter of 16 August 1739, he wrote:

> For it is as true of nominal or degenerate Christians now, as of the heathens of old, that 'having their understanding darkened, they are alienated from the love of God, through the ignorance that is in them, because of the blindness of their hearts ...'[83]

Thus his opinion of the probable lack of active, transforming faith in 'prodigious numbers' of his countrymen was pessimistic and severe. He feared that much of the teaching that people heard in sermons or elsewhere – even in his own preaching – failed to reach below the surface to revive conscience, will and memory.[84] Self-deception might account for many light professions of commitment to the Catholic faith, which some blandly accepted. Jones's uncompromising desire for sincere spiritual convictions echoed rather the urgency of the Collect:

> Mortify and kill all the vices in us, and so strengthen us by thy grace, that by the innocency of our lives, and constancy of our faith even unto death, we may glorify thy holy Name ...[85]

Griffith Jones developed his ministry by using every lawful means to impress minds and wills: catechesis, preaching, religious societies, publishing and pastoral visits to people's homes. He followed the ideal advocated by Bishop Bull: 'Let us study hard, and read much, and pray often, and preach in season and out of season, and catechize the youth.'[86] Jones was not satisfied unless there should be credible evidence of real, repentant, obedient faith. His ambition was for a renewal and awakening from what often appeared dead formalism. He felt strongly the responsibility of clergy to preach awakening:

> Mae'n Ams. Inni ddeffroi, pan fo waith mawr o'n blaen, a pherygl mawr o'n blaen o fod yn esgeulus ynddo. Io, 9.4 rhaid imi weithio & Neh. 3.6
> – pan fo gweinidogion xt yn galw arnom. 2 Cor. 5.
> – pan fo Satan a'i offerynau yn ddeffrous i'n niweidio.
> Ped. byddwch sobr. &[87]

> [It is time for us to wake up, when there should be a great work before us, and a great danger before us of being careless in it. John 9.4 I must work & Nehemiah 3.6
> – when the ministers of Christ call upon us. 2 Corinthians 5.
> – when Satan and his agents are alert to harm us.
> [1st] Peter. [1.13] be sober. &]

Another Collect touched on the same urgency:

> O Lord, raise up ... thy power, and come among us, and with great might succour us; that whereas, through our sins and wickedness, we are sore let and hindered in running the race that is set before us ...[88]

Griffith Jones's opinion of the spiritual understanding of bands of church-attenders was gloomy. He wrote:

> how little it is that prodigious numbers know of the essential doctrines and necessary duties of religion ... having hardly any better account to give of God and his perfections, of Christ and his gospel, of the terms of his salvation, or of their own spiritual state ... than if they had not been born in a Christian country.[89]

It was these 'essential doctrines' and 'necessary duties' that Jones found prominent in the Bible and Prayer Book. He took them as clear-cut priorities for the content of his preaching. He had no time for digressing into broader theological exploration. In this limited conspectus, he was at one with his friend, Sir John Philipps. Sir John reminded himself of the need to stick to the basic points of revelation, for salvation, and not to speculate:

> We have among us a Set of men so foolish & insolent as to unfold ye mysteries of Religion, when, alas! they are at a loss to explain the mechanism of a Mite ... We are poor, weak, shallow Creatures, and what Impudence is it for us to pretend to fathom the depths of Eternity.[90]

PRAYER BOOK CONVERSIONS AND THE DANGER OF ENTHUSIASM

The search for the steady piety necessary to counteract widespread apathy became touched by the mysticism of Continental Halle and Moravian Pietism. Sir John Philipps and other SPCK supporters were particularly impressed by examples of fervent zeal and dedication, and by what they learnt from Continental visitors and correspondence.[91] Influential clerics such as John Wesley or Benjamin Ingham (1712–72) also came to be affected. Besides the influence of Pietism, there were the proclivities of the growing circle of itinerants, including confessedly Arminian preachers, which centred on indiscriminately seeking to procure conversions. The trends, some of which were obviously disruptive of harmony in the Church, prompted caution in Griffith Jones. He seems to have deemed it safer to avoid disagreements – on subjects like millennialism, or the extent of the Atonement – by keeping to the Prayer Book's and Homilies' deliberately limited doctrinal field.[92] Sermons in the books of his sermon transcripts mostly expound the New Testament. Though he did not neglect the Old Testament, Griffith Jones's preaching approached the somewhat simplistic Christocentrism of much later Evangelicalism.[93] His combination of close analysis and aptness of expression produced remarkable effects from his preaching, within a comparatively limited theological range. At length perhaps, such 'narrowing' helped to foster the assumption amongst the new wave of preachers, including uneducated lay 'exhorters', that Gospel preaching consisted intrinsically in evoking instant and climactic changes in the hearers: that is, 'crisis-conversionism', and ideally *en masse* as 'revival'.[94] Amongst his hearers, for individuals, for families, or more widely, Griffith Jones desired above all that their faith might 'live'.[95] For him as a High Churchman, the theme of 'new life', in the sense of renewal from disbelief, lukewarmness, or immorality, to refreshed understanding, zeal, hope and trust, was not foreign to his mind. Rather, it was a prime motive in Jones's efforts. His advocacy of reinvigorated Anglican piety expressed the spirit of the General Thanksgiving:

> And we beseech thee, give us that due sense of all thy mercies, that our hearts may be unfeignedly thankful, and that we shew forth thy praise, not only with our lips, but in our lives; by giving up ourselves to thy service[96]

In keeping with this, Griffith Jones was led to praise Bishop Nicholas Clagett (1685/6–1746) for supporting catechesis.[97] He admired: 'his Lordship's zeal to revive the now much impaired Christian religion among us'.[98] Doubtless, Jones's evangelism envisaged, not inconsistently, numerous conversions, in 'reviving' of the people within the national Church. The Prayer Book gave him encouragement to ask for it, by the words of another Collect, which, if taken seriously, could promote what might look to some dangerously like enthusiasm: 'Grant that we being regenerate, and made thy children by adoption and grace, may daily be renewed by thy Holy Spirit.'[99] His labour to inculcate the basic needs of spiritual life seems to have replicated the urgency of the Collect: 'Graft in our hearts the love of thy Name, increase in us true religion, nourish us with all goodness, and of thy great mercy keep us in the same.'[100] Griffith Jones did not profess to wield the hypothetical range of 'evangelising techniques' for producing conversions alleged by Geraint Jenkins.[101] Furthermore, he struggled to keep other, younger preachers, like Howel Harris, within the conventional bounds of ecclesiastical decency. 'Reviving' could indeed, in the heightened atmosphere of successful evangelism, become infected by embarrassing enthusiasm: ungoverned emotion, fanciful triumphalism and carelessness about sober correctness.[102] Jones felt constrained to be cautious about his links with some Methodist itinerants, though he kept as close to them as caution allowed. He was careful never to mention the word 'Methodism' in letters to the SPCK.[103]

Throughout his notebook, Griffith Jones's sermon sketches followed a catechetical pattern. Each sermon began by a brief question presenting the issue (the abbreviated words given below in full). Thereafter, he divided the answer under sub-headings. This echoed his habitual practice in catechizing. To ask a question in order to arrest the hearer's attention, and fix precisely the topic, is an obvious rhetorical device. He would come straight to the point, for instance: 'Q. Pa Anogaeth, mae Duw yn roi i'r drygionus i adel eu ffordd?' (Q. What Persuasion does God give to the wicked to leave their way?)[104] The answer immediately follows: 'Mae'n addo, y cânt Drugaredd i faddeu eu pechodau. Exod. 34.6–7. Ioan 10.3–8' (He promises they will get Mercy for the pardon of their sins). The verses from Exodus and St John's Gospel, noted lower on the page, would almost certainly have been quoted, adding weight: 'the Lord God, merciful and gracious, longsuffering and abundant in goodness and truth ... forgiving iniquity and transgression and sin'; and 'then said Jesus unto them again, Verily, verily I say unto you, I am the door of the sheep'.

The next paragraph reiterates this reassurance to the repentant: 'Ac y cânt eu harbed rhag y gosb ddyledus am Bechod. Mal. 3. arbedaf hwynt fel &' (And they will be spared from the due punishment for sin.

Malachi 3.17 'I will spare them as a man spareth his own son'). Jones drove home the point by defining the reciprocal doctrine: 'Athrawiaeth 1. Heb Ddychweliad, ni's gellir disgwyl am Drugaredd Duw. Is. 45.22. Act. 3.19. Luc. 3.3 Io. 3.3' (Doctrine 1. Without Turning one cannot expect God's Mercy. Isaiah 45.22, Acts 3.19, Luke 3.3, Gospel of John 3.3). And added:

> Fod Duw o'I Drugaredd yn Nghrist, yn galw pechaduriaid i ddychwelyd: ac yn addo Trugaredd i'r rhai a ddychwelant yn wirioneddol oddi wrth eu ffordd ddrwg. Is. 1.18.

> [That God of his Mercy in Christ calls sinners to return: and promises Mercy to those who truly turn back from their wicked way. Isaiah 1.18 ('Come now, and let us reason together, saith the Lord: though your sins be as scarlet, they shall be as white as snow')]

In Catechism form, another question followed: 'Beth yw gwir Ddychweliad?' (What is true turning back?) The corresponding answer, the second limb of the homiletic syllogism, followed containing Griffith Jones's habitual compulsive summons to repentant faith:

> Ymwrthod yn gwbl a ffordd Pech. fel <u>Ephraim</u>. Hos. 14.8. Troi at Duw a'n holl Gal. Inst. Mab <u>afradlon</u>' (To reject completely the way of Sin like <u>Ephraim</u>. Hosea 14.8 Turn towards God with one's whole heart. Inst. <u>Prodigal</u> son).

This was his foundational formula. In it there is recognizably what became the distinctive thrust of Evangelicalism: a call to 'return' to God with a new purpose of faith and of obedience to his commandments.[105]

As already mentioned, Griffith Jones co-ordinated his parish preaching ministry with that of working through the Church Catechism. This was especially designed for the youth, but their elders often came to listen.[106] Jones was an experienced educator. Education and evangelism seem to have been interwoven in his career from the first. As a newly ordained deacon, he had been recruited by Thomas Philipps as curate and master for the school at Laugharne, where teaching the Catechism would be part of his duties.[107] Though Jones pursued catechesis with unusual diligence, others also followed the practice. The Catechism was warmly recommended on all hands, by prelates and especially by the SPCK, and was promoted as part of the renewing work of the religious societies.[108] Griffith Jones repeatedly affirmed his opinion that catechizing was needed to drive home the lessons of the pulpit: 'Serious men in the ministry have experienced, and complained much of it, that without catechising ... preaching is in a manner lost and thrown away.'[109] His method of expository, systematic analysis in preaching probably gained conviction and structure from his devotion to catechizing. The notebook outlines contain this method throughout. But it is important to remember that he was not original in this; other conscientious and successful clergymen used it. William Gibson wrote: 'Sermons had a clear catechetical purpose, and were widely used in Anglicanism to prepare people for confirmation.'[110] In the sermons transcribed as *Trysor o Ddifinyddiaeth* ('A Treasure of Divinity'), Griffith Jones habitually used question-and-answer. In some, the actual questions were lacking, though the points followed in a logical order. He preached a sermon at Llanllwch on 11 April 1736, on the parable of the royal wedding.[111] In a methodical exposition, he laid out first the main purpose of the parable, with its relation to the Gospel in general:

> Diben mawr yr Efengyl dragwyddol a'r pregethiad o honi yw, dangos i bechaduriaid, nid yn unig eu trueni eu hunain, ond hefyd y wledd ryfeddol o freintiau nefol ag y mae Duw yng Nghrist yn ddarparu ... gan eu gwahodd i ddyfod i gyfammod ag ef ...[112]

> [The great purpose of the everlasting Gospel and of preaching it, is to show sinners, not only their own wretchedness, but also the wonderful feast of heavenly benefits that God is preparing in Christ ... by inviting them to come into covenant with him ...]

The Theology of Griffith Jones and Religious Thought

This introductory paragraph was followed by a numbered list of points in the parable as analysed in order, some couched catechetically as questions:

'Rhannau'r testyn. 1. Y brenhin yn dyfod i weled y gwahoddedigion ...'
[Dividing the text. 1. The king coming to see the guests ...]
3. Beth oedd yn eisiau ar y dyn hwn; sef y wisg brïodas ...
[3. What was needed by this man; namely the wedding garment ...][113]
4. Beth yw atteb y dyn hwnnw drosto ei hun?[114]
[4. What is the man's answer for himself?][115]

After the introductory analysis, the sermon followed with Jones's usual exhaustive dissection into questions, each followed by its answer, with pointed personal application to the hearers and their state:

I. Q: Pa'm y dylai dynion ddyfod pan eu galwer i gyfammod prïodas â'r Arglwydd Jesu?
A: 1. Oblegid cymmaint yw eu trueni tra bônt hwy allan o'r cyfammod hwnnw ...[116]

[1 Q: Why ought men to come when they are called to a wedding covenant with the Lord Jesus?
A: 1. Because their miseries are so many as long as they should remain out of that covenant ...]

Griffith Jones distinguished himself by the simplicity of the basic plan of his preaching.[117] The fact that many were drawn to hear him, and returned often and willingly, attests the powerful attraction of his message. John Morgan-Guy referred to the ideal of simple and comprehensible preaching held by Bishop Bull, who made a seminal impression on Griffith Jones: 'intelligibility was of paramount importance for those occupying parochial pulpits. George Bull ... himself a theologian of international stature, nevertheless intensely disliked "empty and frothy and trifling sermons".[118] The overall emphasis seems clear: that of calling his hearers to a repentance which would be sincere and lasting; that of 'heart religion', rather than bare respectable formality.[119] The fact that this call was made indiscriminatingly, to church-members as well as outsiders, distinguishes Griffith Jones's approach. For him, mere acquiescent church-membership was not enough; the Church itself must be viewed as a due field for evangelism. He vehemently denounced clergy who complacently ignored the low state of piety.[120] Jones held to a visible, inclusive, established Church, but also felt that fervent piety was far from being incompatible with such an institution. This view, however, and his attempt to work within it, clashed with what many came to think proper, in view of the divisive effect of numerous conversions amongst those already confirmed participants in the Church's worship.[121] Griffith Jones's aim in preaching cannot be convicted of departing from the Prayer Book. Though the liturgy was composed with something of an intentional range of interpretability, the Prayer Book's theological and moral themes generally provided the substance of Griffith Jones's sermons. His exhortations expressed no more than the ideals of, for instance, the Collect for all Conditions of men, praying that God would make known:

> thy saving health unto all nations[122] ... we pray for the good estate of the Catholick Church; ... guided and governed by thy good spirit, that all who profess and call themselves Christians may be led into the way of truth, and hold the faith in unity of spirit.[123]

The invidious contrariness that arose from Griffith Jones's fulfilment of the Anglican ministry was not, at root, of his making.

Griffith Jones gave little sign in his writings of being an adventurous thinker. He seems to have clung to early convictions throughout his career, preaching along lines marked out in the established Church. The impressions gained from his upbringing and, in some measure, the ideals recommended by figures of authority, like his bishop, George Bull, were a compass-bearing that he seems never to have felt it necessary to change.[124] His message was absolute in its summons to turn from sin, but also in its reassurance to those who respond in faith and repentance:

111

4. Heb i'r drygionus adel eu ffordd, ni's gall byth gael heddwch â Duw. Es. 57. ult. Rhufeiniaid 8.7–8'

[4. Unless the wicked leave their way, they can never obtain peace with God. Isaiah 57.21 (There is no peace, saith my God, to the wicked). Romans 8.7–8 (Because the carnal mind is enmity against God: for it is not subject to the law of God, neither indeed can be. So then they that are in the flesh cannot please God.)]

5 – ni's gall byth hawl yng Nghrist. Effesiaid 2.12. Eich bod y pryd hyny heb Crist. 2 Corinthiaid 5.17

[5 – they can never obtain a right in Christ. Ephesians 2.12 (ye were without Christ, being aliens from the commonwealth of Israel, and strangers from the covenants of promise, having no hope, and without God in the world.) That you were at that time without Christ. 2nd Corinthians 5.17 (Therefore if any man be in Christ, he is a new creature: old things are passed away; behold, all things are become new.)]

The question arises how, from this convinced High Church standpoint, Griffith Jones became so strongly committed to the primacy of evangelistic preaching.[125] He arrived at the insistence that all conventional religion is insufficient without the experience of 'new birth'.[126] He came to the crucial conviction that the same urgent summons – or pastorly advice – to decisive faith, due to the heathen of Tranquebar, was needed by those in 'the extreamly miserable blindness of his own country'.[127] He early appropriated the dogmatic emphasis in addressing all and sundry with this preceptual demand for undelayed obedience to the call to faith. Along with the demand went denunciation of sin, even to the faces of the rich or his fellow clergy.[128] His seeking for this 'crisis conversion' was, for Griffith Jones, the great deciding point. His use of the conversion formula in numerous sermons made him a leading exponent of this dogmatic emphasis, and an example followed by the rising band of younger preachers. Thus he anticipated something of what was yet fully to be formed as the main identifying feature of the Evangelical strand of British Protestantism. It is aptly named 'conversionism' by David Bebbington.[129] The latter wrote of the developed mentality: 'Conversions were the goal of personal effort, the collective aim of the church, the theme of Evangelical literature.'[130] In Griffith Jones's circles, conversion was often accompanied by an affirmation of experiences of God: a pitch of enthusiasm particularly offensive to many, and hence a focus of their emphatic rejection of all that was coming together under the heading of 'Methodism'.

NOTES

1   NLW, untitled notebook, MS.5920A. Not in the vast corpus of sermons, transcribed by curates, about 1760.

2   There is no page numbering and covers are missing. References below are numbered by counting from the beginning of sermon notes.

3   NLW, notebook, MS.5920A. First leaf recto.

4   Isaiah, prophesying in Jerusalem *c*.740–701 BC. The Old Testament contains a large collection of his narratives and prophecies in the *Book of Isaiah*.

5   G. Jones, 'Letter V. The religion of the age lamented', in *Letters of the Rev. Griffith Jones to Mrs Bevan*, ed. Edward Morgan (London, 1832), p. 26.

6   As attested by the huge corpus of sermon transcripts *Trysor o Ddifinyddiaeth*, in NLW and Cardiff Central Library.

7   *BCP*, 'The Order of the Administration of the Lord's Supper, of Holy Communion'.

8   Francis Sheppard, *London: A History* (London, 1998), p. 156.

9   Quoted in John R. H. Moorman (ed.), *The Cure of Souls* (London, 1958), pp. 155–6.

10   W. K. Lowther Clarke, *Eighteenth Century Piety* (London, 1944), p. 4.

11   Roger Lee Brown, *A Social History of the Welsh Clergy circa 1662–1939* (Welshpool, 2017), part two, vol. 2. pp. 349–62.

12   Roy Porter, *English Society in the Eighteenth Century*, rev. edn (London, 1981), p. 226.

13   John Brewer, *The Pleasures of the Imagination, English Culture in the Eighteenth Century* (London, 1997), p. 170.

14   W. Gibson, 'The British Sermon 1689–1901', in Keith A. Francis and William Gibson (eds), *The Oxford Handbook of the British Sermon 1689–1901* (Oxford, 2012), p. 12.

15   George Bull, *A companion for the candidates of holy orders, or, The great importance and principle duties of the priestly office* (London, 1714).

16   Gwyn Davies, *Griffith Jones, Llanddowror: Athro Cenedl* (Bridgend, 1984), pp. 25–6, 29–32.

17   NLW, untitled notebook, MS5920A, first leaf recto. The Welsh text is quoted here and below with the abbreviations written in full.

18   Julian Hoppit, *A Land of Liberty? England 1689–1727* (Oxford, 2000), p. 237.

19   CUL, SPCK, *Minutes*, 2 February 1700/1, MS A33/1.

20   Julian Hoppitt, *A Land of Liberty? England 1689–1727* (Oxford, 2000), p. 458.

The Theology of Griffith Jones and Religious Thought

21 G. Jones, 'Letter XLII. Bad times – preparation for them', in *Letters to Mrs Bevan*, pp. 134–6.

22 The biblical 'ungodly/wicked' – 'return' – 'righteousness' axis is powerfully expressed in the Welsh Prayer Book: 'Pan ddychwelo'r annuwiol oddi wrth ei ddrygioni ... hwnnw a geidw yn fyw ei enaid.'

23 Denoting Ezekiel 18:27: 'When the wicked men turneth away from his wickedness that he hath committed, and doeth that which is lawful and right, he shall save his soul alive.' (Authorized version) and *BCP*.

24 *BCP*, 'The Order of Morning Prayer, Daily throughout the Year' (1662).

25 *BCP*, 'The Order for Morning Prayer'.

26 This parable is also quoted in the ninth of the eleven opening sentences.

27 Lamentations 3:40: 'Let us search and try our ways, and turn again to the Lord.' (Authorized version)

28 Isaiah 55:7: 'Gadawed y drygionus ei ffordd ... a dychwelyd at yr Arglwydd.' Lamentations 3:40: 'dychwelwn at yr Arglwydd'. Ezekiel 18:27: 'A phan ddychwelo yr annuwiol oddi wrth ei ddrygioni ...'

29 NLW, untitled notebook, MS5920A. Second leaf verso.

30 In English: Isaiah 5:7: 'For the vineyard of the Lord of hosts is the house of Israel, and the men of Judah his pleasant plant: and he looked for judgment, but behold oppression; for righteousness, but behold a cry.' Romans 8:7–8: 'Because the carnal mind is enmity against God: for it is not subject to the law of God, neither indeed can be. So then they that are in the flesh cannot please God.'

31 NLW, notebook.

32 Peter D. Robinson, *http://theoldhighchurchman.blogspot.co.uk/2009/*, 19 December 2009 (accessed 16 November 2017).

33 The word 'reformation' was used of moral improvement, not of an alteration of polity or worship.

34 David Bebbington, *Evangelicalism in Modern Britain* (London, 1989), p. 19; D. Densil Morgan, 'The Emergence of Evangelicalism in Wales', in Michael A. G. Haykin and Kenneth J. Stewart (eds), *The Emergence of Evangelicalism* (Nottingham, 2008), p. 99.

35 Bebbington, *Evangelicalism*, pp. 35–6.

36 John Walsh, 'Origins of the Evangelical Revival', in G. V. Bennett and J. D. Walsh (eds), *Essays in Modern Church History* (London, 1966), p. 154.

37 'The principle that the Church or schools should be independent of the State and supported by voluntary contributions', *OED*.

38 Richard Hooker, *Of the Laws of Ecclesiastical Polity* (1594, 1597; London, 1830), vol. 3, p. 254.

39 '[T]he "gathered church" principle, according to which the regenerate sinners separated from the world into an association of "visible saints"'. Geraint Tudur, *Howell Harris, from Conversion to Separation 1735–1750* (Cardiff, 2000),, p. 33.

40 J. R. Tanner, *English Constitutional Conflicts of the Seventeenth Century 1603–1689* (Cambridge, 1960), p. 128.

41 Walsh, 'Origins of the Evangelical', pp. 139, 161.

42 *BCP*, 'The Ministration of Publick Baptism of Infants', preface, first para.

43 *BCP*, 'A Catechism', answer to second question.

44 Cf. Romans 12:4–5; 1 Corinthians 12:12–14, 27. Richard Hooker, *Of the Laws of Ecclesiastical Polity*, Book V (1594, 1597; London, 1990), vol. 2, p. 325.

45 *Form of Prayers and Ministration of the Sacraments &. of English Congregation at Geneva: and approved by the famous and godly learned man, John Calvin* (Geneva, 1555; Edinburgh, 1577), chapter 7, 'A prayer for the whole estate of Christ's Church', para. 5.

46 NLW, notebook, MS5920A, fourth leaf recto.

47 Hoppitt, *A Land of Liberty*, p. 214.

48 Jacob William, 'Methodism in Wales', in Glanmor Williams et al. (eds), *The Welsh Church from Reformation to Disestablishment 1603–1920* (Cardiff, 2007), p. 165.

49 Particularly Daniel Rowland, Howel Harris and William Williams.

50 John Morgan-Guy, 'The Church in Wales', in Richard C. Allen (ed.), *The Religious History of Wales* (Cardiff, 2014), p. 16.

51 John Tillotson, 'The Advantages of Religion to Societies', in *The Works of Dr John Tillotson*, ed. Thomas Birch (London, 1820), vol. 1, p. 422.

52 G. Jones, 'Letter XXXIX, The character of true godliness', in *Letters to Mrs Bevan*, pp. 127–9.

53 G. Jones, 'Letter LXX, How to know our interest in Christ', in *Letters to Mrs Bevan*, pp. 244–6.

54 NLW, Philipps of Picton Castle mss. GB 0210PICTLE, p. 584.

55 Quoted in W. Moses Williams (ed.), *Selections from the Welch Piety* (Cardiff, 1938), p. 31.

56 Williams (ed.), *Selections*, p. 31.

57 The Church of England Puritans, and other Reformed theologians, held to the so-called 'Regulative Principle'. William Cunningham (1805–61) wrote of it as 'the alleged unlawfulness of introducing into the worship and government of the Church anything which is positively warranted by Scripture, and the permanent binding obligation of a particular form of Church government.' Quoted by I. H. Murray, in *The Reformation of the Church* (London, 1965), p. 38.

58 Josiah Woodward, *Account of the Rise and Progress of the Religious Societies in the City of London, &c. and of their Endeavours for Reformation of Manners*, seventh edn (York, 1800), pp. 78–9.

59 D. Densil Morgan, *Theologia Cambrensis*, vol. 1 (Cardiff, 2018), p. 288.

60 'High-flyer, -flier ... in late 16th and early 18th. One who made or supported lofty claims on behalf of the authority of the Church; a High-Churchman; a Tory.' *OED*, p. 1305.

61 Mary Clement, *Correspondence and Minutes of the SPCK relating to Wales 1699–1740* (Cardiff, 1952), p. 1.

62 G. Jenkins, 'An Old and Much Honoured'; 'Griffith Jones, Llanddowror', *Welsh History Review*, II (1983), 451.

63 Quoted Williams (ed.), *Selections*, p. 19.

64 Williams (ed.), *Selections*, p. 19.

65 D. E. W. Harrison, *The Book of Common Prayer, the Anglican Heritage of Public Worship* (London, 1959), p. 50.

66 *BCP*, 'Morning Prayer', etc.

67 NLW, notebook, MS5920A, third leaf recto.
68 *BCP*, 'The first Day of Lent, commonly called Ash-Wednesday: the Collect'.
69 NLW, notebook, MS5920A, fourth leaf recto.
70 *BCP*, 'Collect for the third Sunday in Advent'.
71 *BCP*, 'Morning Prayer', Psalm 95.
72 NLW, notebook, MS5920A, third leaf recto.
73 *BCP*, 'At Evening Prayer', Psalm 98.
74 *BCP*, Psalm 67.
75 Morgan-Guy, 'The Church in Wales', in R. Allen (ed.), *Religious History*, p. 16.
76 Griffith Jones, *The Welch Piety* (London, 1740), p. 34.
77 Quoted in Keith A. Francis, 'Sermons, themes and Developments', in Francis and Gibson (eds), *The Oxford Handbook*, p. 35.
78 Geraint H. Jenkins, *Literature, Religion and Society in Wales 1660–1730* (Cardiff, 1978), p. 135.
79 Jenkins, *Literature, Religion*, p. 136.
80 NLW, notebook, MS5920A, tenth leaf recto.
81 *BCP*, 'At Morning Prayer', the Creed of Saint Athanasius, Quicunque Vult.
82 Quoted Isabel Rivers, 'Tillotson, John (1630–1694)', *ODNB*.
83 Williams (ed.), *Selections*, p. 26. Griffith Jones was quoting from the *Epistle to the Ephesians*, chapter 4, verses 18–19.
84 G. Jones, 'Letter XLI, Gloomy times – the duty of living to God', in *Letters to Mrs Bevan*, pp. 132–4.
85 *BCP*, 'Collect for the Innocents's Day'.
86 Cf. Bishop George Bull's recommendations of such to ordinands. Bull, *A Companion for the Candidates*.
87 NLW, notebook, MS5920A, ninth leaf recto.
88 *BCP*, 'Collect for 4th Sunday in Advent'.
89 Quoted in Williams (ed.), *Selections*, p. 28.
90 NLW, Sir John Philipps notebook, GB 0210PICTLE 936.
91 D. Ceri. Jones, 'Calvinistic Methodism and English Evangelicalism', in Haykin and Stewart (eds), *The Emergence*, pp. 108–9.
92 *The Two Books of Homilies*, preface p. 4.
93 Cf. 'Christocentrism' under heading 'Crucicentrism' in Bebbington, *Evangelicalism*, pp. 14–17.
94 John Coffey, 'Puritanism, Evangelicalism and the Evangelical Protestant Tradition', in Haykin and Stewart (eds), *The Emergence*, pp. 272–3.
95 G. Jones, 'Letter IX, To live to God by faith in Christ', in *Letters to Mrs Bevan*, pp. 49–50.
96 *BCP*, 'A General Thanksgiving'.
97 Bishop of St Davids 1732–42.
98 Quoted in Williams (ed.), *Selections*, p. 30.
99 *BCP*, 'Collect for Christmas-Day'.
100 *BCP*, 'Collect for the seventh Sunday after Trinity'.
101 Jenkins, *Literature, Religion*, p. 15; and 'An Old and Much Honoured', 456, 457.
102 Jenkins, 'An Old and Much Honoured', 451–2.

103 Mary Clement, *The SPCK and Wales 1699–1740* (London, 1954), p. 64.

104 NLW, notebook, MS5920A, first leaf verso (quoted here in full, where Jones's notes are abbreviations).

105 Isaiah 55:7: 'dychweled at yr Arglwydd'; Lamentations 3:40: 'dychwelwn at yr Arglwydd'; Ezekiel 18:27: 'a phan ddychwelo yr annuwiol oddi wrth ei ddrygioni'.

106 G. Jones, Letter 30 March 1738, in *The Welsh Piety* (London, 1740), p. 19.

107 Clement, *Correspondence*, p. 24.

108 Cf. dedication to Bishop John Hough, in Thomas Bray, *Catechetical Lectures on the Preliminary Questions and Answers of the Church-Catechism* (London, 1703), pp. i–vi.

109 G. Jones, Letter 16 August 1738, *Welch Piety*, quoted in Williams (ed.), *Selections*, pp. 28–9.

110 William Gibson, 'The British sermon 1689–1901', in Francis and Gibson (eds), *Oxford Handbook*, p. 12.

111 Gospel according to Matthew 22:11–13.

112 NLW, G. Jones, *Trysor o Ddifinyddiaeth*, Transcriptions of Collected Sermons 1760, MS 24057B, p. 835.

113 This is a positive statement.

114 NLW, Jones, *Trysor*, p. 836.

115 This is a question, and following points are introduced as questions.

116 NLW, Jones, *Trysor*, p. 837.

117 Jenkins, *Literature, Religion*, p. 23; David Jones, *Life and Times of Griffith Jones of Llanddowror* (London, 1902), p. 149.

118 Morgan-Guy, 'Sermons in Wales in the Established Church', in Francis and Gibson (eds), *Oxford Handbook*, p. 187.

119 G. Jones, 'Letter LXXXII, What religion requires', in *Letters to Mrs Bevan*, pp. 277–80.

120 Jenkins, *Literature, Religion*, p. 451.

121 J. William, 'Methodism in Wales', in Williams et al. (eds), *The Welsh Church*, pp. 176–7; Davies, *Hanes Cymru*, pp. 299–300.

122 Translated in the Welsh Prayer Book as 'dy iachawdwriaeth', that is 'thy salvation'.

123 *BCP*, 'Collect for all Conditions of men' in 'Prayers and Thanksgivings upon Several Occasions'.

124 NLW, notebook, MS5920A, second leaf verso.

125 'Evangelism' defined as a general call to faith in promises contained in the Bible. Cf. in D. J. Tidball, 'Theology of Evangelism', in Sinclair B. Ferguson and David F. Wright (eds), *New Dictionary of Theology* (Leicester, 1988), pp. 240–1.

126 G. Jones, 'Letter XXXIII, The importance of being born again', in *Letters to Mrs Bevan*, pp. 107–11.

127 Clement, *Correspondence*, p. 57.

128 Jenkins, 'An Old and Much Honoured', 451, 462.

129 'Conversionism', a convenient neologism. A necessary category leading to making the inducing of conversions the core of the Church's preoccupations.

130 Bebbington, *Evangelicalism*, p. 5.

Chapter 5

THE THEOLOGY OF GRIFFITH JONES'S PREACHING

PREACHING AND A USE OF THE LITURGY

Griffith Jones's ministry in the Welsh Church arose from the approved practice. His approach, said D. Densil Morgan, was that of a 'Prayer Book Anglican', and 'bore all the marks of the Anglicanism of the golden age'.[1] He conformed to Hooker's concept of the *Ecclesia Anglicana* as held in Wales by such as Rhys Prichard (*c*.1579–1644).[2] This ecclesiology deriving, according to Morgan, obviously from the 'influence of Richard Hooker', accepted:

> the episcopal ministry as a divine ordinance, the validity of hallowed tradition in governing the church, baptismal regeneration as an inference of the tradition of justification by faith alone and a high ideal of eucharistic grace.[3]

His approach in doctrine, worship and practice accorded with Julian Hoppit's assertion: 'Tory or High Church ideology was authoritarian, occasionally dictatorial. It was an ideology of certainty and of a particular truth.'[4] Though Jones's ecclesiology produced notable developments in preaching and charity-schooling, nothing in his work was a deliberate departure from this foundation. The flexible originality of his evolving projects was thus, paradoxically, formed out of a compliant conservatism. Like many others, Griffith Jones equated the Church with the Kingdom of God.[5] In Mat. 13:44, he commented:

> Diben y ddammeg hon yw gosod allan odidowgrwydd yr Arglwydd Iesu Brenhin teyrnas Nefoedd. Teyrnas Nefoedd ar y ddaear yw Eglwys Dduw, a Brenhin y deyrnas hon yw'r Arglwydd Iesu ... ac ynghylch y deyrnas hon y dylai ein holl ymofyniad ni fod; ar ein hawl ynddi y mae'n holl ddedwyddwch ni'n sefyll.[6]

> [The point of this parable is to set forth the excellence of the Lord Jesus, King of the Kingdom of Heaven. The Kingdom of Heaven on earth is the Church of God, and the King of this kingdom is the Lord Jesus ... and about this kingdom our whole inquiry must be; upon our claim of right within it stands our whole happiness.]

This opinion narrows the concept of the 'Kingdom'. From being seen as that which has a wide restorative effect on the whole human person, the 'Kingdom' becomes limited to the narrower channel of special grace, and so tends to view the outside world as a doomed wilderness, to be avoided as a field dangerous to Christian spirituality.[7] Pietistic reaction against sin seeks to defend life within the 'Kingdom' from its ordinary, natural creative activities. Pursuits engaged in by all, whether Christians or not, are distrusted as 'carnal' and at odds with the pursuit of holiness and salvation. Art, music, dance and other creative – and therefore pleasurable – activities are deemed 'worldly' and dangerous to piety, having no rightful, permanent place. Derec Llwyd Morgan described this recourse to an exclusively religious daily life at Herrnhut: 'dalient na allai dyn ei hun wrth ddisgwyl ei achubiaeth wneud dim mwy nag ymdawelu ac ymlonyddu' (they held that man himself, in awaiting his salvation, could do nothing more than remain calm and still).[8] It was a striking example which inspired the idealism of groups like the Fetter Lane Society, a recurring, ascetic concept of Christian life that was to have lasting influence on Welsh Methodism.

Griffith Jones's loyalty to the High Church concept of the Church as an authoritative institution was thoroughgoing. His attitude was like that of William Grimshaw (1708–63), who spoke for a growing body of evangelizing clergymen when he wrote: 'I believe the Church of England to be the soundest, purest, most apostolical Christian Church in the world.'[9] Like other clergy drawn into the pursuit of conversions, Grimshaw kept a high view of the sacraments. Archbishop Hutton of York, in answer to complaints about Grimshaw's alleged itinerancy, said: 'We cannot find fault with Mr. Grimshaw when he is instrumental in bringing so many to the Lord's Table.'[10] The same phenomenon of popular attraction to evangelistic preaching within the setting of the Communion liturgy spread widely in England, and was paralleled also among others than Episcopalians in Lowland Scotland and New England.[11] Griffith Jones excelled as a preacher. His nervous, hypochondriac temperament, tending to be obsessive and prone darkly to dwell on trials and sorrows, coloured his preaching. F. A. Cavenagh commented of Jones: 'Most certainly he needed to tap the "unconscious" energy in order to create some system out of chaos, to work through years of feeble health against apathy and virulent opposition'.[12] His command of the Welsh language and its idioms, together with a melodious voice, made him naturally an attractive public speaker.[13] Jones's serious mind gave intensity to his preaching to the crowds that, from about 1711, eagerly heard his sermons.[14] Though his preaching of the doctrines of heaven and hell was compunctive, his congregations swelled in numbers. Concerning the appeal of his preaching, Geraint Jenkins wrote:

> Jones stands out as a connecting link between the puritan itinerants ... and the early Methodist evangelists ... Excited crowds, many of them bored by the tedious homilies of their pastors, went to some pains to hear him.[15]

But Jenkins's comment is shallow: it was scarcely a flight from boredom that induced increasing crowds to attend his intense, demanding ministry; nor was mere excitement the essence of a deep and lasting effect upon many hearers. Griffith Jones deplored the infectious emotional excesses of some among the new wave of converts.[16] Many might have believed flowery 'testimonies' of alleged experiences, but Griffith Jones was wary of them.[17] Loud professions of faith may grow cool, whereas reticence can mask what turns out to be lasting conviction. In something resembling an evangelistic manifesto, Jones stressed the difference between nominal or transient faith and heart-felt religion:

> Nid Cristianogion mewn enw, fel y mae pawb yn y teyrnasoedd Cristianogol; ond Cristianogion mewn gwirionedd; yn rhai fyddo yn proffesu Crist mewn purdeb a pherffeithrwydd calon; gwedi eu cyssegru gan yspryd Duw i bob duwioldeb a sancteiddrwydd. Dyma'r fath ddynion sydd raid i chwi a minnau fod, os dymunwn ran o'r waredigaeth hon gan Grist.[18]

> [Not Christians by name, as is everyone in Christian kingdoms; but Christians in truth; those who would profess Christ in purity and perfection of heart; having been consecrated by the spirit of God to all godliness and sanctification. That is the sort of men which you and I must be, if we desire part of this salvation by Christ.]

Furthermore, his preaching of faith in Christ did not obstruct Jones's stressing duty:

> Y mae pawb, wyf fi'n dybied yn foddlon ddigon i dderbyn Crist fel Offeiriad, i wneuthur jawn a boddlonrwydd i Dduw dros eu hanwireddau hwynt; ond ni chlywant ar eu calonnau i gymmeryd eu dysgu ganddo, fel y mae'n Brophwyd; nac ufuddâu iddo, fel y mae'n Frenhin.[19]

> [Everyone, I suppose is willing enough to accept Christ as Priest, to make atonement and acceptance with God for their iniquities; but they do not find it in their hearts to receive their teaching from him, as a Prophet; nor to obey him, as King.]

PREACHING ON COMMUNION SUNDAYS

Communion Sundays had a central importance. The monthly observance of Holy Communion was not curtailed in favour of spending more time on preaching. Indeed, the gatherings for 'that blessed Ordinance', with more than one sermon, became a customary feature at Llanddowror.[20] It was even then that the intensity of the religious stirring was most evident.[21] The gatherings attracted large crowds, even from as far as Herefordshire.[22] These popular assemblies seem to have been a perpetuation, in part at least, of the long-standing vernacular Welsh tradition of communal church festive gatherings.[23] What happened on Griffith Jones's Communion weekends was also experienced elsewhere. The example of popular piety on Sacrament Sundays at Llanddowror made an impression, evincing revulsion in some clergy, but imitation by others. Daniel Rowland, curate of Llangeitho was affected by hearing Griffith Jones preach, to the extent that his ministry turned to follow the same pattern of evangelism practised within the constraints of the Prayer Book ordinances.[24] It was reported of Rowland's sacrament administrations: 'It was no uncommon thing for him to have fifteen hundred, or two thousand, or even two thousand five hundred communicants.'[25] People's coming sometimes from great distances for the celebration of communion was notable:

> They would set out on Friday, some on horseback, others on foot, and join in procession to Llangeitho singing ... They were a veritable procession of pilgrims ... to partake of the Living Bread and to drink 'the royal wine of heaven'... Llangeitho Church.[26]

Similar Communion gatherings occurred elsewhere. George Whitefield, in September 1749, wrote: 'I preached ... thrice at Haworth. At his Church, I believe, we had above a thousand communicants, and, in the churchyard, about 6,000 hearers.'[27] The Welsh Methodist custom of large preaching gatherings – 'cyrddau mawr' – reflected the custom of Communion week-end gatherings.[28] Griffith Jones's preaching affirmed an individual believer's personal possession of Christ, in the experience of salvation. There might have seemed the suggestion of an ascetic, Pietistic

The Theology of Griffith Jones and Religious Thought

motive in this ideal: at various times, many have taken 'choosing Christ' to mean literally rejecting human companionship and temporal property.[29] Indeed, the pious combating of the 'world' and the 'flesh' sometimes induced the ascetic depreciation of matrimony, or laying stress on a duty of ritual fasting, by John Wesley and other Methodists.[30] Jones's concept of repentance was drastic:

> troedigaeth oddi wrth bechod. Mae'r dyn edifeiriol yn ymrôi â'i holl galon yn erbyn pechod: Nid yn erbyn rhyw <u>un</u> pechod, ond erbyn pob pechod: Fe ymedy dynion annuwiol â rhai pechodau; ond ni allant ymadael â'u holl bechodau[31]

> [turning from sin. The repentant man stirs up his whole heart against sin: Not against some <u>one</u> sin, but against every sin: Ungodly men depart from some sins; but cannot depart from all of their sins]

In keeping with his alliance with Sir John Philipps, and High Church moralism, Jones's preaching contained a predominant call to a higher morality. He urged both Anglican conformity and rigorous uprightness, built upon a basis of faith and repentance. The virtues proposed by the religious societies and the SPCK received a recommendation amidst other points of application:

> Y rhai a feddant ar y fath ffydd ag a baro iddynt barhâu yn nyledswyddau Crefydd, mewn Gweddi ac Addoliad Duw, a glynu wrtho er gwaethaf pob amheuon a digalondid.[32]

> [Those who possess such faith as should cause them to persist in the duties of Religion, in Prayer and the Worship of God, and cling to it despite all doubts and discouragement.]

Preaching in his parish of Llandeilo Abercywyn, on 11 November 1711, the year of his induction there, and five years before his appointment to Llanddowror, Griffith Jones said:

The Theology of Jones's Preaching

> Ni a ddylem foliannu Rhagluniaeth Dduw am ein danfod ni i'r byd yr oes ddiweddaf hon, o herwydd bod gwaith Iechydwriaeth yn awr yn oleuach, ac yn llawer mwy eglur, na chynt.[33]

> [We ought to praise God's Providence for sending us to the world in this latter age, because the work of Salvation is now more apparent and much clearer than formerly.]

Griffith Jones, it seems, was referring to the contemporary upsurge of serious spiritual interest in Wales, and the accompanying wish for teaching. His apparently optimistic expectation of even greater response amongst his hearers added conviction to his exhortations to faith. He agreed with Josiah Woodward's words concerning the religious societies, of their having: 'contributed towards the increase of Christian Knowledge, the reviving of true Piety, the suppression of Vice'.[34] Jones's assured preaching manner, strengthened by High Church magisterialism, was probably in conscious imitation of the Apostles' authoritative practice.[35] The pattern of his own ministry sought to replicate their 'primitive' announcement of the Kingdom of God:

> Dyma'r testyn ag oedd iddynt helaethu a phregethu arno; sef, fod Crist, y Messiah, wedi dyfod i'r byd, i osod i fynu deyrnas yr Efengyl, gan wahodd dynion iddi trwy edifeirwch a ffydd.[36]

> [This is the text (i.e. Mat. 10:15) that they were to expand and preach upon; that is that Christ, the Messiah, had come to the world, to set up the kingdom of the Gospel, by inviting men to it through repentance and faith.]

His sermons show Griffith Jones's high concept of the office of 'minister of the Word'. A divine calling gave him authority to imitate John the Baptist:

> Mae Ioan yn eu galw dan enw llym, ag sy'n cynnwys ynddo gerydd deffrôus iawn iddynt: Cenhedlaeth gwiberod ... a dyled Gweinidogion yw mynegi hynny yn ddidderbyn wyneb. Ioan 8: 44. Mat: 12:34. 23:33.[37]

125

[John calls them by a harsh name, and which contains in it an awakening rebuke: Generation of vipers ... and the duty of Ministers is to express this without respect of person (i.e. favouritism).]

Jones frequently went as far as to cite the authority of Christ Himself lying behind the words of an appointed preacher like himself, as in:

Ond wrth fod yn ddïofal ac esgeulus chwi ddylech gofio, Mai nid Gweinidogaeth dyn ydych yn ddirmygu; ond amharchu yr ydych Weinidogaeth Crist ei hun.[38]

[But being at your ease and neglectful you must remember, That it is not the Ministry of man that you are despising; but you are insulting the Ministry of Christ himself.]

Moral censure remained part of Griffith Jones's oratory, his reprimands sometimes being remembered as excessive.[39] Nevertheless, he thought a preacher of redemption likely also to be received with apathy and incomprehension. He said:

Er bod y rhan fwyaf o ddynion, fel y mae gwaetha'r modd, â'u clustiau wedi byddaru, fel na fynnant hwy glywed cynghorion nefol; a'u calonnau wedi caledu, yn mogi pob cynhyrfiad da; fel nad yw Gair Duw, na llais ei Yspryd ef yn gallu menu arnynt.[40]

[Though the greater part of men, unfortunately, have ears which are deafened, so that they do not wish to hear heavenly counsels, and their hardened hearts, smothering every good impulse, so that neither God's Word nor the voice of his Spirit can make an impression on them.]

Jones was loath to perform any of his duties in holy orders in a perfunctory way. He likewise solemnly warned his hearers regarding their obligation seriously to heed his teaching. High Church principle itself postulated a high authority for a clergyman. Bishop Bull had stressed an ordinand's need of an inner divine calling before presuming to teach others. Jones said: 'Dylai Gweinidogion dderbyn galwad ac awdurdod oddi wrth Grist i waith y Weinidogaeth' (Ministers must receive a calling and authority from Christ for the work of the Ministry).[41] His perhaps incautious choice of words, at times, regarding his own call, and therefore his authority to teach, were fastened on by John Evans to build exaggerated accusations of bigotry.[42] Griffith Jones indeed himself recognized that some ordained men fell short of the proper standards. There were inequalities amongst ministers.

> Nid oes mo bawb o Weinidogion Crist mor enwog a'u gilydd. Fe enwir Iudas Iscariot yn eu mysg. Cenhadodd Crist i un twyllwr fod yn eu plith, fel y gallai'r byd ddisgwyl clywed, pe buasai dim ffalsder ganddynt.[43]

> [Of all Christ's Ministers not all are as renowned as one another. Judas Iscariot is named amongst them. Christ allowed for one deceiver to be in their midst, even as the world might expect to hear, as though there were no falsehood in them.]

However, the varied quality of its clergy did not, for him, make it any less a true Church and worthy of men's loyalty.[44] Some clergy, like Evans, were inclined to oppose him; and hostility in influential quarters denied him preferment. Jones said: 'Dylai gweithwyr, nid rhedeg i'r cwr a fynnont o'r cynhauaf, ond disgwyl wrth Arglwydd y gwaith i'w danfon lle y mynno efe (Workers ought not to run to the corner of the harvest-field that they may desire, but to expect from the Lord of the work for him to send them where he himself should wish).[45] This perspective, with its allusion to the providential appointment of a clergyman's circumstances, helps to explain Griffith Jones's lifelong acceptance of labour in a relatively humble and unpromising sphere, without preferment. He felt that his 'calling' was to labour there. However, this apparently sincere commitment to serve a designated cure, in an undivided Church, was made somewhat ambiguous by his pastoring 'exercised' converts, extraparochially in select groups. Samuel Wesley had obliquely acknowledged the dilemma for clergymen concerning 'converts', by denying its effect. He wrote of those 'of whose conversion to God there may be hopes.'[46] But Wesley also insisted, unconvincingly, that the aim of the religious societies was 'by no means to gather Churches out of Churches, to foment New Schisms'.[47] Griffith Jones suffered in the same quandary; his establishing of distinct bodies of converts was effectively a step towards creating *ecclesiolae in ecclesia*.[48]

BIBLICISM

Biblicism was central to Griffith Jones's expository preaching, always turning for authority to other, corroborating biblical texts. Of the parable of 'treasure hidden in a field', he said:

> Y maes lle mae'r trysor hwn yn guddiedig yw'r Ysgrythyrau. Athrawiaeth ac Ordinhadau'r Ysgrythyr, yw'r hen Destament a'r Newydd, sydd fel llaeth yn y fron, fel dwfr mewn ffynnon, fel mêr yn yr esgyrn, fel manna yn y gwlith, fel perl mewn cragen, fel mel yn y graig, fel mwyn gwerthfawr ynghalon y ddaear (y mwyn goreu sy ddyfnaf) dyma lle rhaid ymofyn am Gras. Ioan. 5: 39.[49]

> [The field where this treasure is hidden is the Scriptures. The Doctrine and Ordinances of the Scripture are the old Testament and the New, which are like milk in the breast, like water in a well, like marrow in the bones, like manna in the dew, like a pearl in a shell, like honey in the rock, like a precious mine in the heart of the earth (the best mine is the deepest) that is where one needs to seek Grace. John 5:39.]

This extract exemplifies his dense mode of exposition. Its amazing string of natural analogies was all gathered from either of the Testaments, revealing a broad and confident grasp of the content of the Bible. It displays perfectly the same florid currency of scriptural allusion that was not unknown elsewhere, but became habitual amongst adherents to the evangelizing movement, also lending poetic effect to hymns like those of Williams Pantycelyn. Griffith Jones's choice of passages gathered evidence widely, according to the broad tenor of Scripture, so reinforced his urging of personal faith.[50] Thus his choice of matter and treatment betokened

The Theology of Jones's Preaching

something of the formulaic evangelism of later, contrived 'revivalism'.[51] He wrote:

> Er ei fod fel trysor cuddiedig, nid yw ddim dan glô; mewn maes y mae; ac y mae'r maes yn agored, i bwy bynnag a fynno i chwilio am dano. A'r neb a'i caffo a'i piau.[52]

> [Though it is like a hidden treasure, it is not at all locked up; it is in the field; and the field is open, to whoever wishes to look for it. And it is the property of whoever should take it.]

For Griffith Jones, the Christian Gospel contained an emphatic invitation. In this, he was in accord with the Reformers and the Puritans.[53] Along with the broad exhortation, he handled the difficult doctrine of predestination cautiously.[54] His preaching seems to have provided the reassurance of solifidianism for people conscious of their own weak attainments, and to have avoided any clashing allusion to stringent moral standards in a way which might seem to limit the breadth of the offer of forgiveness.[55] This comforting note, accompanying his moralism, must account, in part at least, for Jones's great popularity. His sermons progressed in a series of sections dealing with points arising, each in turn, from the biblical text, in a logical sequence. Each point was followed by a range of detailed biblical references. In the examples above, Jones tied the metaphor of 'treasure' into theology and common Christian experience. The extension of exposition into each component detail was redolent of the best of Puritan preaching.[56] He elaborated the wealth acquired through faith:

> Mae trysor yn gwneuthur y neb a'i caffo yn gyfoethog, er ei fod o'r blaen yn dlawd ac yn anghenus. Mae Crist yn cyfoethogi ei bobl â thrysor o ras, a thrysor o ddoethineb, â thrysor o gyfiawnder a sancteiddrwydd, a thrysor o heddwch, ac etifeddiaeth dragwyddol yn nheyrnas Nefoedd. Eph: 3: 8.[57]

> [Treasure makes rich whoever should get it, despite his being poor and needy before. Christ enriches his people with a treasure of grace, and a treasure of wisdom, with a treasure of righteousness and sanctification,

and a treasure of peace, and an everlasting heritage in the kingdom of Heaven. Eph. 3:8.]

The sermon contains one of Griffith Jones's extended lists: not an unconsidered heap, but a chain of spiritual benefits in a theological order. His implying a distinction between imputed righteousness and sanctification conformed to a basic locus of Reformed theology.[58] He added: 'Mae trysor yn gwneuthur dynion yn anrhydeddus. Dïar: 14: 20. Felly mae Crist yn gwneuthur y neb a'i caffo. Dïar. 8: 35' (Treasure makes men honourable. Proverbs 14.20. Likewise Christ makes anyone who finds him. Proverbs 8.35).[59] He described the social effect of the 'treasure' of grace: 'Mae trysor yn arfer gwneuthur dynion i fod yn fwy gwasanaethgar i eraill' (Treasure tends to make men more prone to serve others).[60] In an age of subordination to superiors, such doctrine was novel for Welsh countryfolk lacking wealth and influence.

Griffith Jones's direct personal exhortation could scarcely have been in more absolute terms. A feature to become standard in Evangelical preaching was the lost and guilty human state, contrasted with that of the renewed and converted person. Many later followed Jones, urging a turning in faith to God, but failing to recognize that conversion may be only temporary. David Bebbington does not seem to be alert to the crucial distinction.[61] To assume conversion always as regeneration remains a recurring feature of Evangelicalism.

> Dal sylw, enaid (nid oes arnaf fi ddim ofn i ddywedyd gair dros Dduw'r Nefoedd) nid oes i ti ac i bob dyn arall, ond un o'r ddwy ffordd hyn ... Ac am hynny edrych attat dy hun mewn pryd, pa un o'r ddau hyn yw dy gyflwr ar dy enaid di. Os ydwyt ti etto heb droi oddi wrth dy ddïofalwch, ac edifarhâu, mae dy enaid mewn cyflwr enbydus a thruenus jawn; mae dy holl ddedwyddwch a'th lawenydd ar ddarfod; ni wyddost ti o awr i gilydd pa gynted y byddi ymhoenau Uffern.
> Mae'r geiriau hyn yn perthyn i bawb o honoch chwi[62]

> [Take notice, soul (I am not afraid to say a word for the God of heaven) you and every other man only have one of these two ways ... And therefore

take notice of yourself in time, which of these two is the state of your soul. If you have still not turned from your carelessness, and repented, your soul is in a perilous and miserable state; your whole blessedness and joy are expiring; you do not know from one hour to the next how quickly you will be in the pains of Hell.

These words relate to each one of you]

The swelling numbers of regular hearers and curious visitors perhaps induced Jones's frequent repetition of this theme. That he could not know each of his hearers personally, nor give private advice, made his pulpit speaking all the more important. Widespread poverty and epidemic illness without hope of cure could induce people to seek solace in the Church. There were serious outbreaks of smallpox (1710, 1714, 1719 and in 1721 to 1723 spreading widely, and in 1751–53).[63] The years 1728–30 included the 'last catastrophic epidemic' of pre-industrial times.[64] Jones wrote in September 1731: 'It is a very sickly time near this neighbourhood, where many die, and many more are sick of a Nervous kind of feavour.'[65] Surprisingly, he preached in his usual manner during this time. On 27 June, during the 1731 epidemic, no special warning was given:[66]

> Gwelwn pa drugaredd ei maint yw cael cyfodiad ar ol syrthio. Syrthiodd dau apostl, <u>Pedr</u> a <u>Judas</u>; ond ni chyfododd ond un, sef <u>Pedr</u>. &. Yr ŷm ni bawb wedi syrthio yn Adda, ac ynom ein hunain. &.
>
> Gwelwn yma diriondeb Duw at ei bobl, yn ewyllysgar i'w derbyn drachefn wedi cwympo, yn barod ac yn ddiddannod. Sal. 32.1,
>
> Gwelwn mor angenrheidiol yw gwir edifeirwch; ni faddewir pechod Apostol hebddo. &.
>
> Cadwed y rhai edifeiriol yn agos at Grist. &. Gocheled pawb y cammau ag sy'n arwain oddi wrth Grist. &.[67]

> [Let us see how great the mercy is in being raised up after falling. Two Apostles fell, <u>Peter</u> and <u>Judas</u>; but only one arose, that is <u>Peter</u>. &. We are all fallen in Adam, and in ourselves. &.
>
> Let us see here God's gentleness towards his people, willingly accepting them straight away after falling, readily and without reproach. Ps. 32.1 &.

131

> Let us see how necessary is true repentance; an Apostle's sin is not forgiven without it. &c.
> Let those who are repentant keep close to Christ &. Let everyone beware the steps that lead away from Christ. &c.]

Perhaps some reference to the devastation of the recent epidemic is observable in what follows: 'Pa fodd y mae y rhai gawsant faddeuant mewn cyflwr cysyrus, pa glefyd neu ofid bynnag fyddo arnynt?' (In what way are those who have received forgiveness in a comforting state, whatsoever sickness or trouble they may have?)[68] In dealing with the biblical narrative, Jones laid out his theology of sin. There is no hint of any special crisis in the sermon. After mention of Adam's sin, he presented the Protestant view of absolute divine forgiveness, adding his usual warning against complacency. The necessity of repentance was affirmed, followed by pastoral exhortation to circumspection in the walk of faith.

Griffith Jones's theological compass was noticeably not far-ranging. He avoided digression on, for instance, the details of eschatology, comment on the social order, or description of the historical background of the narratives expounded. Geraint Jenkins wrote of his being: 'Unrelenting in his stress on man's sin and the need for unqualified repentance.'[69] Jones's concentration on personal renewal to faith and conformity with the moral norm left little scope for wider review. But the growing numbers of his congregations prove the depth of the impression that Griffith Jones's teaching made. Moreover, his carefully reasoned and cautious exegesis of the chosen passages in vivid language kept fresh the repetition of the main themes of sin, repentance, judgement, faith, forgiveness and renewal. In many places, Griffith Jones used the word 'anufudd' ('disobedient' in failing to heed God's call), referring to the dangerous state of being uncommitted towards God.

> Y bydd i Dduw yn nydd y barn gyfrif â dynion, ynghylch y modd y darfu iddynt wrando a derbyn Athrawiaeth yr Efengyl. Hag. 1.6 ... Oh bydd cyflwr pob dyn annuwiol yn ddrwg jawn y pryd hwnnw! etto bydd cyflwr rhai yn waeth na'u gilydd.[70]

[There will be for God in the day of judgement an account with men, about the manner in which they happened to receive the Doctrine of the Gospel. Hag. 1.6 ... Oh the state of every ungodly man will be very bad at that time! still the state of some will be worse than others.]

Preaching on Christ's forgiving the paralysed man brought to Him, he alluded to his sad state:[71]

Os y rhai y maddeuwyd eu pechodau a allant fod yn gysurus ymhob cyflwr, mae y rhai sydd heb faddeuant mewn cyflwr truenus, pa ddedwyddwch neu wynfyd bynnag fô ganddynt. Maent yn agored i bob trueni presennol a thragwyddol.[72]

[If those whose sins were forgiven can be at ease in every condition, those who are without forgiveness are in a sad condition, whatever happiness or blessing they may have. They are open to every wretchedness present and eternal.]

Besides exhorting his hearers, Griffith Jones stressed the divinely appointed order of events. Here he used a question, answered in a list:

Q: Pa lun y mae maddeuant pechod yn dyfod?
A: 1.   Trwy trefniant Duw.
     2   Trwy bryniad Mab Duw.
     3.   Trwy gynhwysiad Yspryd Duw.
     4.   Trwy gyfarwyddyd Gair ac ordinhadau Duw.
     5.   Trwy bregethiad Gweindogion Duw.[73]

[Question: What method does the forgiveness of sin follow?
Answer: 1.   Through God's arrangement.
          2   Through redemption by the Son of God.
          3.   Through reception of the Holy Spirit.
          4.   Through the guidance of the Word and God's ordinances.
          5.   Through the preaching of God's Ministers.]

Jones turned the Transfiguration narrative into a comforting reassurance, as providing evidence of everlasting life:[74]

> Fod y rhai a aethant o'r byd hwn yn fyw'n wastad mewn byd arall. Felly Moses ac Elïas. Am Abraham y dywedir, Efe a fu farw, ac a gasglwyd at ei bobl. Felly hefyd Isaac, Jacob, Aaron, a Moses, &c.
> Fod y duwiolion ar ol mynd oddi yma, mewn 'stad a chyflwr' gogoneddus.[75]

> [That those who went from this world lived constantly in another world. So Moses and Elijah. It is said of Abraham, He died and was gathered to his people. So also Isaac, Aaron, and Moses, &c.
> That the godly after leaving here, are in a glorious 'state and condition'.]

A reassurance of glory for all repentant believers followed, with warning to the careless of judgement:

> Mae cyfnewidiad gwedd, nid cyfnewidiad sylwedd, sydd ar gyrph y Seintiau mewn gogoniant ... Yr un corph, a'r un aelodau a gyfodir o'r llwch ag aeth yno ... Y cyfnewidiad sydd ar y corph; naill ai yn y wedd a'r olwg ogoneddus a ymddengys arno, trwy sancteiddiad Gras[76]

> [It is a transformation of appearance, not a transformation of essence, which is on the bodies of the Saints in glory ... The same body, and the same members which are raised up from the dust as went into it ... be it either in the form and glorious appearance shown on it through the sanctifying of Grace]

This strong assertion of identical bodily resurrection was a trope in early Protestant wills, giving evidence of a Lutheran influence merging with Lollard oral tradition.[77] Reassurance of close communion with Christ was also reiterated: 'Os dywedai Pedr ar ben y mynydd, Da yw i ni fod yma, Oh pa gymmaint mwy da fydd i'r duwiol fod gyd â Christ yn y Nefoedd!' (If Peter said on the top of the mountain, It is good for us to be here, Oh how much better will it be for the godly to be with Christ in Heaven!)[78] Necessary faith and moral duty were always presented in close relation.

134

Mae cariad a thosturi'r duwiol yn peri iddynt ymofyn cymmorth yr Arglwydd i bwy bynnag yn eu teulu a fô mewn trueni ... Hunan-ymwadiad a gostyngeiddrwydd mawr y canwriad dan addewid Crist o'r fath ffafr iddo.[79]

[Love and godly pity cause them to seek the Lord's help for whoever in their family should be in adversity ... The centurion's self-denial and great humility at Christ's promise of such a favour to him.]

Self-examination was thus part of piety, also much emphasized by Puritan preachers.[80] Griffith Jones even seemed to include himself in the exhortation:

A roddasom ni ein hunain i Grist? A ydym ni yn dilyn Crist ynghyngorion ei Air, yn esampl ei fywyd, ac yn nhywysiad ei Yspryd? – Dyma'r ffordd i ni ddyfod i adnabod ein hunain. Y rhan fwyaf a ânt yn golledig trwy gamsyniad &. Nid gwneuthur gwyrthiau yn enw Crist, ond canlyn Crist yw'r peth. & Mat:7: 22, 23[81]

[Did we give ourselves to Christ? Do we follow Christ in the counsels of his Word, the example of his life, and in the leading of his Spirit? – This is the way for us to know ourselves. Most go astray through misapprehension &. Not working miracles in Christ's name, but following Christ is the thing. & Mat. 7:22–3]

Jones presented Christ as the focus of faith, without always relating salvation to the Godhead as a whole. Such 'christomonism' was later to develop strongly as a main emphasis of Methodism and Evangelicalism generally.[82]

Mae Crist, fel trysor cuddiedig, yn guddiedig oddi wrth yr annuwiol: Ni welant mo'i ragoriaeth, er cymmaint ydyw. Can: 5: 9. Luc. 19. Ac y mae mewn rhan yn guddiedig etto oddi wrth y duwiol.[83]

[Christ, like a hidden treasure, is hidden from the ungodly. Song 5:9. Lk 19. And it is in part still hidden from the godly.]

The corresponding devotion to the person of Christ follows the sense of personal possession.

> Mae trysor yn tynnu serch a chariad dynion ar ei ol. Mat: 6: 21. Felly mae holl serch, ac awydd a chariad y duwiol yn cyfeirio at yr Arglwydd Iesu. Sal: 73: 25.[84]

> [Treasure draws men's affection and love after it. Mat. 6:21. So the whole affection, and desire and love of the godly man are directed towards the Lord Jesus. Ps. 73:25]

> Fod Crist y fath drysor i'r Cristion a'i caffo ag a dâl iddo ymadael â phob peth er ei fwyn ef.[85]

> [That Christ is such a treasure to the Christian who may discover him and hold to him so as to leave everything for his sake.]

GRIFFITH JONES'S METHOD OF PREACHING

Griffith Jones's preaching was 'systematic', the product of an active, punctilious but cautiously unadventurous mind. His established custom was orderly exposition of Bible passages, often consecutively. Calvin's example of systematic exposition was widely influential in Protestant Europe.[86] With the Bible as both authority and plentiful fund of material, Jones drew his doctrine, deducing warnings and exhortations, from his chosen passage. To each point he added corroborating citations, showing mastery of detail over the whole range of Scripture.[87] He stood upon this single doctrinal authority, but, as a convinced Anglican, with the assurance that all corroborated the doctrine of the Church of England. Each sermon in turn comprised a distinct event or passage of Christ's teaching, and tended to be expounded as a complete pericope.[88] In this, one may say that his teaching concentrated on detail, whilst having a unifying view of the whole corpus in his evangelistic paradigm. If an 'apostolic' tradition lent coherence to the preaching of such as George Herbert (1593–1633) or Lancelot Andrewes (1555–1626), covenantalism gave a unifying force to the scheme of doctrine of preachers like John Owen (1616–83) or Thomas Watson (1617?–89).[89] Perhaps one can define Griffith Jones's teaching as a non-covenantal but coherent, 'Christocentric' and moralistic evangelism.[90] He followed emphases which were to lead on to modern Evangelicalism.[91] Griffith Jones's preaching was more doctrinally didactic than Whitefield's, and perhaps was most suited to the meditative Welsh mind.[92] After quoting the text of a sermon, Jones analysed the main doctrines in the passage. Each point was carefully isolated and defined, and not without an exhortation to practical application. The text was broken into divisions and subdivisions, somewhat as in Puritan sermons.[93] The implications of each point were shown, with appropriate exhortation. It is not clear how far this structure imitated that of published commentaries, but his own thorough grasp of the Bible is obvious. His catechetical manner caught the hearers' attention by asking an obvious question: 'Q: Pa'm hynny? &. A. 1. Fe roddodd Crist ei hun drostynt hwy' (Question: Why that? & Answer: Christ gave himself on their behalf).[94] The ampersand placed at the end of some sentences seems to denote additional extempore supporting comments: perhaps with the easy fluency for which he became famous.[95] Thus Griffith Jones thought apparently that the importance of these elaborations was only secondary to the doctrinal argument. In contrast, the text of Titus 2:14, being part of God's Word, was then quoted in full from the Welsh Bible. Many quotations followed, each answering a point in turn.[96]

Griffith Jones's sermons were in the orderly Anglican form, as suitable to be read out verbatim or, not infrequently, to be printed.[97] Though delivered without being slavishly tied to the written notes, his preaching avoided the extemporary randomness that some later Welshmen would assume to be the concomitant of a dependence upon the Holy Spirit's guidance. Though he made practical application of each point with urgency, Jones analysed texts, relating their doctrine and example to other parts of Scripture. His assurance of the unity of the Bible and of its consistent, though unfolding, revelation throughout the two testaments, was unfaltering. His use of Welsh for the benefit of the peasantry had a practical intention: to touch the mind and conscience. Jones appears never to have swerved from his single-minded call to faith and the categorical promises of acceptance for every believer. His intense mind worked by a thorough logical progression. In order to reach the individual hearer, each point was reiterated with emphatic application. No hearer could be in doubt about Griffith Jones's own belief in the Christian message of 'everlasting consolation and good hope through grace'.

> Ni wn i lai nad oes rhyw ystyr brophwydol yng-weddnewidiad Crist ar fynydd uchel. Yr oedd yn awr belydr neu ddau o ogoniant teyrnas a brenhiniaeth Crist yn ymddangos ar fynydd uchel, fe allai, i ddal allan ddyrchafiad ei deyrnas ef goruwch holl fynyddoedd, a galluoedd, a brehinoedd y byd hwn, yn ol geiriau'r Prophwyd <u>Esay</u>. 2: 1, 2.[98]

> [I do not know but there was some prophetic meaning in Christ's transfiguration on a high mountain. There were now one or two beams of the glory of Christ's realm and kingship appearing on a high mountain, it could be to set forth the rising of his kingdom above all mountains and powers and kings of this world, according to the words of the Prophet <u>Isaiah</u>. 2:1, 2']99

He pointed out the contrasting qualities of true, but unostentatious, faith:

> Q: Pa fath yw y rhai'ny a fydd flaenaf ger bron Duw, er na bônt, mae'n bossibl, ond digyfrif neu fel yr olaf yngolwg y byd?
> A: 1. Y rhai a fo ganddynt fwyaf o wir ostyngeiddrwydd ... 2. Y rhai a fô'n fwyaf cynnyddus Yngras Duw ac yn ffrwythau o hono.[100]

> [Q. What sort are they will be foremost before God, though they should be possibly only negligible or as the least in the world's view?
> A. 1. Those with the most of true humility ... 2. Those most thriving in the Grace of God and in its fruits.]

Jones pursued the evidence of true faith in a resulting spiritual fruit, and warned of the dangers of superficial and temporary response to evangelism. In keeping with his whole emphasis, he praised the work of grace in the heart of those who seek to follow Christ's way of service:

> Y rhai mwyaf eu zêl dros ryw duwioldeb, ac yn erbyn pechod.
> Y rhai a fô fwyaf parod ac ewyllysgar i weithredoedd o gariad dros Dduw, ac eneidiau dynion ... Os yw sefyll dros achos brenhin daiarol gymmaint o anrhydedd a dyrchafiad, pa faint mwy o anrhydedd yn sefyll dros achos Brenhin y Nefoedd? ... Os yw cael perl a gollwyd yn ynnill mawr, pa faint mwy yw achub enaid colledig? ... Gall y gwannaf a'r tlottaf wneuthur rhan.[101]

> [Those with the greatest zeal for some kind of godliness, and against sin. Those most ready and willing for works of love on behalf of God, and men's souls ... If standing up for an earthly king's cause is so much respect and exaltation, how much more honour standing up for the cause of the King of Heaven? ... If getting the pearl that was lost is great gain, how much more is rescuing a lost soul? ... The weakest and the poorest can take part.]

Many obtained the personal faith constantly preached by Jones, but others were unmoved or even became hostile. For the latter, he felt that warnings were necessary:

> Ni fynnai rhai wrando na derbyn Apostolion Crist, er eu bod yn dyfod dros Grist gyda'r fath awdurdod, a gallu. Sal: 58: 3–5. Y mae y rhai ni fynnant wrando a derbyn addysg, yn peri i'r Efengyl ymadael oddi wrthynt.[102]

> [Some did not wish to listen or accept Christ's Apostles, though they came on Christ's behalf with such authority and power. Psalm 58.3–5. Those who do not wish to listen and receive teaching, make the Gospel depart from them.]

Presumably, he believed, when faith was increasing, that invective against contempt for the 'means of grace' was justified:

> Y mae dirmygwyr Crefydd yn halogi'r llwch dan eu traed: Ac fe all Duw
> ei ddwyn i'r farn, i roddi tystiolaeth yn eu herbyn. Mar: 6:11. Act: 13:51.
> 18:6. Iago.5:3.[103]

> [Despisers of Religion defile the dust under their feet: And God can bring
> them to judgement, to give testimony against them. Mark 6:11; Acts
> 13:51; 18:6; James 5:3.]

To Jones, the danger for those ignoring the call was not trivial. He
sometimes underlined warnings in his notes against the flouting of God's
demand, many biblical passages being quoted verbatim. Presumably these
were to be read out with added emphasis.[104] Other assertive summaries
of doctrine were likewise underlined. The denunciatory note, however,
sometimes was softened by including himself as also needing a reminder:

> Pa edifeirwch mawr a ddylai fod ynom, am ein hanufudd-dod a'n
> hanystyrwch dan Air Duw yr amser a aeth heibio! Dat: 3: 3. Ier: 8: 6.
> Ceisiwn, trwy Ras Duw, fod o hyn allan yn barchus, yn awyddus, yn ofalus,
> ac yn ufudd. &c. Ar hyn y mae'n sefyll holl freintiau Iechydwriaeth.[105]

> [What great repentance needs to be in us, for our disobedience and
> indifference under God's word in time gone past! Revelation 3:3; Jer. 8:6.
> Let us try, through God's Grace, to be from now on reverent, zealous,
> careful and obedient. & Upon this stand all the rights of Salvation.]

Along with the reminder of religious duties, Jones's struggle to make a
lasting impression included warnings against resisting the preached Word.
Failure to act upon the Gospel held shut the door to new life:

> Q: Pa fath fydd cyflwr y rhai a barhânt yn anufudd dan Weinidogaeth yr
> Efengyl?
> A: Oh mor echrydus a fydd! Nid yw debygol (nac yn bossibl chwaith, os
> felly y parhânt) iddynt gael dychweliad nac Iechydwriaeth byth; canys y
> maent yn gwrthod yr unig beth a ddichon eu cadw hwynt. Iago. 1: 21[106]

The Theology of Jones's Preaching

[Q. What will be the condition of those who persist in being disobedient under the Ministry of the Gospel?

A. Oh it will be so shocking! It is not likely (nor possible either, if they persist thus) that they should ever get restoration or Salvation; for they are rejecting the only thing that could keep them safe. James 1.21.]

In his sermon on Mat. 13:44, Griffith Jones returned to the theme of treasure, mentioning things recommended as 'precious' ('gwerthfawr').

Fe sonir yn y 'Sgrythyr am dri pheth gwerthfawr a ddaeth i ni trwy Grist. Gwaed gwerthfawr. 1 Ped: 1: 19. addewidion gwerthfawr 2 Ped: 1: 4. gras gwerthfawr, sef ffydd. 2 Ped: 1: 1.[107]

[In the Scripture three precious things are mentioned which come to us through Christ. Precious blood. 1 Pet. 1:19. precious promises 2 Pet. 1:4. precious grace, that is faith. 2 Pet. 1:1.]

Exhortation usually followed Jones's detailed exposition. He summarized the New Testament Gospel, in a pointed, personal application. This 'personal touch' must explain much of his success in gaining the attention of ordinary countryfolk: 'Cedwch afael yng Nghrist, a glynwch wrtho' (Keep hold of Christ, and stick to him).[108] Sermon 47 exemplifies Griffith Jones's aptitude to lead untutored minds into the realm of theology. He expounded the Transfiguration, so as to enable his hearers to glimpse the event: 'Fe osodir yma beth rhyfedd ac uchel jawn o'n blaen ni, ag a ddylem gyd â pharch a gostyngeidrwydd mawr ystyried. Gwel Exod: 3: 3–5. 1 Ped: 2: 1, 2' (There is placed before us here something wonderful and very high which we must consider with reverence and great humility. See Exod. 3:3–5; 1 Pet. 2:1–2).[109] Jones explained Christ's taking three disciples with Him in terms of the biblical rules of credible witnesses in legal pleadings.[110] He followed this with the question 'why on a mountain?' He answered, typically, by allusion to practical piety:

141

> Er mwyn bod yn ddirgelaidd, ac yn llonydd oddi wrth derfysg ac aflonyddwch ... Dylem dynnu o'r neilldu oddi wrth olwg a rhwystrau'r byd, os synnwn gymmundeb dirgelaidd â Duw.[111]

> [In order to be out of sight, and undisturbed by riot and disturbance ... We must draw aside from the scenes and hindrances of the world, if we are concerned about secret communion with God.]

Griffith Jones was magisterial in propounding doctrine, conscious of the duty of obedience. But he included himself: 'dylem dynnu o'r neilldu', 'we ought'. This contrasts with an aloof clerical manner, like that of James Hervey (1714–58), mentioned by Bob Tennant:

> 'Many of my hearers, I observe, are husbandsmen [sic]' ... and this more remote rhetoric, always reminding the listener, and reader, of the distinction between minister/author and congregation/reader ...[112]

Griffith Jones cited other biblical references to significant happenings on mountains: Sinai, Moriah, the Mount of Olives, etc., in terms of the hearers' personal response. He said that the high lands were always: 'yn fwy derbyniol o Grist a'i Efengyl, na'r bröydd, neu'r dyffrynoedd breision' ('more receptive of Christ and his Gospel than the vales or the plentiful valleys').[113]Perhaps the inhabitants of Welsh hills were here present in his mind.

Griffith Jones's view of his duty of reaching people in their spiritual need seems to accord with his exposition of texts concerning apostolic miracles. For him, kind works towards basic human needs could not be separated from his announcing of the Gospel. Pre-eminently, his educational work for the poor, with its link to the spiritual, expressed this conviction.

> Beth a wnaent; sef selio gwirionedd eu hathrawiaeth, trwy wneuthur gwyrthiau. Nid gwyrthiau o farn, ond gwyrthiau o drugaredd oedd iddynt wneuthur; a'r cwbl yn rhad. Trwy ddangos trugaredd i'r dyn oddi allan, y mae treio dyfod â'r dyn oddi mewn i gael trugaredd hefyd.[114]

[What did they do; that is seal the truth of their doctrine, through working miracles. Not miracles of judgement, but miracles of kindness were what they had to do; and the whole free of charge. Through showing kindness to the outer man, there is the attempt to bring the inner man to find kindness also.]

What follows in this sermon seems, by the very comprehensiveness of its assertion, to confirm Griffith Jones's policy of uncontroversial conformity to the worship and government of the Church of England in his time. He saw personal piety, based on clear faith in the promise of salvation in Christ, as the foundation which he was called to lay. But the question remains about how to distinguish the essential, basic doctrine and message of the Church from what are side matters. Not all those who espoused fervent evangelism would have agreed with Griffith Jones about its answer. In his own mind, as an unyielding devotee to the Church of England in doctrine and worship, he seemed clear:

Dynion o zêl fawr dros ryw bethau neillduol mewn Crefydd (i ddinystr y pethau mwyaf) ... Dylid ystyrio yn dda, nad yw neb defodau, na dyledswyddau, nac egwyddorion mewn Crefydd, yn talu dim ymhellach nag y bônt yn fuddiol i chwanegu ein sancteiddrwydd ni. &[115]

[Men of great zeal over certain particular matters in Religion (to the destruction of the greatest matters) ... One needed to consider well, that there are no customs, not duties, nor principles in Religion, of worth beyond their being successful in adding to our sanctification. &]

Inevitable controversy arose from evangelism which made the Bible a searching judge of men's thoughts and actions. The more exact the search, the broader was the field of disagreement over what were essentials, or what were *adiaphora*.[116] Griffith Jones also called for obedient conformity, but without providing a biblical rationale of compromise.

A BACKGROUND OF DISTRUST AND REJECTION

Griffith Jones persevered in his evangelism amidst a growing public currency of suspicion and the accusation of enthusiasm.[117] He felt a need to warn against the evasions and self-deception committed by church-attending people who had heard his preaching of the Gospel:

> Dynion gwresog mewn Crefydd dros dro ac wedy'n yn llaesu yn ol; naill ai yn llwyr-gilio, ac felly yn llwyr-golli gwobr Crefydd; neu ynte yn llaesu mewn rhan, ac yn colli rhan o'i gwobr; cariad a'u diwydrwydd cyntaf yn oeri ... Dynion llawn hyder, er eu bod yn parhâu o syniad cnawdol a daiarol fel eraill.[118]

> [Men fervent in Religion for a while and afterwards falling weakly back; either be it fully retreating, and so fully losing the reward of Religion; or likely slackening in part, and losing part of their reward; love and their first devotion becoming cold ... Men full of confidence, despite continuing in a carnal and earthly mind like others]

Probably, the bitter retorts of some resentful of his warnings against sin added a personal note in Sermon 25, on Mat. 11.16–17: 'Am fod dynion yn gadael i'r llid a'r digofaint a ddylai godi yn erbyn pechod, gyffroi yn erbyn y rhai a'u rhybuddio yn erbyn pechod' (Because men allow anger and indignation that they ought to raise against sin, to stir them up against those who warn them against sin).[119] His tactless disparagement of less zealous clergy could not win him many friends. Sermon 57 contained an accusation of cold formality, comparing Christ's clerical opponents with formalists of Griffith Jones's time:

> Q: Pa fath rai yw y rhai'ny ag a fyddant olaf yn y dïwedd, ar ol tybied eu bod fel ymysg y blaenaf yn awr?
> A:1. Dynion ffurfiol mewn Crefydd, heb yspryd duwioldeb ganddynt; fel yr Iuddewon gynt, ac eraill yn awr.[120]

[Q. What sort are those who will be last in the end, after thinking that they are amongst the first now?

A. Men formal in Religion, not having a spirit of godliness; like the Jews of old, and others now.]

Griffith Jones insisted that wisdom, with other attainments, is a gift to be sought after. He quoted Prov. 3:15: 'Gwerthfawroccach yw hi nag emmau' [corrected later in the same hand to 'na gemmau'] (It is more precious than gems).[121] Alert to the danger of spiritual pride, he taught the duty of not being censorious: a brake on the naive assumption that one can read the depths of another's mind. This is a particular danger in a time of religious excitement, when extravagant phenomena of conversion can be assumed to be infallible proof of regeneration.

> Dysged hyn ni na byddom rŷ barod i farnu yr hyn na's gwyddom am eu gilydd ... Y mae yn wir rai pethau yn amlwg ymlaen llaw yn y duwiol a'r annuwiol. Edrychwn na bôm o nifer y rhai a fô ymlaen yngolwg dyn, ac yn ol yngolwg Duw ... Er pelled y bôch oddi wrth y blaengaraf ger bron dynion, ymdrechwn yn helaeth ynghylch y pethau a'ch dygo yn y blaen ger bron Duw.[122]

[Let this teach us not to be too ready to judge what we do not know about one another ... There are indeed certain things plain already in the godly and the ungodly. Let us look out not to be among the number of those who might be to the fore in the sight of man, and behind in the sight of God ... However far you might be from the foremost amongst men, let us strive exceedingly for the things which would bring you to the fore in the presence of God.]

Griffith Jones was preaching amidst a growing movement of animated concern over spiritual issues. Despite his call for caution in judging by externals, he fell into transgressing his own rule. One catches him calling motivated believers – such as his own converts – 'duwiol' ['godly'], 'ei bobl' ['his – that is, God's – people'], or simply and exclusively as 'Cristion' ['Christian']. This might seem to imply that he believed all reticent, undemonstrative faith to be false, and only those professing conversion to be true members of the Church. A shallow evaluation of the real, lasting effects of the new evangelism was to foster the facile dictum amongst some zealots that there was little or no 'life' in the Church before the 'Awakening'.[123]

NOTES

1   D. D. Morgan, 'Continuity, Novelty and Evangelicalism in Wales, *c*.1640–1850', in Michael A. G. Haykin and Kenneth J. Stewart (eds), *The Emergence of Evangelicalism* (Nottingham, 2008), p. 99.

2   Geraint H. Jenkins, *Literature, Religion and Society in Wales 1660–1730* (Cardiff, 1978), pp. 153–4.

3   Morgan, 'Continuity, Novelty and Evangelicalism Wales', p. 99.

4   Julian Hoppitt, *A Land of Liberty? England 1689–1727* (Oxford, 2000), p. 196.

5   Unlike much modern Evangelicalism, which recognizes the Church in separated bodies of converted believers, these seek to realize the 'Invisible' Church made 'visible' by including only those recognizably converted and taken to be regenerated. Cf. R. B. Gaffin, 'The Kingdom of God', in Sinclair B. Ferguson and David F. Wright (eds), *New Dictionary of Theology* (Leicester, 1988), pp. 367–9.

6   NLW, G. Jones, 'Sermon on Mat. 13.44. [2 January 1734] the parable of treasure hidden in a field', *Trysor o Ddifinyddiaeth*, p. 43.

7   Brown, 'Pietism', in Ferguson and Wright (eds), *New Dictionary of Theology*, pp. 515–17.

8   Derec Llwyd Morgan, *Y Diwygiad Mawr* (Llandysul, 1999), p. 11.

9   Robert Spencer Hardy, *William Grimshaw, Incumbent of Haworth 1742–1763* (London, 1860), p. 173.

10   Hardy, *William Grimshaw*, p. 232.

11   Cf. Arthur Fawcett, *The Cambuslang Revival, the Scottish Evangelical Revival of the Eighteenth Century* (London, 1971); I. H. Murray, *Jonathan Edwards* (Edinburgh, 1987); I. H. Murray, *Revival and Revivalism* (Edinburgh, 1994).

12   F. A. Cavenagh, *The Life and Work of Griffith Jones of Llanddowror* (Cardiff, 1930), p. 7.

13   Thomas Kelly, *Griffith Jones. Llanddowror, Pioneer in Adult Education* (Cardiff, 1950), p. 17.

14   David Jones, *Life and Times of Griffith Jones of Llanddowror* (London, 1902), p. 36.

15   Jenkins, *Literature, Religion*, p. 15.

16   G. Jenkins, 'An Old and Much Honoured'; 'Griffith Jones, Llanddowror', *Welsh History Review*, II (1983), 452.

17   G. Jones, 'Letter LVII, Questions as to Sincerity', in *Letters of the Rev. Griffith Jones to Mrs Bevan*, ed. Edward Morgan (London, 1832), pp. 190–1.

18   NLW, Jones, *Trysor*, pp. 73–4.

The Theology of Jones's Preaching

19 NLW, Jones, *Trysor*, pp. 74–5.
20 Like all else in Griffith Jones's innovations, it was not original to him, however.
21 G. Jones, *The Welsh Piety* (London, 1740), p. 19.
22 D. Ambrose Jones, *Griffith Jones Llanddowror* (Wrexham, 1923), p. 48.
23 William Jacob, 'The State of the Parishes', in Glanmor Williams et al. (eds), *The Welsh Church from Reformation to Disestablishment 1603–1920* (Cardiff, 2007), pp. 145–7.
24 Eifion Evans, *Daniel Rowland and the Great Awakening in Wales* (Edinburgh, 1985), p. 31.
25 E. J. G. Rogers, 'The Evangelical Fathers and the Liturgy (With particular reference to Holy Communion)', *The Churchman*, 60/4 (1946).
26 Rogers, 'The Evangelical Fathers'.
27 Rogers, 'The Evangelical Fathers'.
28 Jones, *Life and Times*, pp. 178–80.
29 E.g. Benedict of Nursia (480–543). Moravian communalism moved somewhat in the same direction.
30 Frank Baker, *John Wesley and the Church of England* (London, 1970), pp. 27, 40.
31 NLW, Jones, *Trysor*, p. 153.
32 NLW, Jones, *Trysor*, p. 720.
33 NLW, Jones, *Trysor*, Mat. 1:1 [11 November 1711], p. 57.
34 Josiah Woodward, *Account of the Rise and Progress of the Religious Societies in the City of London, &c. and of their Endeavours for Reformation of Manners* (London, 1698), p. 24.
35 David Bebbington, *Evangelicalism in Modern Britain* (London, 1989), p. 36.
36 NLW, Jones, *Trysor*, p. 288.
37 NLW, Jones, *Trysor*, p. 123.
38 NLW, Jones, *Trysor*, p. 64.
39 Jenkins, 'An Old and Much Honoured', 452.
40 NLW, Jones, *Trysor*, p. 63.
41 NLW, Jones, *Trysor*, p. 287.
42 Cavenagh, *The Life and Work*, p. 6.
43 NLW, Jones, *Trysor*, p. 287.
44 Jones, 'Letter XI, The paucity of good men lamented', p. 57: 'Letter XLVIII, Troubles from the Clergy', in *Letters of the Rev. Griffith Jones to Mrs Bevan*, ed. Edward Morgan (London, 1832), pp. 154–5.
45 NLW, Jones, *Trysor*, pp. 287–8.
46 Samuel Wesley, *An Account of the Religious Society begun in Epworth, in the Isle of Axholm Lincolnshire* (1701/2), para. VI.
47 Samuel Wesley, 'A Letter concerning the Religious Societies', appendix to *The Pious Communicant Rightly Prepar'd; or a Discourse Concerning the Blessed Sacrament* (London, 1700).
48 Bebbington, *Evangelicalism*, p. 40.
49 NLW, Jones, *Trysor*, p. 434.
50 Jenkins, 'An Old and Much Honoured', 456–7.
51 Bebbington, *Evangelicalism*, pp. 34–5.
52 NLW, Jones, *Trysor*, Sermon Mat. 13:44, p. 434.
53 Bebbington, *Evangelicalism*, p. 35.

The Theology of Griffith Jones and Religious Thought

54 Cf. *Westminster Confession of Faith* (London, 1646; Glasgow, 1994), ch. 3, para. 8: 'The doctrine of this high mystery of predestination is to be handled with special prudence and care, that men attending the will of God revealed in His Word, and yielding obedience thereunto, may, from the certainty of their effectual vocation, be assured of their eternal election.'

55 Cf. J. Calvin, *Institutes of the Christian Religion*, trans. Henry Beveridge (Geneva, 1559; London, 1962), vol. 2, ch. XXII, para. 10, pp. 221–4; A. A. Hodge, *Outlines of Theology* (1879; London, 1972), p. 446, para. 4; John Murray, *Studies in Theology*, vol. 4 of *Collected Writings* (Edinburgh, 1982), p. 114.

56 Compare John Flavel (1616–83), sermon XXIII on Mat. 26:47–9: *Works of John Flavel* (London, 1820; London, 1968), pp. 283–95.

57 NLW, Jones, *Trysor*, Sermon, Mat. 13:44, p. 436.

58 Cf. *Articles of Religion* (1562), XI and XII; *Canons of Dort.* (1619), heads II and V; *Westminster Confession of Faith*, chs 11 and 13.

59 NLW, Jones, *Trysor*, Sermon, Mat. 13:44, p. 436.

60 NLW, Jones, *Trysor*, p. 437.

61 Bebbington, *Evangelicalism*, pp. 5–10.

62 NLW, Jones, *Trysor*, Sermon no. 57 [Mat. 20:16], p. 143.

63 'History of Epidemics in Britain', *http://www.mongenes.org.uk/epidemics_in_bri.html* (accessed 7 August 2017).

64 Jenkins, *Literature, Religion*, p. 136.

65 Mary Clement, *Correspondence and Minutes of the SPCK relating to Wales 1699–1740* (Cardiff, 1952), p. 163.

66 Note that the numbering is Griffith Jones's own listing of points in order. Not all are quoted here.

67 NLW, Jones, *Trysor*, Sermon no. 84, Mat. 26:74, 75, pp. 1143–4.

68 NLW, Jones, *Trysor*, Sermon no. 19, Mat. 29:2 [24 December 1732], p. 263.

69 Jenkins, *Literature, Religion*, p. 23.

70 NLW, Jones, *Trysor*, Mat. 26:74, 75 [27 June 1731], pp. 289–90.

71 Matthew 9:2.

72 NLW, Jones, *Trysor*, p. 262.

73 NLW, Jones, *Trysor*, p. 262.

74 Matthew 17:1–7.

75 NLW, Jones, *Trysor*, p. 589.

76 NLW, Jones, *Trysor*, pp. 590–1.

77 There is a doubt as to whether that emphasis had continued from the 1520s, and especially whether so in Wales. CUL, Susan (Harding) Howell, 'East Anglia on the Eve of the Reformation' (unpublished PhD thesis, CUL, 1967).

78 NLW, Jones, *Trysor*, p. 591.

79 NLW, Jones, *Trysor*, p. 232.

80 K. Bockmuehl, 'Sanctification', in Ferguson and Wright (eds), *New Dictionary*, p. 613.

81 NLW, Jones, *Trysor*, p. 243.

82 Bebbington, *Evangelicalism*, pp. 14–17.

83 NLW, Jones, *Trysor*, p. 434.

84 NLW, Jones, *Trysor*, p. 436.

The Theology of Jones's Preaching

85 NLW, Jones, *Trysor*, pp. 435–6.
86 T. H. L. Parker, *John Calvin: a Biography* (London, 1975), pp. 91–6.
87 Cf. other preachers of biblicistic outlook, such as John Bunyan (1628–88) or Charles Simeon (1759–1836).
88 Sometimes spread over more than one sermon.
89 *Westminster Confession of Faith*, ch. 7, 'Of God's covenant with Man', pp. 41–5.
90 Cf. Jones's use of 'covenant' elsewhere.
91 Cf. Bebbington, *Evangelicalism*, pp. 2–10.
92 Morgan, *Theologia*, p. 289.
93 E.g. William Perkins (1558–1602), William Ames (1576–1633).
94 NLW, Jones, *Trysor*, p. 115.
95 Morgan, *Theologia*, p. 281.
96 NLW, Jones, *Trysor*, p. 115.
97 The *Trysor* transcribed sermons sometimes are headed with later notes of being preached again, subsequently, after Jones's death.
98 NLW, Jones, *Trysor*, January and February 1736, p. 587.
99 Isaiah 2:2, a prediction of large movements of Gentiles to faith in the God of Israel, using the metaphor of Mount Zion rising up.
100 NLW, Jones, *Trysor*, p. 719.
101 NLW, Jones, *Trysor*, p. 720.
102 NLW, Jones, *Trysor*, 2 September 1733, p. 289.
103 NLW, Jones, *Trysor*, p. 289.
104 NLW, Jones, *Trysor*, September 1736, p. 717.
105 NLW, Jones, *Trysor*, p. 307.
106 NLW, Jones, *Trysor*, p. 305.
107 NLW, Jones, *Trysor*, Mat. 13:44, p. 438.
108 NLW, Jones, *Trysor*, Mat. 13:44, p. 441.
109 NLW, Jones, *Trysor*, Mat. 17:1–3, January and February 1736, p. 581.
110 Deuteronomy 17:6; Matthew 18:15.
111 NLW, Jones, *Trysor*, Mat. 13:44, p. 586.
112 Bob Tennant, 'The Sermons of the Eighteenth-Century Evangelicals', in Keith A. Francis and William Gibson (eds), *The Oxford Handbook of the British Sermon 1689–1901* (Oxford, 2012), p. 123.
113 NLW, Jones, *Trysor*, p. 587; Griffith Jones or his amanuensis, altered 'bröydd' ['vales'] by adding an 'n', to write 'bronydd' ['hillsides']. It perhaps speaks of Jones's meticulous revision of his transcriptions, although the alteration still seems to be the mistake of a busy man.
114 NLW, Jones, *Trysor*, Mat. 10:15, 2 September 1733, p. 288.
115 NLW, Jones, *Trysor*, Mat. 20:16, p. 718.
116 Gomer Morgan Roberts, *Bywyd a Gwaith Peter Williams* (Cardiff, 1943), pp. 42–5.
117 John Evans, *Some Account of the Welch Charity-Schools, and the Rise and Progress of Methodism in Wales* (London, 1752); Morgan, *Theologia*, pp. 281–2.
118 NLW, Jones, *Trysor*, pp. 718–19.
119 NLW, Jones, *Trysor*, Mat. 11:17, 13 January 1733/4, p. 305.
120 NLW, Jones, *Trysor*, p. 715.

121 NLW, Jones, *Trysor*, Mat. 13:44, p. 437.

122 NLW, Jones, *Trysor*, p. 721.

123 Richard Bennett, *Blynyddoedd Cyntaf Methodistiaeth* (Caernarfon, 1909), p. 43.

Chapter 6

GRIFFITH JONES'S MORALISM AND THEOLOGY

GRIFFITH JONES AND BISHOP GEORGE BULL

Griffith Jones retained a great respect for Bishop George Bull and the pastoral encouragements that he gave when Jones was ordained.[1] Jones is unlikely not to have become aware at some time of a difference between the widely held view of good works expressed in Bull's doctrine of justification, and that of the Church's Reformers. He could scarcely have been ignorant of the ardent controversy within the Church of England and elsewhere on this topic.[2] Griffith Jones was an uncompromising moralist in denouncing sin and demanding holiness as an essential fruit of faith in the Christian, but he avoided insisting on accomplished good works as the first proviso to the offer of salvation.[3] In Griffith Jones's lifetime, the persisting distrust of the Prayer Book's doctrine of justification by many in the Church of England, including John Wesley, was not easily to be removed by the biblically based arguments of men like James Hervey.[4] Such men as these latter were explicitly accused of heterodoxy in their teaching of solifidian justification. In St Edmund Hall, Oxford, in 1768, an over-reaction to the discovery of the presence of six Methodistic students led to their investigation and expulsion from the university for gatherings involving reprehensibly talk of 'regeneration, inspiration and drawing nigh unto God'.[5] The charges against the men began with the accusation of 'Holding the doctrines of Election, Perseverance, and Justification by Faith without Works': all contain in the Articles to which every Anglican ordinand was obliged to subscribe.[6] Griffith Jones emphatically preached a solifidian offer of forgiveness, along with a teaching which revealed him, nevertheless, to be a pronounced moralist.[7] The theme of 'reformation' was of long standing in the Church of England. Jones stood aloof from demands, such as those for further reformation in components of worship and polity that had been made by the Puritan party before 1660. He was at one, however, with the wish even in the most powerful circles for a 'reformation of manners', for a change in public opinion about immorality and common decency. John Spurr wrote of:

> the 'godly revolution', the publicity campaign that portrayed the 1688–89 Revolution as a work of piety and the Williamite court as a vehicle for national moral and religious renewal ... and (to give the impression of a will) to reconnect the Church of England with what they saw as its roots in the sixteenth-century Reformation.[8]

The baton of agitation for public morality passed after 1660, notably to the Societies for the Reformation of Manners, in which High Churchmen – including Samuel Wesley – were prominent.[9] Sir John Philipps, who was at one with Griffith Jones's ideals, exemplified the trend and was noted in Parliament as 'run mad for reformation'.[10] In Jones's preaching, the demand for holiness as essential to the Christian life, and the denouncing of sin in thorough detail, were prominent. Moral behaviour was, however, posited, not as in itself earning salvation, but rather as a consequence and evidence of faith in the Gospel, and a test of Christian discipleship.[11] In contrast, the offer of forgiveness itself was always immediate and absolute:

> Mae Crist yn tynnu ymaith y gosp, sef y farn a'r felldith, y digofaint a'r ddamnedigaeth ag y mae pechod yn haeddu. Rhuf: 8:1 Nid oes gan hynny yn awr ddim damnedigaeth i'r rhai sy yng Nghrist Iesu.[12]

> [Christ takes away the punishment, that is judgement and curse, the anger and damnation which sin deserves. [He then quotes the Bible:] Romans 8:1 'There is therefore now no condemnation to them which are in Christ Jesus.']

But Jones preached the necessity of good works with equal emphasis. For instance, a sermon about attending the Holy Communion included: 'Chwiliwch eich calonnau, i wybod pa bechodau ydych yn fwyaf euog o honynnt, ac yna edifarhêwch a galarwch am danynt (Search your hearts, to know of which sins you are the most guilty, and then repent and mourn over them).[13]

A noticeable loosening in the consistency of Anglican adherence to the Reformed system had happened regarding the key doctrine of justification, after the accession of James I in 1603. It was redoubled after 1660. Peter Nockles wrote:

> The later Caroline Divines, such as Jeremy Taylor and George Bull reacted against what they perceived as the excesses of Puritan covenant theology in the Commonwealth era. For the later Carolines, the mid-century Puritan divines had fallen into the error of Solifidianism[14]

The theological issues are too complex to be discussed fully here. But it can be argued that the most influential breach in general acceptance of the Church's teaching as found in the Articles resulted from a re-evaluation of the received doctrine of justification.[15] The explicit Reformed definition of justification, contained especially in Articles X to XIII, is constitutive of a whole theological scheme.[16] But the doctrine incited an aversion in some High Churchmen, who sought to promote an interpretation that might leave room for a dependence on human ability and moral effort. However, the attempt was, correspondingly, strongly denounced by some leading English divines, notably George Morley (1598?–1684), bishop of Winchester.[17] George Bull's Latin works made him a leading exponent of a certain High Anglican postulation of orthodoxy in the later seventeenth century. His repute as a theological paragon was tempered, however, by his first book, the *Harmonia Apostolica* (1670). In it, he refused to accept the categorical divine imputation of righteousness through faith alone, but propounded a view of justification as an attempted resolution of the alleged contradiction between the Apostle Paul in Ephesians 2, and James in his Epistle 2.[18] Bull proposed that justification was indeed an act of God's grace, imputing righteousness freely, and received by faith. But he added the arbitrary proviso that one must prepare for such reception by diligent acts of 'evangelical obedience'.[19] In his sermon on Hosea 10:12, he wrote:

> God indeed, is infinitely good and merciful, and it is out of that infinite goodness and mercy, that He bestows the gift of eternal life upon any man; but God is also infinitely wise, and righteous, and holy; and therefore will not (I think I may say He cannot) confer the rich donative upon any unholy or unrighteous person.[20]

This antithetical 'harmonizing' must be deemed as impossible to be reconciled with the core of Anglican soteriology as stated unambiguously in the Articles, Prayer Book and Homilies. Bull's theory overrode the New Testament's treatment of causality, and had the effect of discrediting the classic Protestant doctrine of justification. Stephen Hampton wrote:

> When George Bull published the *Harmonia Apostolica* ... he was spoiling for a fight ... Since solifidianism ... had been the near-unanimous teaching of English divines until the 1640s ... and was commonly understood to be the position endorsed by the Thirty-Nine Articles, Bull was being wilfully, indeed outrageously, provocative.[21]

Bull's daring soteriology was evidence of a weakening of the confidence of some High Churchmen in the key Reformed doctrine of justification. The trend, sometimes called 'English Arminianism', is not to be equated fully with any present-day category. It did express a recoil from what some deemed to be an over-systematizing in the 'Genevan' covenantalism, taught pre-eminently by the school having Theodore Beza (1519–1605) as an early exponent.[22] In the attempt to integrate the whole corpus of doctrine, Anglican anti-solifidianists tended to assume ecclesiology, rather than covenantalism, as providing the necessary unifying dogmatic matrix. They did this whilst contending, nevertheless, for important aspects of Reformed theology, such as divine sovereignty, biblical authority and revealed religion.[23] The theological issues are complex. But is seems clear that a weakening of dependence on the Church's Articles as a whole necessarily came by this slackening of commitment to a doctrine which incited in the 'Arminians' an understandable reactive moralism and suspicion of antinomianism. These men insisted that the teaching of absolute justification through faith was an inevitable and fatal disincentive to good works in believers.[24] This fear came to be sharply expressed in John Wesley's teaching, in which he, and his many followers, denounced the doctrine of the imputation of Christ's works of righteousness as antinomian.[25] When James Hervey (1714–58) published *Theron and Aspasio* in 1755 as a defence of the Reformed doctrine of imputation, Wesley initiated an injurious pamphlet debate against its doctrine. He wrote:

> Then for Christ's sake, and for the sake of the immortal souls which he has purchased with his blood, do not dispute for that particular phrase, the *imputed righteousness of Christ*. It is not scriptural, it is not necessary ... But it has done immense hurt[26]

L. E. Elliott-Binns wrote of *Theron and Aspasio*: 'Its views aroused a small war of pamphlets, and it was ardently defended by Cudworth.'[27] Nevertheless, John Wesley was not consistent. Revealing a muddled incompetence in handling the biblical data, he strongly preached immediate forgiveness through faith. Indeed, his 'new-birth' conversionism posited a due assurance of this: 'I mean a sure confidence, that by the merits of Christ he [i.e. a believer] was reconciled to the favour of God.'[28] Seeking to co-ordinate the importance of faith with the postulated contribution of righteousness through good works to the believer's justification, Wesley – like others – was led crucially into the expedient of lowering the standard of perfection, in order for one to be able to reach it.[29] This was the 'evangelical obedience' proposed by Bishop Bull.[30] Wesley denounced the preaching of Christ's vicarious good works as 'downright antinomianism'. He insisted, concerning Christ's works for believers, that:

> the nice, metaphysical doctrine of imputed righteousness, leads not to repentance, but to licentiousness ... that foundation is already laid in the merits of Christ. Yet we obey, in order to our final acceptance through his merits. And in this sense, by obeying we lay a good foundation, that we may attain eternal life.[31]

No less than George Bull, John Wesley was magisterial in his denunciation of clergy who offered salvation in terms which were, in fact, consistent with Articles XI and XII. He coolly affirmed that his own teaching wholly conformed to the Anglican formularies, writing of an open-air sermon at Abergavenny in 1739: 'I simply described the plain old religion of the Church of England which is now almost everywhere spoken against under the new name of Methodism'.[32]

BISHOP BULL AND ANTINOMIANISM

George Bull's dissent from the Protestant doctrine of justification went so far as to imply that all Anglicans who preached justification as not dependent upon preparatory good works were prodigious deviationists:

> Among us Protestant, there have been many (too, too many) that have taught for pure, yea, the purest Gospel, such doctrines as these; 'That the faith whereby we are justified, is nothing else but a recumbence or reliance upon Christ ...' The men that taught these sad propositions, were called Antinomians; whose name indeed is now every where odious and decried[33]

Bull thus touched on a sensitive nerve. Some sectaries, such as the Ranters, of the 1650s had indeed taught that God's forgiveness of sins freed believers from any obligation to keep the moral Law.[34] This had lent plausibility to anti-Puritan polemics, lumping all solifidians, including

Griffith Jones's Moralism and Theology

many respected Anglican divines, together as antinomian. Sir John Philipps revealed some awareness of the current antinomian controversy, in a passage in a private notebook, made some time after 9 January 1724:

> if Pelagians, & Arminians, did not stand up to so much for free-will, there wd not be so many Antinomians, who hold that all is done by God & nothing the creature.[35]

His remark seems to reflect a common misunderstanding: that a rejection of Pelagianism and Arminian semi-Pelagianism must entail a denial of the necessity of good works. In Reformed thought, justification is, by definition, entirely an act of divine grace.[36] Good works necessarily result from justification, but do not purchase it.[37] Probably Sir John was influenced by the moral panic of the time, which included a justifiable fear of heterodox libertinage. Bishop Bull and others felt led to employ the fear of antinominanism to evade the full force of the Church's soteriology. The rejection of loose living was a strong motive also for the SPCK, and appears prominently in the moralism of Griffith Jones's sermons; indeed, as an integral fibre of his evangelistic preaching. Sir John's imprecise definitions help to provide an understanding of his generous devotion to the works for social improvement, and especially his approval of Griffith Jones. The unbroken like-mindedness of this apparently disparate partnership in Christian service seems anchored in this theological outlook, though Jones would perhaps not have fully agreed with his patron's inept misstatement. Bull reinforced his own deprecation of the received doctrine of justification with dark references to the bitter resentments still felt against the victorious side in the Civil War:

> And the same men, (when they are now not only not licensed, but themselves forbidden to preach,) are the only men that still maintain and strenuously propagate those pernicious doctrines in the schismatical assemblies.[38]

George Bull attempted here to preclude solifidians by a disputational artifice. But disfranchised Presbyterian divines were not 'the only men' to hold the classic Protestant soteriology; many, including some unimpeachable leading Anglican theologians still also taught it. Strong Anglican complaints arose against George Bull's anti-solifidianism: from Charles Gataker (1613–80), rector of Hoggeston, Buckinghamshire, in 1670,[39] and from Bishop George Morley (1598?–1684), who went so far as to forbid his clergy even to read the *Harmonia* or preach on it.[40] Thomas Tully (1620–76), principal of St Edmund Hall, Oxford, called it 'heretical'.[41] Thomas Barlow (1608/-9–91), bishop of Lincoln, called the book Socinian and 'parricidal'.[42] John Spurr quoted Barlow regarding Remonstrant doctrines, refuted by the Synod of Dordt (1618–19): 'did not the Church of England, and all her obedient sons till 1626 or 1628 (both the universities) approve the doctrine of that synod?'[43] He wrote: 'Barlow leaned ... towards a high Calvinist theology ... increasingly unfashionable in 1630s Oxford'.[44] Despite this Oxonian trend, many others persisted in rejecting Bull's teaching. Discounting the opinion of leading Anglican theologians, Gilbert Sheldon (1598–1677) recommended the *Harmonia*, which was reprinted and became an accepted textbook. This serious doctrinal rift in the Church continued unresolved, into the time of Griffith Jones's ministry.

Griffith Jones must have been aware of the differences of opinion in the Church, for and against the advancing neonomianism.[45] The perseverance of some, including dissenters, in Wales in an unmodified Reformed soteriology may have influenced Jones's view of the doctrine. D. Densil Morgan alluded to an important fact in the Welsh Church, likely to have had an influence upon the course of Griffith Jones's ministry. Of a prayer of Edward Wynn (1618–69), a 'conformist, moderate Puritan', he wrote:

> This is a good example ... of so-called 'Anti-Arminianism' or traditional Reformed churchmanship ... [despite] a renewed Laudian-type prelacy ... the significance of Wynn's brand of piety should not be discounted. It would help ensure the remarkable success of the SPCK in affording godly literature ... and provide the impetus ... for the educational and

Griffith Jones's Moralism and Theology

evangelistic labours of Griffith Jones. Not all Anglican theology in Wales
... would be dry, formalist and Arminian.[46]

Despite Thomas Barlow's standing as an Oxford divine, and the
controversy about what should be held as the Church's received teaching
on justification, Griffith Jones gave no sign of lessening respect for George
Bull. Jones was reputedly well read in theological literature. The *Sketch*
stated that: 'Mr Jones made the Study of Divinity the main Point of his
Pursuit ... [and] became well versed in the Writings of the most eminent
Divines, whether at home or abroad'.[47] There may be over-generosity in
this praise, and wide reading does not necessarily ensure discernment
of theological subtleties. But Griffith Jones did have a useful grasp of at
least a department of theology, together with a most thorough working
knowledge of the Bible's contents. He is likely to have had respect for
divines whose theology he steadily seconded in his sermons – but,
apparently, without mentioning any by name. It is perhaps surprising that
Jones seems to have been slow to make any overtly partisan defence of this
pivot of Protestant doctrine. Forbearing to comment on Bull's tendency, he
largely avoided controversy, whilst persisting in his affirmative evangelism
throughout his career.[48] Despite any misgivings that he may have had,
he apparently saw no reason to draw attention towards any weakness in
his mentor's writing. It seems characteristic of Griffith Jones to avoid
controversy by simply pressing ahead with his task, as when accusations
were made against him in print, he wrote on 29 July 1736:

> how much my late friends have endeavoured to possess the Bishop and
> Chancellor with prejudice against me ... left to stand alone, without any
> encouragement ... from my brethren the clergy; yet this, methinks, is an
> advantage to make me proceed with so much more sincerity, with respect
> to God.[49]

Geraint Jenkins wrote that he 'deliberately kept a low profile, choosing to
labour self-effacingly in the rural fastnesses of Carmarthenshire'.[50] Though
he was disposed to follow Bull's example and precepts, it is through the
fine difference in his view of justification that Jones set out on a diverging

path. Despite whatever may have been Jones's inclination, the absolute teaching of justification could only lead to the creation of an opposing, and often indignant, body of opinion, in the contemporary upsurge of revived popular religion.[51] For George Bull, a demand for holy living dominated his theory of justification and the 'hope of glory'. His recorded deathbed words evoke the conventional search after peace of conscience through good works:

> I most firmly believe, that as I yield a stedfast Assent to the Gospel of Christ, and as I work out true Repentance by that Faith, shaking off by the Grace of God the Yoke of every deadly Sin, and in earnest devoting my self to the Observation of his Evangelical Law; I shall obtain by the Sovereign Mercy of God the Father, for the Merits only of Jesus Christ his son, and my Lord and Saviour, who offered up himself unto the Father a truly expiatory Sacrifice for my sins, and for the Sins of the whole World, the full Remission of all my past Sins be they never so many and great.[52]

By these words, Bull appears to have been unable to put trust in a complete remission of sins and justification by divine imputation in Christ alone. He could cling to some hope of forgiveness of 'past Sins', but seems to have lacked confidence for the future. His statement continued:

> But then I have no otherwise any Confidence of my Sins being forgiven me, or of my being in a State of Grace and Salvation, but as by a serious Examination of my Conscience ... there shall be Evidence of the Sincerity of my Faith and Repentance, and while I not only abstain from those Crimes, which according to the Gospel exclude a Man from Heaven, but do diligently likewise exercise my self in Good Works ... so long I may preserve the Grace that is given me, of Remission and Justification: And that if I *die in this State*, I am in the way of obtaining it by the Mercy of God, an eternal Life and Salvation for the sake of Jesus Christ.[53]

This poignant statement implies a conviction that a believer's state before God may be precarious and liable to being overturned by lapses into sin – which are, of course, inevitable.[54] Bull thus appeared unable fully to rely on a perfect atonement made by Christ on his behalf, so as to feel confident that all his sins were covered.[55] His view of justification was that his security continued to depend on his good works of religion and charity, by the 'Observation of his [God's] Evangelical Law'. Like Samuel Johnson (1709–84), Bull appeared to have felt obliged to try, by strenuous efforts, to 'preserve the grace' given to him, which could easily be lost.[56] Bull's view of grace and justification – held by many others – thus touched the same point of contention which drove Martin Luther to publish his own opinion in 1517.[57] The doctrine of salvation was prominent in the formularies of the reformed English Church being based upon justification as an 'act of God's free grace'.[58] Article XI states: 'that we are justified by Faith only is a most wholesome Doctrine, and very full of comfort'.[59] Alongside this, Article XII sees 'good works' nevertheless as arising 'necessarily of a true and lively Faith; insomuch that by them a lively Faith may be as evidently known as a tree discerned by the fruit'.[60] Prayer Book soteriology is oriented upon these cardinal points, and was employed as a persuasive offer of full remission of sin and divine adoption in Griffith Jones's preaching.

THE PREACHING OF REDEMPTION

Faith in the divine promise, as proposed by Griffith Jones, consisted in the embracing of an absolute offer of redemption, usually received through preaching.[61] Preaching acted, conformably, as a tool to inform and give 'assurance': strengthen a person's sense of his or her security under the provisions of divine grace, leading into the future.[62] Preaching was necessary at every stage: begetting faith, but also nurturing the whole Christian life. Thus, whilst always evangelizing, Jones preached equally to inform his hearers of the importance of growth in knowledge, and of pious works as a 'fruit' of faith. As to justification, he appears to have adhered consistently to the received Reformation doctrine, whilst in ecclesiology, he remained completely at one with the High Church party: 'Os Xt yw Craig Iecht ei bobl, Pa mor anhebygol o gael Iecht. yw'r rhai sy'n sylfaeni eu Gob. ar eu Moesoldeb eu hun. &' (If Christ is the Rock of Salvation of his people, <u>How unlikely to get Salvation are they who base their Hope on their own Morality)</u>.[63] The Reformation had established an emphasis on the Gospel as the prime public declaration, somewhat eclipsing thereby all other religious observance.[64] This concept of the Christian message was the core of Griffith Jones's preaching, promising reconciliation, forgiveness, adoption and blessings of the Holy Ghost. Divine gifts were emphatically taught as being all of 'grace': that is, by free gift, without any payment by the recipients.[65] Hence came the paradox that a 'new life' was offered to persons who were actually unworthy of it, merely on condition of believing and trusting God's promise.[66] The promised grace included a divine strengthening to live a new life of obedience to God's moral law; but the resulting deeds were explained as not being any part of a purchase of God's favour, which was entirely 'free', given in Christ the 'Redeemer'.[67] This proposition – of 'substitutionary atonement' – was supremely the substance of Griffith Jones's preaching and teaching, but remained an obstacle to his being fully at one with the ministry of such Methodists as John Wesley and his followers.[68] From the standpoint of the Church's Articles, therefore, one can argue that Griffith Jones was not an innovator in preaching an absolute offer of justification. John Spurr pointed out that, as a writer, Bishop Bull represented an innovating movement in the Church of England, the effect of which was to obscure: 'the theological distinction between justification and sanctification'.[69] Robert Cornwall wrote:

> Bull did in an academic context what parish clergy always did, and that was to recognize the difficulty of distinguishing between faith and works. Although Bull was assuredly more Arminian than Calvinist[70]

In fairness to Bull, it must be acknowledged that innate human moral instinct can, nevertheless, find the unmodified doctrine of free justification repulsive. Awareness of one's moral failures naturally tends to breed uneasiness and a desire for a reassuring sense of creditable achievement by good works.[71] Hence, the Reformed doctrine of substitutionary atonement was – and remains – often baffling, and mistrusted by some as apparently a dogmatically antinomian disincentive to moral effort.[72]

Evangelicalism, as a distinct movement, coalesced out of the leading ideas and practices current in the religious quickening from the 1730s.[73] In its preaching, the message of prime importance was directed towards urging commitment from those lacking a personal profession of faith and, more importantly, lacking the conscious experience of 'conversion': a drastic break with one's former life.[74] This conversionistic trend has come, in more recent times, predominantly to be an appeal to the mass of non-churchgoing 'outsiders'.[75] Griffith Jones consistently practised the pragmatic call to faith, though still largely amongst those within the body of the Church as 'members'.[76] In a time of rising popular religious interest and crowded services, it was understandable that Jones's ministry should develop under the impetus of this evangelistic model, with the intent of re-establishing a Christian posture of morality in the land, as well as fostering individual salvation.[77] His addresses were replete with arguments drawn exhaustively from Scripture, whilst he kept to the Prayer Book liturgy. He also took the opportunity, however, to hold extra week-day services, and advocated the establishing of extra lectures by other clergy.[78] A more general, rising popular mood of religious enquiry perforce begot a new sense of urgency to 'lift up a standard' by more evangelistic preaching. This had the aim of gathering back into the Church the 'strayed sheep' of Wales.[79] Crowds were attracted to Griffith Jones's preaching, as his enemy John Evans reported, and many responded to his call for confident self-commitment.[80] It is not a disparagement, therefore, to describe Jones's application of the biblical text as intensely personal. In preaching, his habit was to comment on the broader doctrinal conspectus of a text, but then to proceed to a narrowing of attention to the details of personal understanding and piety. This evangelistic approach, and the tradition that Jones helped to foster thereby, was a response to circumstances as they developed, as in all his enterprises, rather than the application of some prescribed, textbook method.[81] The Prayer Book makes little use of the word 'conversion', and so avoids the confusion of conversion with divine regeneration.[82] The course of departure in Britain from the theology and practices of the Reformation can be traced partly in the conflation of the two concepts. Evangelical 'Revivalism' and Fundamentalism are partly an outcome of this theological confusion.[83] It seems advisable to avoid using the term 'conversion' to denote the two different, though often connected, things. An observable psychological change does not necessarily announce or ensure a lasting spiritual renewal.[84] Deep religious changes are by nature invisible, and are often unspoken and gradual. Jonathan Edwards (1703–58) related cases of conversion, as examples of a surprising revolution of faith in individuals. These were observable facts: ascertainable changes of mind and habit. Edwards, like Griffith Jones, did not instigate a movement, employing novel means of exciting repentance, faith and uprightness in his hearers. But even Edwards also incautiously used the same word 'conversion' of a presumed inner renewing by the Holy Spirit: 'Conversion is a great and glorious work of God's power, at once changing the heart, and fusing life into the dead soul.'[85] He might have done better to suggest that there is a reasonable hope that the personal revolution of 'conversion' would prove the result of a corresponding permanent divine work of 'regeneration'. The former is observable; the latter unverifiable to men, albeit made probable by a lasting improvement in life and character. This is not to suggest that Jonathan Edwards was unaware of the distinction, but in a time of unusually widespread, eager popular response to preaching, the distinction may be overlooked. In Griffith Jones's time, as in ours, the ill-instructed or 'enthusiastic' could be recklessly incautious over the distinction. Some fervent responses to Griffith Jones's preaching were conversions, but still lacked permanence, as he himself acknowledged: 'evidence of your sincerity, even while I have reason to lament the too much want of it in myself and many others'.[86] A strong moral persuasion can easily wear off, and the old convictions and lifestyle regain control. The psychological impressions may have been valid as far as they went; fundamental change is validated by its full perseverance.[87]

In the debate over the relation of faith to personal morality, there was a reaction of bitter recriminations to the increase in the numbers of new adherents to an undiluted Reformed view of justification.[88] Complaints were to persist against the prominent teaching of justification through God's free imputation, to the wholly undeserving, of Christ's perfect human works of righteousness.[89] There was a particular offence, moreover, in its being treated by the new wave of evangelism as always

Griffith Jones's Moralism and Theology

dependent upon a sudden, critical 'new-birth' experience. The exhilarant, 'enthusiastical' conviction of a convert's new assurance of inner light, guidance and forgiveness alarmed churchmen like Edmund Gibson.[90] One of George Whitefield's (1714–70) many references to the offence caused by his preaching on the 'new birth' was, in 1737:

> Two clergymen sent for me, and told me they would not let me preach in their pulpits any more, unless I renounced that part of my sermon on regeneration, wherein I wished, 'that my brethren would entertain their auditories oftener with discourses upon the new birth'. This I had no freedom to do, and so they continued my opposers.[91]

Whitefield was influential in pressing the teaching of 'new-birth' crisis-conversions distinctly further. He led the trend of itinerating and preaching publicly to sometimes impromptu, unregulated gatherings.[92] His ministry lacked an appointed sphere of duty or formal accountability, thus fostering an impression of reckless innovation and insubordination in practice and doctrine. He preached often in the open air, not taking much care to avoid the offence given to the settled clergy by an appearance of deliberate social disruption, and flouting of ecclesiastical authority.[93] Even his Tabernacle in Tottenham Court Road and other buildings were non-parochial meeting places for mixed throngs of followers.[94] When there, he preached very successfully, but much towards people who were strangers to him, and not formally – nor practically – under his pastoral care. The contrast with Griffith Jones's strict adherence to his own legal parochial duties is clear; but Jones's congregations also included many unknown visitors, some from great distances.[95] In some later Evangelical opinion, only when it was given within such a situation – and often in a trite, over-simplified formula – did the Christian message even deserve the name of 'Gospel'.[96] This is perhaps the most persistent and problematic feature of that tradition in the English-speaking world, which was to evolve eventually, partly from the practice of such as Griffith Jones.[97] The disagreements about justification by faith remained a feature of the evangelistic movement, and continued thereafter in John Wesley's denunciation of its alleged antinomianism.[98] This theory of justification was the boundary between two disparate theological systems, and was later to kindle an unbridgeable contrariety between Anglican Evangelicals, like James Hervey, and the Wesleyans.[99] The fact that Griffith Jones came to place himself, without ostentatious provocation, on the opposite side of the divide from men like Bull is crucial to understanding his motives and lasting significance as an Anglican loyalist. His work helped to lay a foundation upon which the future Welsh Evangelicalism grew.[100] For those later called Calvinistic Methodists, solifidianism was a locus formative of their whole system of theology.[101] Its importance came to be overshadowed, however, as Reformed covenantalism was gradually lost sight of. D. Densil Morgan wrote of Timothy Thomas's *Y Wisg Wen Ddisglair* of 1759, which expressed the standpoint of the older Dissent, that it:

> was on the doctrine of justification by faith alone; it placed regeneration in the context of justification and emphasized the objective facts of the gospel and their appropriation through faith rather than through subjective religious experience.[102]

Morgan went on to cite Lewis Edward's trenchant opinion that this crucial article of faith: 'was, by the late-eighteenth century, being eclipsed by the evangelicals' conviction concerning the need to be born again.'[103]

FROM CONVERSIONISM TO REVIVALISM

The very force of conversionism's grip on minds, promising salvation through a conventionalized 'subjective religious experience', portended the waning of full Reformed orthodoxy, and the predominance of Arminian Evangelicalism.[104] To attribute to Griffith Jones the same outlook, by calling him a 'revivalist' or even an 'Evangelical', is somewhat misleadingly anachronistic. The influence of crowd-emotion, especially on volatile temperaments, can mask the true underlying effects of preaching. Emotional excitement in tears or cries of joy can be a mere passing mood. Griffith Jones himself spoke caustically of the excesses of noisy self-expression, sometimes even deliberately cultivated.[105] The Reformers themselves had acknowledged that some conversions failed to make a radical change.[106] They described an unfathomable inner renewal producing a lasting change as a divine work beyond human power of inspection. It was named 'effectual calling', 'regeneration' or 'new birth'.[107] Griffith Jones believed it beyond any mere human power to produce this transformation. He wrote:

> The Spirit of God is the parent that produceth spiritual appetites; it is from the spirit of adoption put into their hearts, that the saints do long for God, and cry unto him Abba, Father ...

> That the Spirit of the living God ... recover, revive and raise up to life, the souls of men, out of their wretched state of death and darkness[108]

But although acknowledging that mere human effort cannot induce an inner spiritual renewal, Griffith Jones believed that the preaching was God's appointed tool to instil a permanent spiritual effect. He was optimistic about projects for more preaching therefore, writing to Mrs Bevan:

> I am more and more convinced, that the joint and resolute endeavours of several clergymen would have a good effect, by the blessing of God, towards reforming a wicked world.[109]

It is surprising that, despite the very unusual effect of his ordinary preaching in winning acceptance, Jones was, at the height of his success, far from showing the triumphalism typical of some later revivalistic preaching.[110] His proneness to pessimism made him almost morbidly sceptical of its permanence because of the failures of himself and others: 'we have reason to fear that God is now about leaving our land and departing from us ... we should stir ourselves up to ... solicit his return and stay with us'.[111] Contrastingly, the success of some later preachers in winning converts out of their numerous hearers was to breed a lack of caution. Latterly, it produced the assumption that conversion with racked compunction, followed by jubilant peace of mind, was the norm. Regeneration was assumed to be validated by such excitement as that called by Bishop J. C. Ryle 'infectious ... sham, sensational Christianity'.[112] An example of a contrastingly more cautious view of conversions as evidence of divine regeneration is found in reports of Cambuslang and elsewhere in Scotland in 1741:

> That there are some who do not cry out in the congregation ... have been under a law-work for some months, and are, as far as we can know the state of another, savingly converted.[113]

The proviso 'as far as we can know' acknowledged that signs of apparent divine grace lay beyond any human authentication. The later prejudice of much of Evangelicalism was to lead to the assumption that a conversion is always a spiritual renewal by God, and therefore demonstrably complete and genuine. Elliott-Binns wrote of: 'Differences ... over the doctrine among Evangelicals ... arisen through confusing regeneration and conversion.'[114] 'Conversion' (an observable event) and 'regeneration' (inner renewal) were then treated as identical, and assumed to be induced by oratory and playing upon emotions. A 'new birth', it came to be assumed, could be engineered by provoking a 'decision'. As a later and more simplistic manifestation of the trend, Fundamentalism came to allege all converts as 'born-again believers', and therefore fully 'saved'.[115] Those without such conversion could, accordingly, not be called 'Christians', or acknowledged as members of the true Church. Griffith Jones held a different view of regeneration:

> The spirit is the Author of the new birth, and it is by him that the work of regeneration must be carried on to perfection. It is he who gives that clear light, far above the best natural capacities[116]

The later ascendancy of revivalism, stimulated after 1859 in Wales, militated against the theory of regeneration held by Griffith Jones.[117] The theological 'downgrade' that accompanied much revivalism in the next century hastened the withering of the more conservative theology that Jones had held.[118] The trumpeted concentration in Wales upon mass evangelism, lasting till 1904 – and almost exhausted thereafter – exemplified a law of diminishing returns. Past evangelistic successes are, in the present day, related by some with hagiographical nostalgia, and the aims and method of revivalism are fathered unjustly on Griffith Jones. Ivor Bromham wrote of Jones: 'He may more accurately be described as "Preacher and Teacher" rather than as "Revivalist".[119] Griffith Jones kept to the single purpose of performing the clergy's conventional functions. He was neither a Puritan, nor a reckless innovator, intending no move from his doctrinal position as a High Church Anglican. In his evangelistic preaching, he stood within the Church's settled practice; and even his 'innovations' – such as Circulating Schools – arose under the constraints of circumstances, in an attempt at an orderly application of Anglican principles, and usually following a precedent set by others.

NOTES

1   Anonymous (Henry Phillips?), *A Sketch of the Life and Character of the Reverend and Pious Mr Griffith Jones, late Rector of Llanddowror in Carmarthenshire* (London, 1762), p. 4.

2   D. D. Morgan, 'The Welsh Sermon 1689–1901', in Keith A. Francis and William Gibson (eds), *The Oxford Handbook of the British Sermon 1689–1901* (Oxford, 2012), pp. 202–3.

3   G. Jones, 'Letter I, Directions for improvement – The Christian armour', in *Letters of the Rev. Griffith Jones to Mrs Bevan*, ed. Edward Morgan (London, 1832), pp. 2–4.

4   James Hervey, *Theron and Aspasio* (London, 1755), pp. 268–73.

5   Oxford Bodleian MSS St Edmund Hall 56; L. E. Elliott-Binns, *The Early Evangelicals, a Religious and Social Study* (London, 1953), pp. 353–6.

6   Elliott-Binns, *The Early Evangelicals*, p. 354.

7   Emphasizing care about keeping the moral law, and so making preaching the Bible's moral teaching and self-examination important parts of his work, alongside the promise of forgiveness. But moralism was at the heart of SPCK.

8   John Spurr, *The Post-Reformation. Religion, Politics and Society in Britain 1603–1714* (Harlow, 2006), pp. 203–4.

9   Henry D. Rack, 'Wesley, Samuel', *ODNB*.

10 D. W. Hayton, 'Philipps, Sir John, fourth baronet (*c*.1666–1761)', *ODNB*.

11 'Of Good Works', XII, *Articles of Religion* (1562).

12 NLW, G. Jones, *Trysor o Ddifinyddiaeth*, MS 2.162, p. 10.

13 NLW, Jones, *Trysor*, MS 2.162, p. 355.

The Theology of Griffith Jones and Religious Thought

14 Peter Nockles, *The Oxford Movement in Context, Anglican High Churchmanship, 1760–1957* (Cambridge, 1994), p. 257.

15 Alister E. McGrath, 'The Emergence of the Anglican Tradition on Justification 1600–1700', *The Churchman*, 98/1 (1984), 28–43. Justification: the imputation of Christ's righteousness to sinners, freely on account of his perfect Atonement, and received only by faith; not conditioned by their works of righteousness, but nevertheless, as a result of regeneration, producing holiness in them.

16 As it is in the Pauline Epistles.

17 Charles Gataker (1613–80), George Morley (1598?–1684), Thomas Tully (1620–76) and Thomas Barlow (1608/9–91).

18 *Harmonia Apostolica, or Two Dissertations: The Doctrines of St James on Justification by Works is Explained and Defended; The Agreement of St Paul with St James is Clearly Shewn.*

19 George Bull, *The English Theological Works of George Bull D.D.* (Oxford, 1844), p. 349; Thomas Nelson, *The Life of Dr George Bull, Late Lord Bishop of St. David's* (London, 1713), p. 133.

20 Bull, *The English Theological*, p. 5.

21 Stephen Hampton, *Anti-Arminians. The Anglican Reformed Tradition from Charles II to George I* (Oxford, 2008), p. 39.

22 P. A. Lillback, 'Later developments in covenant theology', in Sinclair B. Ferguson and David F. Wright (eds), *New Dictionary of Theology* (Leicester, 1988), pp. 175–6.

23 Bull and others, however, did reveal a tendency to a serious lapse from orthodox Christology, towards subordinationism. Hampton, *Anti-Arminians*, pp. 176–7.

24 Hampton, *Anti-Arminians*, p. 27.

25 John Wesley, *The Journal of the Rev. John Wesley A.M.* (London, 1867), vol. II, pp. 10, 212, 233.

26 Hervey, *Theron and Aspasio*, pp. 467–8.

27 Elliott-Binns, *The Early Evangelicals*, p. 147.

28 John Wesley, *The Journal of the Rev. John Wesley A.M.*, ed. N. Curnock (London, 1938), vol. 2, p. 333.

29 Frank Baker, *John Wesley and the Church of England* (London, 1970), pp. 71–2; David Bebbington, *Evangelicalism in Modern Britain* (London, 1989), p. 153.

30 Bull, *The English Theological*, p. 349.

31 Hervey, *Theron and Aspasio*, pp. 468–9.

32 John Wesley, *Journal*, entry for 15 October 1739; quoted in A. H. Williams, *John Wesley in Wales 1739–1790* (Cardiff, 1971), p. 2.

33 Bull, *The English Theological*, p. 6.

34 Spurr, *The Post-Reformation*, pp. 131–3.

35 NLW, Sir John Philipps's pocket notebook, PICTLE584. Sir John sometimes added thoughts to passages later than the first entries.

36 N. T. Wright, 'Justification', in Ferguson and Wright (eds), *New Dictionary*, pp. 359–61.

37 'Of Good Works', XII, *Articles of Religion*.

38 Bull, *The English Theological*, p. 7.

Griffith Jones's Moralism and Theology

39 He wrote an introduction to *An Antidote Against Errour, Concerning Justification* of his father, Thomas Gataker (1574–1654). Bull answered this in 1675 by the *Examen censurae.*

40 George Morley, bishop of Winchester. Hampton, *Anti-Arminians*, pp. 77–8.

41 Bull answered Barlow and Tully in 1674 with his *Justificatio Paulina sine operibus, ex mente ecclesiae Anglicanae.*

42 He was also Lady Margaret Professor of Divinity and Provost of Queen's College, Oxford.

43 John Spurr, 'Barlow, Thomas (1608/9–1691)', *ODNB.*

44 Spurr, 'Barlow, Thomas (1608/9–1691)'.

45 Adaptations of the doctrine of justification which gave credit to faith itself as being a good work, and – in some theories – reducing the scope of good works to a manageable number to be kept in 'evangelical obedience'. An important example mediating between Puritan covenantalism and Evangelical Arminianism is Richard Baxter (1615–91); cf. J. I. Packer, 'Baxter, Richard', in Ferguson and Wright (eds), *New Dictionary*, pp. 82–3.

46 Morgan, *Theologia*, pp. 168, 169–70.

47 Anon., *A Sketch*, p. 5.

48 Bull himself had written controversially, at length, as a literate, though a respected author. Jones was a literate, and belonged to the inferior clergy, but seems not to have been intimidated from confident speaking and writing.

49 G. Jones, 'Letter XLVIII, Troubles from the Clergy', in *Letters to Mrs Bevan*, p. 154.

50 G. Jenkins, 'An Old and Much Honoured'; 'Griffith Jones, Llanddowror', *Welsh History Review*, II (1983), 449.

51 D. C. Jones, 'Calvinistic Methodism and the Origins of Evangelicalism in England', in Michael A. G. Haykin and Kenneth J. Stewart (eds), *The Emergence of Evangelicalism* (Nottingham, 2008), pp. 113–14.

52 Nelson, *The Life*, pp. 463–4.

53 Nelson, *The Life*, p. 464.

54 Cf. *BCP*, mention of persisting sin in Morning and Evening Prayer, Sentence: 1 St John 1:8, 9; and Communion office, prayer of approach to Lord's Table, 'We do not presume to come.'

55 'Substitutionary Atonement': 'a sacrifice or satisfaction or (as it may be called) amends to his Father for our sins', 'Sermon of the Salvation of Mankind', *The Two Books of Homilies, Appointed to be Read in Churches* (Oxford, 1859), p. 24.

56 Samuel Johnson, *Prayers and Meditations Composed by Samuel Johnson A.M.*, ed. George Strahan (London, 1785), no. V: 'Grant O my God that I may improve the year which I am now beginning, and all the days which thou shalt add to my life, by serious repentance and diligent obedience, that, by the help of thy holy Spirit I may use the means of Grace to my own salvation, and at last enjoy thy presence in eternal happiness, for Jesus Christ's sake. Amen.'

57 N. T. Wright, 'Justification', in Ferguson and Wright (eds), *New Dictionary*, p. 630.

58 *Westminster Shorter Catechism* (London, 1648), question 33.

59 *Articles Agreed upon by the Archbishops and Bishops of both Provinces, and the Whole Clergy* (London, 1562), art. XI.

60 'Of Good Works', XII, *Articles of Religion.*

The Theology of Griffith Jones and Religious Thought

61 G. Jones, 'Letter LX, Union of the Clergy in preaching weekly lectures', in *Letters to Mrs Bevan*, p. 197.

62 R. W. A. Letham, 'Assurance', in Ferguson and Wright (eds), *New Dictionary*, pp. 51–2. Cf. J. Wesley's experience: Baker, *John Wesley*, p. 54.

63 NLW, G. Jones, notebook, MS 5920A, leaf 20, verso.

64 Euan Cameron, 'The Power of the Word: Renaissance and Reformation', in Euan Cameron (ed.), *Early Modern Europe* (Oxford, 2001), p. 92.

65 G. Jones, 'Letter LXXXIV, Encouragement to pray for the Holy Ghost', in *Letters to Mrs Bevan*, p. 282.

66 Cf. John Bunyan, *Grace Abounding to the Chief of Sinners* (1666), based on *1ˢᵗ Epistle to Timothy*, 1.15.

67 *Articles of Religion*, XII; *The Two Books of Homilies*, p. 31.

68 James Hervey, *Mr Wesley's Principles detected: or a Defence* (Edinburgh, 1765), pp. 10–12.

69 J. Spurr, *The Restoration Church of England, 1646–1689* (New Haven, CT, 1991), p. 312.

70 Robert D. Cornwall and W. Gibson (eds), *Religion, Politics and Dissent 1660–1832* (Farnham, 2010).

71 E. D. Cook, 'Conscience', in Ferguson and Wright (eds), *New Dictionary*, pp. 161–2.

72 P. S. Watson, 'Justification', in Alan Richardson (ed.), *Dictionary of Christian Theology* (London, 1969), pp. 184–5.

73 Andrew C. Thompson (ed.), *The Oxford History of Protestant Dissenting Traditions* (Oxford, 2018), vol. II, pp. 226–9.

74 Evangelical emphasis on Gospel as directed personal appeal rather than the Church's 'kerygma' or corporate 'confession'. C. C. Smith, 'Confession', in J. D. Douglas (ed.), *New International Dictionary of the Christian Church* (Grand Rapids, 1974), pp. 250–1.

75 Cf. Whitefield an early example of practice. Cf. John Walsh, 'Origins of the Evangelical Revival', in G. V. Bennett and J. D. Walsh (eds), *Essays in Modern Church History* (London, 1966), pp. 145–6.

76 Thomas Kelly, *Griffith Jones. Llanddowror, Pioneer in Adult Education* (Cardiff, 1950), pp. 20–2.

77 D. D. Morgan, 'Continuity, Novelty and Evangelicalism in Wales', in Haykin and Stewart (eds), *The Emergence*, p. 99.

78 G. Jones, 'Letter LX, Union of the Clergy in preaching weekly lectures', in *Letters to Mrs Bevan*, pp. 196–7.

79 G. Jones, 'Letter IV, The infidelity of the times', in *Letters to Mrs Bevan*, pp. 20–1.

80 John Evans, *Some Account of the Welch Charity-Schools, and the Rise and Progress of Methodism in Wales* (London, 1752), pp. 17–19.

81 For example, Griffith Jones's establishing Circulating Schools. Cf. G. Jones, *The Welsh Piety* (London, 1740), p. 19.

82 Cf. collect and proper lessons for 'Conversion of Saint Paul', *BCP*.

83 Keith J. Hardman, *Charles Grandison Finney* (Darlington, 1987), pp. 104–32; George M. Marsden, *Fundamentalism and American Culture* (Oxford, 2006), pp. 43–5.

84 A dogmatic materialist will, of course, deny the possibility of the latter factor, and attribute conversion entirely to psychological causes.

172

85 Jonathan Edwards, *A Narrative of Surprising Conversions* [1736], in *Select Works of Jonathan Edwards* (London, 1965).

86 G. Jones, 'Letter XXXII Growing in love', in *Letters to Mrs Bevan*, p. 105.

87 *Articles of Religion*, XII.

88 Bull, *The English Theological*, pp. 6–7.

89 *Epistle to the Romans*, ch. 4:24–5; *2nd Epistle to the Corinthians*, ch. 5:19, 21.

90 Norman Sykes, *Edmund Gibson* (Oxford, 1926), pp. 319–20.

91 George Whitefield, *Journals*, pub. separately 1738–41, unabridged edn (London, 1960), p. 90.

92 Bebbington, *Evangelicalism*, p. 20.

93 Bebbington, *Evangelicalism*, p. 23.

94 E.g. The New Room at Bristol built for Whitefield, 1739.

95 Kelly, *Griffith Jones Llanddowror*, pp. 17–18.

96 Bebbington, *Evangelicalism*, p. 118.

97 Marsden, *Fundamentalism*, p. 252.

98 George M. Ella, *James Hervey: Preacher of Righteousness* (Eggleston, Co. Durham, 1997), pp. 261–301.

99 Wesley, *The Journal*, vol. ii, pp. 32, 212, 233, 270.

100 Morgan, *Theologia*, pp. 304–5.

101 *Cyffes Ffydd* (Confession of Faith) of Calvinistic Methodists, 1823; Eryn M. White, *The Welsh Bible* (Cardiff, 2007), pp. 79–83.

102 Morgan, 'Continuity', in Haykin and Stewart (eds), *The Emergence*, p. 97; Timothy Thomas, *Y Wisg Wen Ddisglair, Gymmwys i fyned i lys y Brenhin Nefol* (Carmarthen, 1759).

103 Morgan, 'Continuity'.

104 Haykin, 'Evangelicalism and the Enlightenment', in Haykin and Stewart (eds), *The Emergence*, pp. 59–60.

105 Jenkins, 'An Old and Much Honoured', 452.

106 Mere temporary conversions are recognized in the Bible. Cf. *The Parable of the Sower*, Matt. 13:3–9, 19–23; Acts 8:13–21.

107 *Westminster Confession of Faith* (London, 1646; Glasgow, 1994), ch. 10: 'Effectual calling', pp. 53–5; Shorter Catechism, q. 31, p. 295.

108 G. Jones, 'Letter XLIV, The Spirit in the new birth', in *Letters to Mrs Bevan*, pp. 138–40.

109 G. Jones, 'Letter XXVI, Praying for revival – mutual prayer', in *Letters to Mrs Bevan*, p. 86.

110 Jones, 'Letter IV, The infidelity of the times', pp. 20–2; and 'Letter V, The religion of the age lamented', in *Letters to Mrs Bevan*, pp. 23–7.

111 G. Jones, 'Letter XXVI, Praying', in *Letters to Mrs Bevan*, p. 87.

112 John Charles Ryle, *Christian Leaders of the Eighteenth Century* (London, 1885), p. 183.

113 James Robe, *Narratives of the Extraordinary Work of the Spirit of God at Cambuslang, Kilsyth, & Begun 1742* (Glasgow, 1790), p. 47.

114 Elliott-Binns, *The Early Evangelicals*, p. 394.

115 Charismaticism proposing a second conversion, the next step of receiving the Holy Spirit, significantly in independent of preaching.

116 G. Jones, 'Letter LXIV, The Spirit in the new birth', in *Letters to Mrs Bevan*, p. 138.

117 Donald W. Dayton, 'Revivalism', in Douglas (ed.), *New International Dictionary*, p. 844.

118 Gwyn Davies, *Golau Gwlad, Cristnogaeth yng Nghymru 200–2000* (Bridgend, 2000), pp. 94–100.

119 Revd Ivor J. Bromham, 'Welsh Revivalists of the Eighteenth Century', *The Churchman*, 72/1 (1958).

Chapter 7

CATECHIZING, BAPTISM AND THE TREND TOWARDS EVANGELICALISM

THE SPCK'S EDUCATIONAL AIMS

Founded in the hope of a national religious and moral renewal, the SPCK aimed to encourage the creation of schools where children would learn to read the Bible and recite the Catechism. The aim was especially, as John Spurr wrote, to 'educate the English into religion rather than to prosecute them until pure'.[1] The example of Hermann Franke's account of the success of pietistic schools at Halle strengthened the society's hope of repairing the prevailing public ignorance of the Church of England's teaching.[2] Some promise was entertained that charity-schools could give a child 'the means by which, with God's grace, he could prepare his soul for salvation'.[3] A prime policy of the society was the development of Thomas Bray's scheme, used in Maryland, of lending libraries for hard-up parsons needing aids for sermon preparation.[4] So consistently was the Protestant emphasis on preaching pursued, that the charity-schools' anniversary meetings were a public display with pupils marshalled in ordered ranks, ready to hear an appropriate sermon: for instance, an 'Excellent Sermon' by the bishop of Chester, on 30 April 1713.[5] The society also distributed collections of sermons, along with other useful books.[6] Such were best-sellers, for the English had an appetite for sermons both heard and read.[7]

The SPCK was indefatigable in providing cheap New Testaments and whole Bibles. From June 1713, Griffith Jones adhered to SPCK aims, as a very active advocate and agent of these literary projects in Wales.[8] In this, he was supporting the inclination of other Welsh parsons to obtain as many books as they could afford from their usually meagre incomes.[9] He continued to pursue the production of Welsh editions of the Bible, and their provision by the society in sufficient numbers, at prices affordable to the poor.[10]

Consultations in the 1690s had reiterated the need to teach the Church Catechism.[11] Catechesis continued to be accepted, without dispute, as the main tool for restoring common Christian knowledge, and undoing the irreligion of the age.[12] The High Church ideal stated by George Herbert (1593–1633) in his *Priest to the Temple, or the Country Parson*:

> The Countrey Parson values Catechizing highly: for there being three points of his duty ... a competent knowledge of salvation in ...; to multiply, and build up this knowledge; the third, to inflame this knowledge, to presse, and drive it to practice, turning it to reformation of life[13]

To the SPCK, it was 'the scandalous and heightened enormities of these latter days' that threatened the well-being of the whole nation.[14] The promoting of regular catechizing of the young, and provision of suitable literature auxiliary to it, were a stated aim from its foundation.[15] Samuel Wesley exemplified the zeal of SPCK supporters for catechesis. Henry Rack wrote: 'Initially he catechized all the year round though later, as was customary, only during Lent.'[16] Arthur Middleton referred to Thomas Bray's (1658–1730) influential book on catechizing:

> Catechizing by teaching and discussion was serious work with the grading of different groups and Bray compiling collections of prayers from the Bible, Psalms and Prayer Book, and requiring Confirmands to keep a quiet day before taking their vows.[17]

The SPCK assumed the use of the Catechism also to be an instrument of mission to the heathen. The minutes of December 1712 mentioned the supplying Catechisms to India:

> 200 Single Catechisms be stitched up in Stiff marble paper to be sent with Mr. Berling for ye Schools at Tranquebar ... 100 Single Catechisms ... for the Schools at Fort St. George.[18]

Besides the provision of the Catechism itself, the SPCK's correspondence recorded distribution of more than one exposition of the Church Catechism, including that by Griffith Jones.[19] The use of such expansions of the Catechism itself conformed to the Prayer Book's injunction: 'That none hereafter shall be Confirmed, but such as can say the Creed ... and can also answer to such other Questions, as in the short Catechism are contained.'[20] Amongst the most popular expositions were those of Bishops Thomas Ken (1637–1711), John Williams (1633–1709) and of John Lewis (1675–1747). It is relevant to the bitter contentions over the need for conformity that, although Dissenters were denounced to an extreme for their departures from the Church's appointed forms, there appears to have been no complaint whatsoever that these private complementary works lacked full legal sanction.[21] No one seems to have seen their use as an acknowledgement that the Church Catechism, alone, was inadequate for full, proper instruction in the faith.

Jean Frédéric Ostervald (1663–1747), theologian and author, attained a prominent position in Europe, and gained especial respect among SPCK supporters. As a pastor at Neuchâtel, he was one of the 'Swiss Triumvirate' with Jean Alphonse Turretini (1671–1737) of Geneva and Samuel Werenfels (1657–1740) of Basel.[22] Ostervald's writing and lecturing had great influence in the Reformed churches of Switzerland, France, the Netherlands and Palatinate. He followed Moses (Moïse) Amyraut (in Latin, Amyraldus) (1595–1664), popularizing, amongst a younger generation of ministers, a revision of Reformed, 'federal' theology leaning decidedly toward Arminianism. In response, a restatement of the Reformed view of the disputed doctrines, the *Consensus Helveticus* (1675), was drawn up, as a theological standard for ordinands, in an attempt especially to ban Amyraldianism and its universalism.[23] Meanwhile, Amyraut continued to be viewed with suspicion by several older theologians, who stood apart from the popular trend amongst younger ministers.[24] Influenced by Amyraldianism, Ostervald's exposition stood as being much less than fully orthodox, from the standpoint of strict adherence to the Articles of the Church of England.[25] It is very surprising, therefore, that Ostervald became a respected correspondent with the SPCK from 1701, and that works of his were received, it appears, without reserve by its members, being translated into English and Welsh.[26] Especially influential among Ostervald's writings was his Catechism.[27] As a completely separate work, and not a mere commentary upon an official Catechism, this of Ostervald seems doubly a violation of Anglican orthodoxy. The whole development of SPCK work, and the thinking of its members, including that of Griffith Jones, could hardly be expected to remain fully immune from the effects of Ostervald's teaching, and other liberalizing ideas, which were being given such wide currency.[28] Moreover, a European pietistic tendency, which seemed to promise reinvigoration of religion, also had weight as against a flagging insistence upon a faith based merely in systematic biblical instruction. Hoppit referred to the exhaustion of confidence in customary methods: 'Attempts ... to promote religious homogeneity and orthodox spiritual intensity that had begun at the Reformation had now reached their limit.'[29]

CATECHIZING IN WALES

From its foundation, the SPCK received many requests for copies of the Church Catechism, Bibles, New Testaments and collections of prayers for use on special occasions.[30] For much of its early life, it devoted most of its financial support, surprisingly, to Wales. From the society, Griffith Jones channelled much literature into the work in Wales to renew religion in the parishes.[31] The welcome given to the various books and primers that were provided attests the growing appetite for religious knowledge in Wales.[32] This activity proves that the conventional narrative – specially in Calvinistic Methodism historiography – of a general inertness in the Church before the rise of Methodism is an oversimplification of a complex series of causes and effects on the Church in the time of Griffith Jones, and later.[33] The religious renewal after 1730 was an increase in pace of what was already under way in Wales and other parts of Britain. It was built particularly upon the groundwork done by the religious societies and the SPCK. Griffith Jones and preachers who followed him nurtured an existing work, which was promoted especially by the SPCK. The society also showed a similar generous concern for the concurrent work outside Britain. The minutes mention Irish charity-schools, recording that Sir John Philipps: 'intends to throw his mite in towards encouraging Mr Richardson's proposal and is glad to hear it has made so far a progress'.[34] The Revd John Richardson (1668–1747), rector of Belturbet, wrote in 1712 *A proposal for the Conversion of the Popish Natives of Ireland to the Protestant Religion by printing in the Bible, Liturgy & in Irish ... also by erecting Charity Schools for the Education of the Irish Children gratis in the English Tongue and Protestant Religion.* He liaised with the SPCK and arranged for an Irish translation of John Lewis's Exposition of the Church Catechism, with appended grammatical and spelling notes, together with Morning and Evening Prayer in Irish.[35] The approach to the needs of speakers of other languages than English in the king's dominions, and beyond, was one of kindly solicitude for the people's needs, mainly the religious ones.[36] A contradictory element in this benevolence must be taken into account: a colonialist presumption of a need ultimately to wean them away into using English. Griffith Jones had himself to contend with a benign condescension from friends who could not conceive of there being any value in Welsh. But his major achievement succeeded, by tact and ingenuity, in inducing his English donors into active support of the language.[37]

The poverty in Wales, and sparseness of printed books are not evidence of any lack of appetite there for Christian literature.[38] Such works included aids to catechizing. There had been a warm welcome shown even before 1699 to books like Rees Prichard's *Cannwyll y Cymry*, and to translations of devotional works from English, such as Lewis Bayly's *Practice of Piety*, rendered as *Yr Ymarfer o Dduwioldeb* by its translator, Rowland Vaughan.[39] In a letter of 1 March 1699, the Revd James Harries (1663–1728), whom Geraint Jenkins calls 'the industrious vicar of Llantrisant',[40] reported that he had 'Catechetichal Lectures in the several Chappels of his great Parish & hopes to carry them on, together with the Schooling of Poor Children'.[41] In a letter of 29 April 1700, a Mr Price reported that 'the Clergy of Denbighshire, Flintshire and Montgomeryshire are united in Societies'. Besides the decision to set up free schools for the poor children, these clergymen had 'resolved to be diligent in Catechizing the Youth and designed to Spend ye Summer Season therein and had unanimously agreed to use BISHOP WILLIAMS' Exposition'.[42] Their schools even anticipated Griffith Jones's use of the Welsh language for teaching. John Williams (1633–1709), bishop of Chichester (1696–1709), wrote a *Brief Exposition of the Church-Catechism* (1689), which was translated into Welsh by John Morgan.[43] In 1708 the SPCK distributed throughout Wales copies of a popular exposition of the Church Catechism by William Beveridge (1637–1708).[44] It had been translated into Welsh by Thomas Williams, and was mainly intended as an instruction manual for schoolmasters and heads of families.[45] A feature of this didactic component of Welsh church life was a measure of unanimity between most Churchmen and Dissenters, as well as the methodistical evangelists, about the authority of the Bible and moral standards. There was, despite an element of mistrust and recrimination, an overlap of beliefs and aims.[46] Robert Nelson noted that, surprisingly, Bishop Bull did not dilate on the subject of the Catechism: 'As to Catechising, he just hints at the Necessity and Usefulness of it'.[47] The Catechism was the unquestioned remedy for ignorance of Christian teachings, and so perhaps scarcely seemed to need any lengthy recommendation. George Bull's suggestions merely reiterated the Prayer Book rubric which called for teaching of children: 'by the Curate, until such time as they have learned all that is here appointed for them to learn'.[48] Griffith Jones, and the younger preachers who followed his example, used the same teaching methods and expounded the body of doctrine found in the Church's formularies, which Jones described as 'a Scripture Body of Divinity, in a catechetical method'.[49] The rapidly growing but, by some, distrusted, evangelistic movement watered seeds already widely sown in the Church by the common enterprise of catechesis.[50] Jones's own pessimistic words about the religious state of his age are rather a measure of his high standards of piety, and must not

Catechizing, Baptism and Evangelicalism

be taken as proof of a lack of progress. In August 1735, he wrote, with characteristic exaggeration:

> we have reason to fear that God is now about leaving our land and departing from us ... It is now, if ever, we should stir ourselves up to lay hold of him, and ... solicit his return and stay with us.[51]

He had seen evidence of good fruit from his preaching since at least 1711, but was cautious not to misrepresent his successes as a bright new awakening after a complete deathly night in the Church. For Anglicans like Jones, apparent conversion to new faith needed to undergo the test of time, and prove itself by uprightness: 'that the rest of our life hereafter may be pure, and holy; so that at the last we may come to his eternal joy'.[52] He continued to labour steadily with conviction, persistently following the policy set by the SPCK.[53]

Griffith Jones stated that his schools grew out of his catechizing.[54] His culminating venture of the Circulating Schools was not a diversion from promoting his ideal of the Church of England and a Christian society. Rather, it was a manifestation of it.[55] His venture in specifically Welsh-language catechizing schools began in a small, exploratory way about 1731, growing in number to thirty-seven schools in 1738.[56] The Circulating Schools, as an innovating scheme of circulating literacy classes for all ages – but mostly adults – and both sexes, plainly applied, with confidence, what he had learnt hitherto of school-mastering throughout his adult life.[57] Mary Clement mentioned the important fact that, despite his bent towards teaching, his energies were turned mostly towards other things, such as the Welsh Bible or relief of the Salzburgers, until his proposal of a Welsh school at Llanddowror in 1731.[58] Griffith Jones's thinking evolved slowly, without sudden revolutions, but, once he was convinced, his intense temperament impelled him in his decided course with constant energy and optimism.[59] In a letter of 24 December 1744, he wrote a brief, illuminating account of the beginning of his Circulating Schools:

> The occasion, which through the Grace of God, led gradually to thought of them, was a catechising exercise after the second lesson in Divine Service

upon Saturdays before the monthly Sacrament Sundays, when several adult and elderly as well as young people (particular as desired to partake that blessed ordinance) were examined, not only in the Catechism, but also in a brief system of divinity, and discoursed in an easy, familiar, and very serious way, about every answer, they made, explaining it clearly to their understanding, and strongly applying it to their consciences.[60]

This explanation throughout reflects Jones's unambiguous commitment to Anglican practice, including the prominent place claimed for solemn, regular observance of Holy Communion.[61] In any case, he was not inclined to dabble in novelty. He kept to a settled path of undemonstrative service, disinclined by character to imitate any new departures made by others, as he showed in his lifelong commitment to the national Church.[62] Jones's preaching was the fixed path of his long ministry. Exhaustively detailed, unremitting in exhortation, and with its constant evangelistic application, it was never displaced.[63] The prescribed round of services and other secondary pastoral duties – such as household visitation – was, it seems, also kept up with assiduity.[64] His schools emerged from an unoriginal extension of clerical duties. These he promoted persistently, though organizing them demanded much wisdom and skill in lengthy planning, negotiation and finding finance, accommodation and suitable teachers.[65] They came into being in a steady, pragmatic evolution, rather than as a revolutionary flash of experimentation. Not even Griffith Jones's love for the Welsh language was itself the spur of the Circulating Schools; but his concern was to edify people whose adherence to 'experimental' Christianity was weak. He wrote of:

> nominal or degenerate Christians ... [asking] Will not these poor wretches ... continue 'to walk according to the course of this world ...?' Unless the zealous and charitable followers of God ... do all that is practicable towards 'opening their eyes that they may be turned from darkness to light (they will remain so)'[66]

The path linking catechizing with schooling was well trodden before Jones felt induced to extend his lessons beyond service-times within his churches' walls. Even his first step, in 1731, towards organizing Welsh-language schools was a generation later than those of Dr John Jones (1650–1727), dean of Bangor, and of others in north Wales.[67] But, once convinced of their effectiveness, he pursued his plan with characteristic assiduity. Even through the crisis from 1742 to 1744, caused by his Circulating Schools' alleged attachment to the mistrusted movement in the Church newly labelled 'Methodism', Jones continued to promote them.[68] He managed to avoid controversy with the society by never mentioning Methodism in correspondence, and continuing to be their 'best customer' for Welsh books for his schools.[69] Griffith Jones's wisdom and tact also preserved friendship and trust with Sir John Philipps, when the latter himself cooled towards charity-schools after 1714. Mary Clement suggested that Philipps:

> like the Society, as a body, abandoned the schools to avoid taking part in a bitter sectarian struggle. Many of his schools came to an end during his lifetime, and all finished with his death in 1737.[70]

> Jones, understanding their great value, was able to increase the number of his own schools, without friction.[71] After 1731, he laid down a founding principle, overriding any prejudice amongst his supporters, in insisting, albeit tactfully, that Welsh should be the medium of instruction where that was the language of the community.[72]

THE BAPTISMAL VOW AND 'MODERATE CALVINISM'

Griffith Jones published *The Christian Covenant, or the Baptismal Vow, as stated in our Church Catechism* (1761).[73] In the preface, he firmly placed himself within the tradition and practice of the Church of England:

> Among all the various Methods of Catechising, it seems to be the best, and most agreeable with the constant practice of the Primitive Church, to begin, as our Church does, with the Breviate of the Baptismal Covenant ... that after the Foundation is well laid, the Catechumens may advance regularly in every necessary degree of Christian Knowledge and Practice.[74]

183

C. Morgan-Richardson stressed the Anglican basis of Griffith Jones's educational work:

> In the many volumes which contain the history of the Welsh Piety, and which were published year after year by the Rev. Griffith Jones, the evidence that this charity was founded by the Church of England, and for the Church of England, is so clear and so conclusive.[75]

Preaching on Christ and the Church, Jones referred to baptism as effecting union in Christ. This firmly fixes his standpoint most strongly in orthodox Anglicanism.

> Yr ydym ni trwy'n bedydd (chwi a wyddoch) neu yn hytrach trwy'r Cyfammod newydd o ras yn cael ein cyfrif yn aelodau i Grist. Mae Crist megis yn ben i'r Eglwys, a ninnau megis yn aelodau iddo; ac chwi wyddoch pa beth bynnag yw'r corph neu'r pen, fod yr aelodau mewn mesur yr un peth.[76]

> [We are through our baptism (you will know) or rather through the new Covenant of grace are counted as members for Christ. Christ as a head for the Church, and ourselves as members for him; and you will know whatever the body or the head are, that the members in a measure are the same thing.]

In the same sermon also, he said:

> Fel y darfu iddo ef orchfygu ei elynion, felly y dylem ninnau ymddrechu, trwy gymmorth Gras, i orchfygu ein nwydau a'n chwannau cnawdol, a rheoli ein hunain i fyw yn ofn Duw. Dyma'r gelynion ag ŷm ni ym rhwym i ryfela yn eu herbyn trwy adduned ein bedydd; ac oni bydd i ni mewn pryd eu marweiddio, fe fydd iddynt ein damnio ni. Rhuf: 8:13. Col: 3:9.[77]

> [As it fell to him to defeat his enemies, so also must we ourselves strive, through the help of Grace, to overcome our passions and fleshly appetites, and control ourselves to live in the fear of God. These are the enemies against whom we are bound to wage war through the pledge of our baptism; and unless in time we come to mortify them, it will be for them to damn us.]

Like Sir John Philipps and others, Jones saw his hearers' baptism as their pledge of commitment to serve God in obedience.[78] In this sense, it was looked on as a 'covenant', and was the concept of baptism held, more or less defined, by others at the time. The SPCK minutes referred to literature on a 'Baptismal Covenant'.[79] John Lewis (1675–1747), vicar of Margate, wrote *The Church Catechism Explain'd* in 1700.[80] This influential book was translated into Welsh in 1713.[81] Baptism was assumed as, on one side, a person's covenant made with God to follow Him, rather than, from the other side, as God's sign of engagement to be Saviour.[82] Griffith Jones's application of the doctrine in his texts was to spur his hearers to self-examination. On Mat. 5:20, he said:

> Yn y bennod hon a'r pennodau sy'n canlyn fe ellir canfod pwy sy wynfydedig. &c. Pa fodd mae jawn-gyflawni dyledswyddau, megis rhoddi elusennau, gweddïo, ymprydio, &c. Gyd â pha fath dymmer y dylid trin y byd. &c. A pha fodd y dylid ymdrechu am heddwch Duw a theyrnas Nefoedd mewn pryd ac amser.[83]

> [In this and the following chapters one can find who is blessed. & What way rightly fulfils duties, such as giving alms, praying, fasting. &. With what kind of disposition one ought to treat the world. &. And in what way ought one to strive for God's peace and the kingdom of Heaven in good time.]

In *The Christian Covenant*, Jones described baptism as committing even an infant to a 'covenant': a binding obligation.[84] He acknowledged the important fact that those baptized in infancy could not make commitments for themselves.[85] He accepted that vows were therefore made on a child's behalf by godparents.[86] Griffith Jones made no objection either to paedobaptism or sponsorship. Rather, he developed his exposition upon the need for one baptized in infancy to make good, as an adult, the obligations taken upon him by his sponsors. Hence, in his mind, the existence of a 'covenant', engaged in by a binding vow made on behalf of the child, added valid, biblical force to the evangelistic call.[87] The solemn baptismal covenant could only be fulfilled by faith, repentance and obedience when the child had come to an age of understanding.[88] Baptism into the Church was consequently seen as a pledge of commitment, the seal of a binding engagement to serve God in obedience. This High Church concept, in keeping with the Prayer Book service, held also by Sir John Philipps, was fully aligned with Jones's evangelistic emphasis in preaching.[89] The SPCK's minutes referred the 'Baptismal Covenant', on 3 June 1714, recording a request: 'Upon reading a Letter from Mr Weller of Maidstone desiring a Packet of the Society's Books relating to the Baptismal Covenant.'[90] Thus, in the circumstance of the SPCK's efforts to re-establish active piety in the land, it was promoting an evangelistic emphasis which was bound increasingly to lose favour amongst many of the clergy when incorporated as a distinguishing element of enthusiastical Methodism.

The covenant made with God by baptism, for the candidate, offered moral compunction obliging him to follow God truly, by faith and upright behaviour. This view was quite compatible with the Prayer Book, Catechism and Articles. The doctrine of baptism held by some Reformed theologians, however, rested more on a somewhat different argument, which was, nevertheless, not incompatible to the former interpretation. Baptism, in this theory, was seen as God's own pledge of his eternal Covenant to be the Saviour of the person baptized, on condition of faith and repentance.[91] Griffith Jones wrote:

> Q. Where in the Catechism are you taught the Christian Covenant?
> A. In the first Part of my Catechism, called the *Baptismal Vow*.[92]

Thus, his exposition of the Church Catechism founded the catechumens' obligation on the vow made for them to God vicariously. Upon this ground, he built his teaching of all the spiritual duties of vital Christianity. But he also understood a corollary of the doctrine of the covenantal vow: Christ's receiving believers reciprocally into his 'Covenant of Grace'.

> Q. How is the Christian Covenant called in Scripture?
> A. It is called the *New Covenant*, and the *New Testament in Christ's Blood*, and the *Covenant of Grace*.[93]

Catechizing, Baptism and Evangelicalism

In keeping with the general Reformed explanation of the Covenant, Griffith Jones posited Adam's original dependence on perfect obedience as another covenant, the 'Covenant of Works', which failed by mankind's falling into sin. This failure contrasted with the effective saving plan of the New Covenant:

> Q. Wherein does the Covenant of Grace, and of Works differ?
>
> A. 1. The Covenant of Works was made with us in Adam, our natural Head, in whom we fell under Sin and Condemnation; but the Covenant of Grace is made with us in Christ, our spiritual Head, by whom we are redeemed and saved. *Isa.* xlii. 6. I *Cor.* xv. 22.
>
> 2. The Covenant of Works requireth perfect Obedience; but the Condition required in the New Covenant of Grace, is Faith working Repentance and new Obedience. *Acts* xvi. 31. chap. xx. 21. *Rom.* xvi. 26
>
> 3. The Scripture saith, that the New Covenant is better, bringing in a better Hope. *Heb.* vii. 19, 22. chap. viii. 6.[94]

This thoughtful exposition of the Catechism was in line with the Prayer Book, and was biblical. It was in conformity with the idea of covenant found in John Calvin's *Institutes*.[95] But it did not develop the supplementary biblical teaching of an 'Eternal Covenant' made by God, in Christ, towards man.[96] It can be argued that the wording of the Church Catechism avoids going so far as this wider view of baptism, though being compatible with it:

> Question. What meanest thou by this word *Sacrament?*
>
> Answer. I mean an outward and visible sign of an inward and spiritual grace given unto us, ordained by Christ himself, as a means whereby we receive the same, and a pledge to assure us thereof.[97]

It was also consistent with the Prayer Book for a response of faith and obedience towards God by persons, now come to an age of discretion, to be seen as the keeping of a covenantal vow. Griffith Jones's view of the significance of baptism as a person's covenant, with a binding obligation to follow by faith was also held by other prominent churchmen. Josiah

Woodward (1657–1712) extolled the benefits to children of the religious societies' catechizing:

> youth ... between the age of ten and sixteen ... be brought to a sense ... of the great Obligations and Advantages of our Baptismal Vows; in order to their personal Covenanting with God through our Lord Jesus Christ, first by the Solemnity of a public Confirmation, afterwards at the Lord's Table.[98]

The demand for the Covenant to be fulfilled, in obedience to God's law, was thus taken as stemming from the human commitment made in a sponsors' vow. The 'Covenant of Redemption' – of covenantal or 'federal' theology – in contrast, posited an eternal decree of the divine will.[99] Griffith Jones's somewhat narrower view of the Covenant in baptism laid the emphasis on personal, individual commitment to faith in a new life of obedience, thus promoting a leading component of the future Evangelicalism.[100]

The doctrine of a 'Covenant of Redemption' posited an eternal, overall governance of Creation and Providence mediated by Christ, and pledged in the sacraments. Beza, Turretin and other later Reformed theologians elaborated this doctrine.[101] The 'Eternal Covenant' articulated the theory of divine sovereignty, the central idea of 'Calvinism'.[102] Though not contrary to Prayer Book doctrine and Griffith Jones's baptismal covenantalism, the eternal 'Covenant of Redemption' does not appear to have been part of his theological range.[103] His view seems thus to reflect a broader range of possible interpretation. Jones, perhaps unintentionally, did hint at the possibility that a pre-existing Covenant of Grace in Christ was the foundation a believer's well-being: 'our union with Christ Jesus; from which fountain of all comforts, flow our covenant relation to God ... and every thing that pertains unto it'.[104] There may be a hint that Griffith Jones was making an effort to avoid seeming out of step with respected High Church sacramentalism. Tactful avoidance of too much further elaboration of doctrine was an approach likely to help fellow feeling between churchmen. As a pastor, he was aware of the dangers of unnecessary, divisive controversies, which went often above the heads of the ordinary folk whom he sought to help.[105] High Church opinion naturally assumed that it held the historic, orthodox interpretation of the doctrinal standards of the Church of England. Though Jones was sincerely intent on remaining within the Church and its teaching, he knew that the consistent preaching of the overriding need of personal conversion was bound to cause a certain tension, to say the least. Exasperation at the disparagement, stated or implied, of clergy not of his convictions was expressed most violently in a pamphlet, with extreme invective, by John Evans.[106] An unavoidable difficulty was particularly created by Griffith Jones's strenuous affirming the unsatisfactory state of one lacking the experience of a 'new birth', due to be 'cast away as Branches of the Vine that bear no Fruit'.[107] He was demanding an inner spiritual renewal in those who were, however, already counted as Christians, and who had been formally accepted in many cases, by confirmation, as members of the Church. Among the inclusive membership of the Church, such a compunctious assertion could not but be resented by some.

Griffith Jones may be classed amongst the churchmen of his age who tended to a less highly developed Protestant theology, though he does not seem to have rejected precision as unspiritual and unnecessary intellectualism. Thomas Owen wrote:

> most of the Methodist fathers [of Wales] had been associated with, and were disciples of the Rev. Griffith Jones, Llanddowror they could not have been expected to have done otherwise. Yet it is apparent that their Calvinism, from the beginning, never tended to any extremes but was remarkably moderate.[108]

Jones did consistently show a careful comparative analysis of Scripture, but his theological interest, not unusually, covered a far narrower range than that of some earlier 'scholastic' Reformed theologians.[109] Michael Haykin made the important observation that fully developed Evangelicalism was affected by the 'Enlightenment' distaste for elaborated metaphysical systems. The 'Enlightenment' favoured the rationalistic amassing of physical observations, 'somewhat impatient with the systematizing of earlier Protestant generations, in particular that of the Puritans'.[110] Griffith Jones was indefatigable in amassing biblical data in support of his preached offer of salvation. His intellectual persistence was rigorous in this.[111] But he seems consciously – or temperamentally – to have avoided leading his hearers into extended systemizing or speculation, despite his reportedly being, 'by a close and diligent Application ... well versed in the Writings of the most eminent Divines, whether at home or abroad'.[112] He was probably shrewd enough to foresee the danger from a mass of new converts' being diverted into a field of unhelpful contention. They should: 'rest their Hope ... in a Matter of the greatest Consequence, to be well informed about it'.[113] Haykin further alluded to the absurd dictum of John Newton (1725–1807) that 'Calvinism should be ... like a lump of sugar in a cup of tea; all should taste of it, but it should not be met with in a separate form'.[114] Newton was not original in making a virtue of avoiding theological precision and thorough consistency. 'Moderate Calvinism' became for many merely the general acknowledgement of some aspects of divine sovereignty, along with an emphatic assertion of justification by faith.[115] It failed amongst Anglicans like Griffith Jones, to be an elaborated and coherent theological system. Doubtless, Jones wisely saw safety in dwelling on the Articles and Catechism, and a lively morality based upon them. The fringe sects under the Commonwealth were a warning of what to avoid. Contemporary Dissenters, on the other hand, were divided, with most at various stages of departure from their former covenantal orthodoxy, as evidenced at the 1719 Salters' Hall conference.[116] The editors of Woodward's *Account* in 1800 commented:

> We are they whom the rigid Calvinists would deem Arminians; and the strict Arminians, on the other hand, would term Calvinists; but who, in fact, trouble ourselves neither with Calvin not Arminius. Taking the Scriptures alone for our guide[117]

An avoidance of stringent theological systemization is understandable as a conscious avoidance of extremes such as those of the bitter controversies of the previous century. A predominating wish to foster strong personal faith and holiness seemed to offer a happier avenue. 'Experimental preaching' was to become the firm, predominating ideal of much later Evangelicalism.[118] Griffith Jones's extended and meticulous exposition sought to lead his hearers to acquire: 'the Scripture Character of all that are encouraged to hope for Salvation through Him' (i.e. Christ).[119] In this aim he had much success. But nevertheless, his approach was not exactly that either of the Puritans or present-day Evangelicalism.[120]

NOTES

1   John Spurr, *The Post-Reformation. Religion, Politics and Society in Britain 1603–1714* (Harlow, 2006), p. 212.
2   W. O. B. Allen and Edmund McClure, *History of the Society for Promoting Christian Knowledge 1698–1898* (London, 1898), pp. 10–11.
3   M. G. Jones, *The Charity School Movement: A Study of Eighteenth Century Puritanism in Action* (Cambridge, 1938), p. 37.
4   Allen and McClure, *History of the Society*, p. 23; Leonard W. Cowie, 'Bray, Thomas (bap. 1658, d. 1730)', *ODNB*.
5   CUL, SPCK, *Minutes*, April 1713, SPCK.MS.A 1/6.
6   Some in Welsh; cf. Mary Clement, *The SPCK and Wales 1699–1740* (London, 1954), pp. 166–71; Geraint H. Jenkins, *Literature, Religion and Society in Wales 1660–1730* (Cardiff, 1978), pp. 312–17.
7   John Brewer, *The Pleasures of the Imagination, English Culture in the Eighteenth Century* (London, 1997), pp. 170–1.
8   Clement, *The SPCK and Wales*, p. 28.
9   Jenkins, *Literature*, p. 280.
10   Jenkins, *Literature*, pp. 265, 273; Clement, *The SPCK and Wales*, pp. 22, 38, 78.
11   Jones, *The Charity School Movement*, p. 14.
12   Not until the nineteenth century did catechizing lose its prime teaching position, being replaced by Sunday-school, child-centred sentimentalism. Nevertheless, the seeds of change were evident even in the eighteenth century. Cf. W. K. Lowther Clarke, *Eighteenth Century Piety* (London, 1944), p. 8.
13   George Herbert, 'The Parson Catechizing', ch. XXI, *Priest to the Temple, or the Country Parson, http://www.ccel.org/ccel/herbert/temple2.xxiii.html* (accessed 31 July 2017).
14   Josiah Woodward, *Account of the Rise and Progress of the Religious Societies in the City of London, &c. and of their Endeavours for Reformation of Manners*, seventh edn (York, 1800), p. 27.
15   Allen and McClure, *History of the Society*, p. 15.
16   Henry D. Rack, 'Wesley, Samuel', *ODNB*.
17   Arthur Middleton, 'Thomas Bray', *Anglican History site, anglicanhistory.org/essays/middleton/bray.pdf* (accessed 31 January 2019).
18   CUL, SPCK, *Minutes*, December 1712, MS A 1/6.
19   Griffith Jones, *Instructions for the young Christian, or, An exposition of the church catechism: by way of question and answer: confirmed by Scripture proofs, and adapted to the meanest capacity / by a minister of the Church of England = Addysg i'r Cristion*

The Theology of Griffith Jones and Religious Thought

jeuangc: neu, Eglurhâd ar gatecism yr eglwys: mewn ffordd o holiad ac atteb: wedi ei brofi allan o'r Ysgrythur Lan, a'i gymhwyso i'r gwaelaf ei ddyall / gan weinidog o Eglwys Loegr (Llundain, 1750).

20 Preface to the Order of Confirmation, *BCP* (1662).

21 The Westminster Shorter Catechism was favoured, Dr White calling it and other documents: 'little garrisons against Popery'. Sermon 16 May 1706. The society issued a Welsh translation of a Westminster Assembly document in 1707.

22 Thomas A. Howard, 'Religion and the Rise of Historicism', W. M. L. de Wette, *Jacob Burckhardt and the Theological Origins of Nineteenth-Century Historical Consciousness* (Cambridge, 2006), p. 202.

23 The *Consensus Helveticus* was drafted as a denial of the doctrine taught by Amyraut in the University of Saumur. Its authority was only in Switzerland; *https://biblehub.com/library/various/creeds_of_christendom_with_a_history_and_critical_notes/_61_the_helvetic_consensus.htm* (accessed 20 February 2020).

24 Friedrich Spanheim (1600–49) and Francis Turretin (1623–87) led accusations of heresy against Amyraut.

25 For much of its early life, the SPCK devoted most of its financial support to Wales. Ostervald's *Catechism* is mentioned in the SPCK list of circulated books. CUL, SPCK, *Minutes*, 5 December 1711, MS A33/1.

26 Mary Clement, *Correspondence and Minutes of the SPCK relating to Wales 1699–1740* (Cardiff, 1952), p. 111 n.

27 Clement, *Correspondence*, p. 111.

28 Gerald Robertson Cragg, *From Puritanism to the Age of Reason* (Cambridge, 1950), p. 60.

29 Julian Hoppitt, *A Land of Liberty? England 1689–1727* (Oxford, 2000), p. 241.

30 Clement, *The SPCK and Wales*, p. 22.

31 Jenkins, *Literature, Religion*, p. 265.

32 E.g. Letter of response to distribution, 25 March 1720; Clement, *Correspondence*, p. 111.

33 William Gibson, *The Church of England 1688–1832* (London, 2001), p. 4.

34 Clement, *Correspondence*, pp. 49–50.

35 Toby Barnard, 'Richardson, John', *ODNB*.

36 Jones, *The Charity School Movement*, pp. 8–9, 36–9.

37 W. Moses Williams (ed.), *Selections from the Welch Piety* (Cardiff, 1938), pp. 52–9.

38 Jenkins, *Literature, Religion*, pp. 9–10.

39 Jenkins, *Literature, Religion*, p. 52.

40 It is noted in Clement, *Correspondence*, p. 4, that Harries was a fellow of Jesus College Oxford 1687–98, vicar of Llantrisant 1698–1728 and prebendary of Llandaff in 1704. He was the chief worker for the SPCK in Glamorgan from 1699 till his death; he founded the first two charity-schools in Wales in 1699.

41 Clement, *Correspondence*, p. 4.

42 Clement, *Correspondence*, pp. 5–6.

43 J. S. Chamberlain, 'Williams, John (1633x6–1709)', *ODNB*.

44 Bishop of St Asaph 1704–8.

45 Jenkins, *Literature, Religion*, p. 81.

Catechizing, Baptism and Evangelicalism

46 William Jacob, 'The Restoration Church', in Glanmor Williams et al. (eds), *The Welsh Church from Reformation to Disestablishment 1603–1920* (Cardiff, 2007), pp. 71–2.

47 Nelson, *The Life*, p. 420.

48 *BCP*, Catechism, second rubric.

49 G. Jones, Letter II, 16 August 1739, *The Welsh Piety* (London, 1740), p. 33.

50 Jacob, 'The Welsh Clergy', in Williams et al. (eds), *The Welsh Church*, pp. 125–6.

51 G, Jones, 'Letter XXVI, Praying for revival – mutual prayer', in *Letters of the Rev. Griffith Jones to Mrs Bevan*, ed. Edward Morgan (London, 1832), pp. 86–7.

52 Prayer of Absolution, 'The Order for Morning Prayer', *BCP* (1662).

53 First mentioned in SPCK records, 24 October 1712, elected member 18 June 1713. Cf. Clement, *Correspondence*, p. 52 n.

54 Jones, Letter I, 30 March 1738, in *Welsh Piety*, pp. 19–20.

55 Cavenagh, *Life and Work*, p. 37.

56 Jones, Letter I, p. 20.

57 W. Jacob, 'Methodism in Wales', in Williams et al. (eds), *The Welsh Church from Reformation*, p. 160.

58 Clement, *The SPCK and Wales*, p. 22.

59 G. Jenkins, 'An Old and Much Honoured'; 'Griffith Jones, Llanddowror', *Welsh History Review*, II (1983), 451–3.

60 Letter quoted in C. Morgan-Richardson, *History of the Institution once called 'The Welsh Piety', but now known as Mrs. Bevan's Charity* (Cardigan, 1890), p. 12.

61 He was an advanced clergyman in the 1720s, in holding Holy Communion once a month in his congregations, rather than following the common custom of four times a year, or even less frequently.

62 Jenkins, 'An Old and Much Honoured', 451.

63 Jenkins, *Literature, Religion*, p. 23.

64 Anonymous (Henry Phillips?), *A Sketch of the Life and Character of the Reverend and Pious Mr Griffith Jones, late Rector of Llanddowror in Carmarthenshire* (London, 1762), pp. 17–20.

65 Jacob, 'Methodism in Wales', 160.

66 G. Jones, Letter 16 August 1739, in *Welsh Piety*, pp. 26–7.

67 Clement, Abstract of letter 202, 21 June 1700, *Correspondence*, pp. 2, 7.

68 Jacob, 'Methodism in Wales', p. 161.

69 Clement, *The SPCK and Wales*, pp. 65–6, 82.

70 Clement, *The SPCK and Wales*, p. 15.

71 Jacob, 'Methodism in Wales', pp. 162–3; numbers of schools and pupils.

72 Williams (ed.), *Selections*, pp. 37–53.

73 *The Christian Covenant, or the Baptismal Vow, as stated in our Church Catechism* (London, 1761).

74 Jones, *The Christian Covenant*, second edn (London, 1762), preface iii.

75 Morgan-Richardson, *History of the Institution*, p. 6.

76 NLW, Jones, *Trysor*, p. 94.

77 NLW, Jones, *Trysor*, pp. 99–100.

78 G. Jones, *The Christian Covenant*, first edn (London, 1761), pp. lii–vi.

79 CUL, SPCK, *Minutes*, 3 June 1714, MS A33/1, P. 179.

80 John Lewis, *The Church Catechism Explain'd by Way of Question and Answer* (London, 1700).

81 Trans. John Richardson, *Catecism yr Eglwys wedi ei Egluro Trwy Holion ac Attebion* (Shrewsbury, 1713).

82 Jones, *The Christian Covenant* (1761), p. 10.

83 Jones, Mat. 5:20, *Trysor*, p. 167.

84 Jones, *The Christian Covenant*, pp. 23–5.

85 Jones, *The Christian Covenant*, p. 25, first and second questions.

86 Jones, *The Christian Covenant*, p. 25, third question.

87 Jones, *The Christian Covenant*, pp. 33–4, second question.

88 Cf. Lewis, *The Church Catechism Explain'd*, pp. 44–5. (Translated into Welsh by Ellis Wynne, 1713.) Note that Lewis saw the sacrament as an engagement for the child at length to fulfil its obligations; but he was closer to actual covenantalism than Jones, seeing in baptism God's making covenant with baptized persons, including infants.

89 Also a secondary implication seen in baptism by Puritans. Cf. *Westminster Shorter Catechism* (London, 1648), Q. 94.

90 CUL, SPCK, *Minutes*, 3 June 1714, MS A33/1, p. 179.

91 'Covenant', also translated as 'Testament', from Hebrew תירב, Greek Διαθηκη.

92 Jones, *The Christian Covenant*, p. 10

93 Jones, *The Christian Covenant*, p. 100.

94 Jones, *The Christian Covenant*, p. 22.

95 J. Calvin, *Institutes of the Christian Religion*, trans. Henry Beveridge (Geneva 1559; repub. London, 1962), vol. I, ch. X, para. 1–4, pp. 369–71.

96 Cf. Louis Berkhof, *Systematic Theology* (London, 1958), pp. 265–71; Charles Hodge, *Systematic Theology* (London, 1960), vol. II, pp. 362–72; Heinrich Heppe, *Reformed Dogmatics* [trans. *Of Reformierte Dogmatik*] (London, 1950), pp. 371–487.

97 *A Catechism, that is to say, an instruction to be learned of every person, before he be brought to be confirmed by the bishop.* Question on Sacraments.

98 Woodward, *Account of the Rise*, p. 71.

99 Hodge, *Systematic Theology*, vol. II, p. 358; Herman Bavinck, *Gereformeerde Dogmatik*, trans. William Hendriksen, *The Doctrine of God* (Edinburgh, 1977), III, p. 240.

100 David Bebbington, *Evangelicalism in Modern Britain* (London, 1989), p. 3.

101 Berkhof, *Systematic Theology*, p. 265; John Owen, *Works of John Owen* (London, 1967), vol. X, pp. 168–9.

102 Cf. *Epistle to the Romans*, chs 8, 28.

103 Incidentally also, it was not largely developed by Calvin.

104 G. Jones, 'XLV, the study of the scriptures most useful', in *Letters to Mrs Bevan*, p. 216.

105 Jenkins, 'An Old and Much Honoured', 456–7.

106 John Evans, *Some Account of the Welch Charity-Schools, and the Rise and Progress of Methodism in Wales* (London, 1752).

107 Jones, *The Christian Covenant*, p. 27.

108 Thomas Owen, *The Atonement Controversy in Welsh Theological Literature and Debate, 1707–1841* (Welsh, 1874; trans. John Aaron, Edinburgh, 2002), p. 9.

109 E.g. John Owen (1616–83).

110 Haykin, 'Evangelicalism', in Haykin and Stewart (eds), *The Emergence*, p. 42.
111 Cf. detailed referencing in transcribed sermons: NLW CMA 8326; Cardiff Central Library, MSS 2.162, 2.1103.
112 Anon., *A Sketch*, P. 5.
113 Jones, *The Christian Covenant*, preface, p. iv.
114 Haykin, 'Evangelicalism', p. 42.
115 Roger Thomas, 'Parties in Nonconformity', in C. G. Bolam (ed.), *The English Presbyterians* (London, 1968), pp. 103–4.
116 Thomas, 'Presbyterians in Transition', in Bolam (ed.), *The English Presbyterians*, pp. 160–5.
117 Woodward, *An Account of the Rise*, p. xxiii.
118 'Experimental' in the sense of dwelling upon the subjective experience of individual believers, not on speculative experimentation.
119 Jones, *The Christian Covenant*, preface, p. vi.
120 David Ceri Jones, *The Fire Divine* (Nottingham, 2015), p. 34.

Chapter 8

GRIFFITH JONES'S MINISTRY AND THE WELSH LANGUAGE

OFFICIAL AMBIVALENCE: THE BIBLE AND THE BOOK OF COMMON PRAYER IN WELSH

The 'Act of Union' of February 1535/6, and statute of 1542, incorporated Wales into the kingdom of England. Henceforth, all legal business was to be in English, 'and ... no Person or Persons that use the *Welch* Speech or Language, shall have or enjoy any manner Office or Fees'.[1] The Act thus laid the foundation for creating an anglicized gentry in Wales, and Griffith Jones's efforts to retrieve the use of Welsh were achieved in the face of legal disadvantages and English prejudices. Worship in the Church was, however, where the official attitude to Welsh came to contradict itself. In 1558, the Protestant constitution of England had seemed very precarious. It appeared important that Anglican corporate worship and doctrine should be strengthened as a focus of social cohesion and political stability. So, contrary to the policy of speeding the demise of Welsh, an Act of Parliament of 1563 ordered the translation of the Book of Common Prayer and the Bible into Welsh.[2] Moreover, apart from political expediency, there was an argument for this in the core of Anglicanism itself. The Protestant emphasis on faith, and the consequent need for teaching and understanding of doctrine, promoted the argument that worship and preaching must be in a language understood by the people. The Book of Homilies stated: 'we have both the plain and manifest words of the Scripture, and the consent of the most learned and ancient writers, to commend the prayers of the congregation in a known tongue'.[3] The Welsh Prayer Book and New Testament were published in 1567. In 1588, a version of the whole Bible in Welsh was issued, ironically with conspicuous royal approval.[4] Also, Edmund Prys (1543/4–1623) was to produce a complete version of the Psalms in metre in 1621, necessary for congregational singing.[5] Griffith Jones was primarily of a conformist mind, willing to acquiesce to the conventions of the society in which he ministered. He expressed High Church loyalty to the 39 Articles and Prayer Book, to the king, parliament and constitution, which was part of the submissive orderliness of behaviour to be enjoined upon his hearers. He even marked his loyalty, according to Williams Pantycelyn, by preaching once before Queen Anne.[6] One people, one church – and in many cases, one language – was a governmental aspiration. But Jones had the astuteness and courage to exploit the political inconsistency in the interest of Welsh religion and culture. Though his leading motive was religious, not cultural, his work had radical effects on Wales.[7] He was a submissive, conservative 'revolutionary'. In 1701, nine-tenths of its population, which was mostly monoglot Welsh-speaking, estimated at a mere 420,000 people, had been baptized as members of the established Church of England according to its appointed rites.[8] Welsh speakers thus in a measure, remained apart, despite being deemed an inseparable part of the one English realm and people.[9] By 1700, many of the Welsh gentry had adopted the use of English as its first language. Along with this, they had merged with English ruling circles, often marrying English heiresses, as seen in Sir John Philipps's family connections.[10] They had long been preparing their sons for public office by sending them to English schools, the universities and the inns of court or of chancery.[11] The separation from their tenants was thus widened, leaving most of the inferior Welsh population without the prominent cultural leadership that any society and its language need. An effect of Griffith Jones's promotion of the language in his schools, along with the work of Welsh-speaking preachers, was to restore a measure of public respectability and prestige to the use of Welsh.[12] Especially in his provision of literacy in

Welsh by the Circulating Schools, Jones showed an unusual combination of gifts. His tact, practicality and mildly stated patience enabled him to keep building the system for thirty years – eventually to pass the growing movement into the hands of Bridget Bevan (1698–1779), who carried it on into greater success until her own death in 1779.

The expansion of his Circulating Schools meant that Griffith Jones continually needed to solicit donations, especially from his wealthy English contributors. He wrote: 'there are no certain Funds nor Annuities to defray the Expence of them for one Year'.[13] He had launched out in 1731 without reserves of money, or any guarantee that the costs of an expanding project could be covered. However, Bridget Bevan's support included frequent contributions.[14] The approach of Captain Thomas Coram (1668–1751) to establishing a contemporary educational charity contrasts strikingly with Griffith Jones's: they were both what J. S. Taylor called: 'a blend of Christian benevolence, practical morality, and civic spirit'.[15] In 1722, Coram decided to establish the Foundling Hospital in London for abandoned infants. Unlike Jones, he waited for guarantees of finance and official approval. In July 1737 – fifteen years later – Coram petitioned the king in council who appointed 375 governors.[16] The hospital opened on 25 March 1741, when Jones's Circulating Schools had been already at work for ten years. The Circulating Schools were a masterpiece of practicality, maintained by unmatched persistence. Sir John Philipps's own conviction of the usefulness of charity-schools, however, faltered to some extent.[17] Jones, on the other hand, began with a small venture in Llanddowror, but continued to manage yearly growth. He pressed on against all setbacks and the difficulties of managing and financing increasing numbers of learners, teachers, accommodation and supplies, until he died in 1761, leaving it a thriving and still-growing work. Huge numbers of men, women and children attended the Circulating Schools. Until his death in 1737, Sir John Phillips had remained a faithful friend and patron of Griffith Jones's ministry, being his brother-in-law from 1720.[18] After 1737, Jones enjoyed loyal support from 'Madam' Bridget Bevan of Laugharne, Carmarthenshire, who agreed with Jones's whole school policy, including the use of Welsh.[19] This like-mindedness must have begun well before 1731. As a young woman, Mrs Bevan had been deeply affected by hearing Griffith preach in Laugharne church, where he was curate from 1708.[20] Her father John Vaughan of Derllys (1663–1722) was himself a strong supporter of the SPCK and overseer of its schools in Carmarthenshire from 1700 to 1722.[21] He thus would have known Jones, when acting as supervisor to who Jones was then schoolmaster at Laugharne. From her girlhood, Bridget Bevan was acquainted with him by these connections. Her commitment to his Circulating Schools, once begun, was founded on a familiarity with his practice and, evidently, with an intelligent grasp of matters as an educator in her own right.[22] She had a conviction of the work's religious value.[23] Bridget Bevan became a regular attender at Jones's preaching, when at home, a confiding correspondent and, after 1731, the leading patron and trusted collaborator for his Circulating Schools.[24] So great was Jones's confidence in her judgement and abilities, that he eventually passed on control of the growing school movement entirely to Bridget Bevan. After his death, her able organizing ensured that the schools should flourish even more, so much that the whole Circulating School movement became attributed to her. Griffith Jones's memory as the pioneer was eclipsed by its being given the name 'Mrs Bevan's Charity'.[25] She was an example of the many 'strong women' in this phase of church history in Britain. Mary Clement alluded to: 'the group of which she was only the most prominent member'.[26] Clement mentioned: 'over thirty women patrons in Wales from 1699 to 1740', supporting schools in Wales.[27] Her mutual understanding with Griffith Jones, and the bond of friendship that many admirers also acquired with him, were particularly shown in their correspondence.[28] This seems to be proved poignantly by Bridget's wish to be buried beside him in Llanddowror church, although her predeceased husband Arthur was buried in their local church in Laugharne.[29]

THE SIGNIFICANCE OF GRIFFITH JONES'S CIRCULATING SCHOOLS

Between 1699 and 1737 the SPCK founded ninety-five charity-schools in Wales, and twenty-nine other schools were privately endowed. It also distributed in Wales, either free of charge or very cheaply, thousands of devotional books and tracts both in Welsh and English, and sponsored two editions of the Welsh Bible (totalling 30,000 copies). Yet a prevailing illiteracy still hindered the purpose of imparting an understanding of the faith. Griffith Jones had resolved, by 1731, that the people must be taught to read; this had to be in Welsh, the language that they understood best. Others had already recognized this and founded schools to teach in Welsh, like that of Dr John Jones at Aber, Caernarfonshire in 1719.[30] In this, as in other things, Jones was not an innovator, but adopted methods that he saw to be needful, and believed to be feasible. His schools were at first a cautious step further from his parish catechizing.[31] They continued the policy of inculcating the doctrines of the Church of England, but the true novelty was Jones's driving tenacity in its accomplishment. He was 'a man of inexhaustible energy'.[32] His success became unparalleled. As might be expected, he set up the first school in his own parish of Llanddowror in 1730, and within nine years thirty-seven schools had been established by him in north and south Wales.[33] Without their own permanent buildings and individual staff, his schools might rather be called peripatetic literacy classes. They were open to all ages; both sexes were included.[34] The schools answered a desire for literacy – to read the Bible primarily – amongst people affected by the growing movement of popular piety. They were free to all, even the books being provided without charge. As the schools became better known, collections were made in many parish churches to help defray the cost. The masters were all churchmen, and some mistresses were employed.[35] To fill the posts, Griffith Jones even set up a 'college' at Llanddowror to give training for masters.[36] His classes remained three, four or even five months in a parish, and then moved to another parish, hence the title 'Circulating Schools'. Between 1737 and 1761, 3,324 schools were held and 153,835 pupils passed through them.[37] This number does not include the unregistered adults who attended at nights, estimated by Jones as twice or three times as many as the day pupils.[38] Thomas Shankland asserted that Jones's successful Circulating Schools caused the decline and gradual disappearing of the SPCK's charity schools; this Mary Clement denied.[39] Not only was Griffith Jones a pioneer of modern education for the Welsh, but he helped to make them a Bible-reading people, and facilitated the work of later evangelists and revivalists.

The charity-schools of Thomas Gouge (1605–86), and of Sir John Philipps, had sought to graft children into an Anglican understanding and loyalty. However, their teaching in English, a language that most pupils could not understand, naturally obstructed the desired result.[40] The SPCK had sympathy for the Welsh poor.[41] But, schooling in English was failing to enable many to study the Bible for themselves and so obtain the desired grasp of Protestant piety.[42] Derec Llwyd Morgan wrote of the SPCK:

> rhwng 1699 a 1727 agorodd hi gant namyn pedair o ysgolion yng Nghymru, a rhwng 1699 a 1738 b'un gyfrifol am gyfieithu a/neu gyhoeddi 31 o gyfrolau defosiynol i'r Gymraeg, gweithgarwch clodfawr, a rhyfedd o ironig ar un olwg, gan mor gyndyn ydoedd i drefnu ysgolion Cymraeg.[43]

> [between 1699 and 1727 it opened 96 schools in Wales, and between 1699 and 1738 it was responsible for translating and or publishing 31 devotional volumes into Welsh, a praiseworthy effort, and strangely ironic from one point of view, in that it was so reluctant to set up Welsh-language schools.]

In contrast, comprehensible teaching in Welsh by the Circulating Schools coincided with the governmental wish for the Welsh people to be integrated as loyal subjects of Hanoverian rule. Sadly, such assimilation, and allowance for language and culture failed to happen in much of Ireland.[44] In the minds of English benefactors there were scruples about supporting the Welsh language.[45] Nonetheless, it was kindly Englishmen, so obstinately slow to admit the value of Welsh, whom Griffith Jones charmed into protracted, generous financial support of his schools, and consequently the enabling of the survival of Welsh language and literary culture. Most of Jones's main donors were English, with few or no Welsh connections, but who, like other Englishmen in the previous century, had a sympathy for the poor neglected peasantry of Wales.[46] The undaunted Griffith Jones engaged in the unpromising task of persuading these English philanthropists of the benefit of using the strange-sounding language for his great educational venture. He was signally persuasive in getting donations during his regular visits to patrician assemblies in Bath. From 1737, Jones circulated annually to his supporters *The Welch Piety*, a printed report on the progress of his Circulating Schools.[47] Of the core of his regular lay donors, whose names appeared in the annual *Welch Piety*, only one was a Welshman, Thomas Jones, an official in the Exchequer office at Westminster.[48] The rest were disinterested English philanthropists, with no imperative obligations to Wales. John Thorold (1703–75), from 1748 the eighth baronet of Cranwell, Lincolnshire, was a wealthy landowner. He seems to have come to know Griffith Jones through Sir John Philipps.[49] Dr James Stonhouse (or Stonehouse) (1716–95) of Northampton, a notable philanthropic physician and cleric, was also a baronet. He had connections with James Hervey and Lady Huntingdon in pious and aristocratic circles.[50] The Revd James Hervey, rector of Collingtree and Weston Flavell, Northants, was a prominent defender of solifidianism against, amongst others, John Wesley. Dr Stephen Hales (1677–1761), born in Bekesbourne, Kent, became perpetual curate of Teddington, Middlesex, in 1719. He was a respected scientist and inventor, distinguished also for support of various charitable causes.[51] The Revd James Sparrow (1703?–1763?) of whom little is known, resided in or near Bath, where a number of supporters were centred or met Griffith Jones during the season.[52] William Butler, was an 'obscure country gentleman' of Audlem, Cheshire, of whose life and connections no records can be found.[53] Sir Francis Gosling (1719–68) was a wealthy City banker and alderman.[54] Slingsby Bethell (1695–1758), London MP and inheritor of a large fortune, was a supporter of many good causes, including the SPG (The Society for Propagating the Gospel in Foreign Parts), as its treasurer.[55] Like the supporters of Thomas Gouge's Welsh Trust in the previous century, these men had sympathy for the neglected state of the Welsh peasantry.[56] Jones was persuasive in getting donations, and it was his custom to meet the main donors during the annual assemblies at Bath.[57] Their names recur annually in *The Welch Piety*, and they all remained supporters, once they had been included in the list.

From about 1749, the names of supportive north Wales clerics also appear in *The Welch Piety*: an indication of Griffith Jones's eventual success in winning over more of the clergy to favouring his schools, and the use of the Welsh language. These men acted as collectors from their local gentry.[58] They were Thomas Ellis, lecturer at Holyhead; Robert Williams, of Bangor; D. Morris, rector of Ffestiniog; Humphrey Morris, rector of Llanfaethlu, Anglesey; W. Wynne, rector of Llanfair, Merioneth; John Kerrick, vicar of Llangernyw, Denbighshire; and Andrew Edwards, rector of Edern, Llŷn.[59] All this is evidence of Jones's happy ability of making and keeping social contacts, and reassuring other clergymen of his conformist intentions. Gradually, the value of his schools was recognized as reaching the approved goal of strengthening the people's grasp of Christian knowledge. The weight of clerical support further helps to prove the existence of a persisting body of diligent and pious, albeit overlooked, clergy in Wales. The very obscurity of some zealous clergymen meant that their work could be neglected by historians, thereby favouring acceptance of the allegation of there being nothing but inactivity, ignorance and impiety among the Welsh clergy.[60]

In *The Welch Piety*, Griffith Jones needed, besides retaining the support of his largely English donors, to defend his work against the recurring imputation of its being an engine secretly intended to promote 'methodistical' enthusiasm.[61] His writing reveals Jones's motives and principles concerning his schooling and, thereby, what ideals could be persuasive to contemporary pious Anglicans. In a letter of 11 October 1739, he forestalled any opponents by himself alluding to arrogations of the superiority of the English language.[62] He raised what was a main obstacle to progress, quoting his opponents' own words: 'The disagreeable novelty of setting up schools in the Welsh tongue.' He added: 'That these Welsh Charity-Schools are Means to continue the Use of the Welsh Tongue, and to keep the Natives in Ignorance of the English.'[63] Robert Lowth (1710--87) was later one who expressed a common opinion by extolling the special qualities of English: 'The English language hath been much cultivated ... considerably polished and refined.'[64] Educated Englishmen could hardly be expected to find reasons for exempting Welsh from unfavourable comparison with the language so exaltedly praised by Lowth. Rather, Jones's promotion of Welsh might easily seem an obstinate provocation. Liberal studies in the Classics naturally tended

Griffith Jones's Ministry and the Welsh Language

to prejudice educated Englishmen against what seemed to some outsiders 'the uncouthness and ungrammaticalness of the [Welsh] language'.[65] Some referred, with careless disdain, to 'that uncouth ungenteel lingua'.[66] Griffith Jones strove to prove foremost, therefore, the immediate practical need of teaching in Welsh, leaving an assertion of the language's peculiar qualities till later. Among his English sympathizers, he attempted to reassure doubters, who, in 1739, must have still been numerous, by the effective ploy of saying: 'They have now pretty well got over such Prejudices that we were afraid would be most fatal to them.'[67] In fact, he still needed to wield effective arguments to deflect 'such prejudices' that persisted against the use of Welsh. The letter reveals Jones's tact and skilfulness of argument in presenting Welsh as a 'special case'. Griffith Jones's simple, flexible scheme of teaching literacy quickly accumulated numbers of pupils and schools, but also the accompanying financial demands. Detractors could easily foment suspicions about this distinct movement employing novel methods of instruction.[68] Facing the possibility that his insistence on using Welsh might exasperate some supporters, who could easily turn their charity to some other worthy cause, he emphasized the daunting financial obstacles to a change to English:

> how much less would the Benefit of them be in *English* than now it is in the *Welsh Tongue* ... three of four Months, in which Time the People learn to read well their own *Language* ... and the three or four Years they must be to learn an unknown Language ... for the same Money there could be but *One* taught to read *English* for *Twelve* that are now taught *Welsh*.[69]

The argument was unanswerable. It was too easy, even for these benevolent outsiders, to overlook the urgent goal of reaching the Welsh with the Gospel in their own language. Remembering this priority, Griffith Jones chose to remind his readers of the damage to the cause of the Church of England in Wales done by clergymen ministering in English to uncomprehending congregations. They had not learnt Welsh, nor had the people English: 'This has, in too many Places, reduced the Country into Heathenish Darkness and Irreligion and ... into different Communities and Separations from the *Established Church*.'[70] Jones's

205

emphatic reasoning seems alarmist – and perhaps exaggerated, but the issue was crucial. If only his donors pondered the dire results of neglecting Welsh, it would be a strong dissuasion to them from risking a change in his policy. Griffith Jones added to his pleas a shaming comparison with Roman Catholicism, the feared rival to English Protestantism.[71] Even that church showed greater wisdom, despite using the 'dead' imperial language in its services: '[Concerning the] Latin service in the Church of Rome ... [the Pope] ordains that preaching be in the known tongue through all his provinces.'[72] Jones's words may also have reminded some donors of the fact that Rome's numerous missionaries at the time were going to lengths to convert the heathen, using the native languages, and succeeding.[73] The inept approach in Wales of teaching through the English language typified the overall failure of Protestantism to fulfil its calling in the world at large – the Danish Lutheran mission at Tranquebar in India being a petty exception.[74] The numerical victories of Rome brought a chastening dubiety to Protestant assumptions of theological superiority deriving from the successes of the Reformation.[75]

THE ARGUMENT FOR SPECIAL TREATMENT FOR THE WELSH LANGUAGE

Griffith Jones had to tackle the obvious objection that Welsh ought not to be dealt differently from the other languages of the king's dominions. He commended the suppression of Irish, Scots and Manx Gaelic, failing blatantly to apply his own argument for the practical religious necessity of using the mother tongue.[76] His general willingness to conform to the mores of the English-speaking gentry – into which he himself had married – perhaps induced Griffith Jones to countenance the destruction of Gaelic language and culture. But his appreciation of Welsh, of which he was a masterly exponent, could not allow him to welcome its destruction.[77] He had, consequently, to plead for special-case treatment. Jones softened his own inconsistency by the rhetorical quoting of his would-be opponents' own argument: 'why must the King's Subjects in Wales be the only Persons with whom little or no Pains are taken to make them learn the English

Tongue?'[78] Jones blandly sidestepped this question, professing, with mild disingenuousness: 'I am not at present concerned what becomes of the language, abstractly considered; nor design to say anything merely to aggrandize or advance its repute.'[79] But his writings do show him warmly favouring Welsh. Nevertheless with his important donors, he built his advocacy upon the pragmatic necessity of the language as a vehicle of reading – pre-eminently of the Bible – but also other edifying literature.[80] He and they were moved with an urgency to bring, as they saw it, a message of hope for people lost and without the knowledge of salvation.[81] Here, and throughout the rise of the evangelizing movement, this was necessarily a predominating motive.[82] This simple basic plea was an irresistible appeal to Jones's supporters' Christian convictions: 'please to consider the Weight and Importance of saving four or five hundred thousand Souls (more or less) now living in *Wales*; and their future Descendants.'[83] Indeed, this object was precisely what members of the SPCK, SPG and the religious societies, all devoutly sought. Preaching to the Welsh ought not to be put off until they learnt English, insisted Jones: 'What Length of Time ... how many hundred Years, must be allowed for the general Attainment of the *English* and the dying away of the *Welsh Language*.'[84]

Griffith Jones adroitly wielded the biblical concept of Providence in his pleading for the use of Welsh. The doctrine had convincing force with his donors, especially at that very time, when it was being contested by Deists and Pelagians.[85] He tactfully introduced it, suggesting need for caution about removing Welsh: 'May we not therefore justly fear, when we attempt to abolish a Language ... that we fight against the Decrees of Heaven, and seek to undermine the Disposals of Divine Providence?'[86] This admonition accorded with the received ideal of dutiful submission to divine authority. Unexpected turns of events were seen as being 'of God'. The bounds of duties in church and state were set by the sovereign disposer of all things for mankind.[87] On the strength of this, Jones was able to add further considerations intended to dissuade his supporters from favouring: 'abolishing the *British Language*'. He urged them to: 'consider, whether there are not some particular Advantages designed us by Providence, in continuing the Use of it'.[88] Addressing men who were avid Bible-readers, he cited the familiar account of the Tower of Babel, where the hubristic building attracted the dividing of languages.[89] Jones conceded that difficulties caused by unintelligibility of language were indeed a 'sore evil', but, ingeniously, he suggested that there were also some advantages: 'His [that is, God's] temporal Judgments are often turned into Mercy.'[90] This description of the confusion of language as 'providential' would have seemed a reasonable proposition to his donors.[91] Trust in divine Providence to bring blessing out of trouble was, for such men, an essential component of true Christian faith.[92] Bishop George Bull wrote: 'Trust and dependence on the Divine Providence is every where in Scripture recommended as our great duty and only security.'[93] 'Providence' implied God's even wielding the reckless entanglements and miseries of wilful human sin as an instrument with a purpose of good outcomes.[94] According to this doctrine, though men built the tower for their own blameworthy ends, the plot was 'providential', serving God's far-reaching plans to advance his Kingdom throughout the world. For example, Alexander Nowell (1516?–1602), dean of St Paul's, had written to the same effect in his celebrated Catechism.[95] SPCK members would be aware that Deists were especially averse to the doctrine of God's over-all sovereignty.[96] The Prayer Book, Catechism and Articles describe God as 'Creator and Preserver of all things',[97] and 'our God, who upholdest and governest all things by the word of thy power'.[98] Sir John Philipps, for one, noted that God's purposes being worked out in Providence are impenetrable: 'We may believe God when he tells us ye Secret Things belong to Him.'[99] Jones praised the Welsh language for being more than a mean rustic dialect. He argued that the division into separate languages – by which Welsh came to exist – kept individual systems of error from gaining complete control of men's minds.[100] This was a much more powerful argument for his supporters, fearful of the circulation of dangerous ideas, than it might be for present-day Christian philanthropists.[101] According to Jones, through history, a valuable body of divine revelation:

> kind Providence made these disagreeing Parties mutual Guards and Watches upon one another; not only to secure the whole Body of Religion,

that no Part should be lost, but likewise to preserve the Holy Scriptures sound and whole[102]

Limitations on the exchange of ideas were indeed greater at a time of poor communications, and the largely oral culture of monoglot Welsh society had a greater conservative effect.[103] Perhaps Griffith Jones was conscious of somewhat exaggerating. Erasmus Saunders reported the continuance of remnants of pre-Reformation ideas and customs.[104] In the people's joy of singing, and of its use as prayer, 'their Ejaculations to invocate, not only the Deity, but ... *Mair-Wen, Jago, Teilaw-Mawr*' disprove Jones's suggestion that the linguistic separation had safeguarded an intelligent understanding of the faith.[105] It seems rather that the later consolidation of biblical knowledge, and popular Protestant understanding in Wales came actually by the recent translation of Christian books from English, such as John Bunyan's *Pilgrim's Progress*.[106]

Griffith Jones suggested that keeping Welsh as the common language of Wales had benefits, in that it was a barrier to the people from leaving their humble callings.[107] The view was then much promoted, in the interest of freedom from disruption, that one's 'station' was appointed by Providence, and therefore to be accepted submissively.[108] By his favourite method of teaching – catechetical question and answer – Jones proposed the startling suggestion of positive advantages:

Question: Wherein is the benefit of retaining the Welsh tongue?
Answer: If all of us spoke the same tongue with you, the common and labouring people would soon desert their callings in low life here, and seek abroad for better preferments in English countries ... and then hands would be much wanted here to cultivate our grounds ... to the great and speedy impoverishment of the whole principality.[109]

This is not a convincing argument for us today, but, though far-fetched, it did touch on serious concerns at the time about the stability of a society depending on everyone's keeping submissively in his appointed rank and calling. English society was in fact comparatively fluid, with opportunities of rising in wealth and social position.[110] Jones himself was proof that there was no absolute hindrance for even a Welsh farmer's son's rising to find acceptance in the higher gentry, and move easily amongst society in Bath and London.[111] There was still concern about society's depending on each keeping to his allotted place. Roy Porter cited misgivings in the century about increasing flexibility: 'Subordination is sadly broken down in this age,' bemoaned Dr Samuel Johnson (1709–84), 'there are many causes.' The lower orders were often observably improvident and unreliable.[112] The maintenance of an orderly society needed all to be content with their lot, even if toiling on the land for small and precarious rewards. If the lowliest learnt English and seized the chance of better circumstances in England, Jones warned that there would be 'great and speedy Impoverishing'.[113] Between April 1740 and January 1741, at the time Griffith Jones wrote these words, serious riots over food prices were happening in England and Wales.[114] The widespread poverty and labouring people's proneness to restless discontent would certainly have been known to Jones's wealthy supporters.[115] His alarmist warnings would therefore not have seemed unreasonable. Henry Newman, secretary of the SPCK expressed the same frank will to keep the poor charity-school pupils in what was deemed the place of servitude appointed by Providence. The children 'whether it were possible to "inure them to labour" or not, should be prepared for servile work'.[116] For continued donations to his schools, Griffith Jones needed to avoid any alienation of English feeling. He reminded his readers of the fact that Welshness had not hindered his people's political loyalty: 'the kings of England have found us to be of untainted loyalty and obedience'.[117] Jones argued from history that their difference of language had not dissuaded the Welsh from co-operating loyally within the Tudor state and Church:

> Ever since Henry the Seventh ... the kings of England have found us to be
> of untainted loyalty and obedience ... Are we not your fellow-members ...
> of the same mystical and political body?[118]

At the time that he wrote, Britain was at war with Spain, and soon would be fighting France in the War of Austrian Succession (1743–8). The country would also be reminded of the Jacobite danger by the French expedition to install Charles Edward Stuart in 1744, and by the uprising in 1745. The solid refusal of the Welsh to aid the Jacobite cause naturally strengthened the contention that it was safe to assure them their language. Even Sir Watkin Williams Wynn, leader of the Jacobite Cycle of the White Rose, in 1745, offered no support to the Pretender, but 'felt justified in his desertion of north Wales for London at that crucial time'.[119] Moreover, Jones referred emotively to the living unity existing in Church and state: 'Are we not your Fellow-Members ... of the same Mystical and Political Body? Many of our Nation are intermixed with You ... Union and Affinity do increase more and more.'[120] This latter appeal may have been convincing to his patrons, and thus a fitting argument for allowing the language of Wales a place in the whole nation. There was a strong moral motive, with a political addendum, in Griffith Jones's linking the English benefactors with the schools and their pupils in a joint cultural and spiritual venture, with the Welsh language as its matrix. He strengthened his argument with allusion to the Christian duty of diligence: 'Gifts and graces not properly used, fade, or vanish; but if we traffick well with a few talents, we shall soon be trusted with more.'[121] Jones thus used an acceptable compunction, implying that all ought to consent to the idea of 'trafficking well' with the Welsh language. In effect, he was inviting English friends to feel even a political inducement to support his cause. Griffith Jones summed up his earnest exhortations with a cautious measure of mutual congratulation:

> it is time ... to tell our benefactors in England, that thousands here ... are bound to join with me, to thank God always for you; and I hope it will not be disbelieved, that what has been said about charity is intended to seek fruit that may abound to your joyous account, as well as your assistance every where to perishing souls to come at their saviour.[122]

WELSH AND ANTIQUARIANISM

Antiquarianism, in linguistics as well as other branches of study, had a strong place in contemporary educated thought and culture, along with Classicism.[123] The work of Edward Lhuyd (1660–1709) represented a growing field of scholarly interest.[124] The idea that Welsh especially was a remainder from the remote past had a strong appeal, later to be augmented by Romanticism. The latter influenced the formation of Evangelicalism.[125] Griffith Jones was wise enough to exploit this, whilst yet avoiding any hint of questioning the existing English political and cultural ascendency: 'The greatest philologists of England and France ... have maintained that to be the chief remains of the Celtique which is spoken in Wales, Cornwall, and Bass Bretagne.'[126] Hence, citing the antiquity of Welsh, Jones found an argument for recommending its preservation. He chose discreetly to invoke the authority of a prominent Englishman: Edmund Gibson (1669–1748), bishop of London. Using it also to affirm the sanction of God's purpose in Providence, he wrote:

> I cannot omit what is asserted ... by the learned Dr Gibson, the present Bishop of London ... 'We cannot but much admire and celebrate the divine goodness towards our Britains [sic], the posterity of Gomer; who, though they have been conquered and triumphed over successively by the Romans, Saxons, and Normans, yet hitherto they enjoy the name of their ancestors, and have preserved entire their primitive language, although the Normans set themselves to abolish it, making express laws to that purpose.'[127]

Gibson, as an influential prelate, having the ear of the government, was respected for several reasons. Whilst at Oxford he had become a knowledgeable Anglo-Saxon and Norse scholar, which perhaps helps to explain his surprising esteem of another native language than English, together with antiquities.[128] The existence of the language for long in the island of Britain would tend to weaken the conception of the Welsh and their speech as being alien and a threat to English national integrity. Rather, Griffith Jones's appeal to the authority of Gibson, with the added weight of Camden's *Britannia*, appears to have contributed to making Welsh seem a significant part of the common heritage, worthy of respect.[129] But Griffith Jones had to employ all his powers of argument against a countervailing linguistic naivety – even among some having the contemporary education in the Classics. Against the way Welsh sounded to unfamiliar ears, or to counter the alleged difficulty of learning it, he wrote: 'Some indeed have complained of its being harsh and rough; it may be so to such as have no mind to learn it.'[130] He recommended the qualities of Welsh:

> Its grammar rules are easy, exact, and less in number than are incident to many other languages; ... the Hebrew, to which it is nearly related... Let who pleases compare the Welsh and Hebrew Old Testament with this view, he will be surprized with the great number of words and expressions he will observe to have a near affinity in their pronunciation and meaning[131]

Jones surely exaggerated the simplicity of Welsh grammar; but another very telling point with his pious readers was the stress on the similarities with Hebrew – which indeed are not imaginary.[132] One must remember that, at the time, a knowledge of Hebrew also was a standard requirement for any serious scholar.[133] The language of the Old Testament had come to be considered a pillar, with Latin and Greek, of the liberal education provided by the English universities.[134] He wrote:

> the *British Language* may be fairly supposed to be one of these which sprung out of the *Hebrew* at the Tower of *Babel*; consequently may be said to have God Himself for immediate *Author* of it[135]

This was an arresting point, even to supporters who were not keen linguists. The alleged derivation from Hebrew would certainly have inclined his classically educated Protestant patrons to view Welsh in a more favourable light. It implied that Welsh was part of their cultural – and, more importantly, their spiritual – legacy, not to be lightly cast aside, though Jones's cavalier theory of origins outran the evidence.[136] He further made Edmund Gibson a powerful ally, in alleging Welsh as 'mother tongue' to Latin. Cognate forms were assumed to prove that Latin, the main Classical language, derived from Welsh in some way. Gibson had written: 'I thus endeavour to derive *Latin Words* from the *Welsh* ... and [the words] were probably in Use in these Islands before *Rome* was built.'[137] Citing as authority yet another English scholar, Jones mentioned that, besides its language, Wales had other venerable connections with past ages:

The Theology of Griffith Jones and Religious Thought

> many *Monuments* of *Antiquity*; considerable numbers of *Manuscripts* of *ancient Dates* do still remain ... 'Where shall we so properly search (*says Mr.* CAMBDEN) as in our *British Language*, which is so pure, unmixt, and extremely ancient?'[138]

Here, Griffith Jones was digressing from the practicalities of basic literacy for Welsh peasants, but he had good reason to believe it necessary to raise his donors' esteem of the language as a cultural medium. Jones implied that educated Christians beyond Wales might rightly feel a duty of care. He cited Camden: 'For ancient languages [continues the author] are highly serviceable to the finding out the first original of things.'[139] Jones's detailed pleading for the whole providential deposit of the Welsh language must have seemed to him a persuasive buttress to his advocacy of his countrymen's access to literacy and the Bible. Since the Classics especially were the main element and standard of gentlemanly education, Welsh needed some semblance of an attachment to them, at least in the minds of his donors. For Englishmen uneasy about showing Christian favour to a despised vernacular, here was some reassurance of their remaining within the bounds of respectable scholarship and gentility, whilst still, in effect, financially supporting the survival of Welsh.

Griffith Jones's argument for schooling in Welsh did not militate against learning English. He stated what ought to have been obvious to any educated person: 'Sure I am, the *Welsh Charity-Schools* do no way hinder to learn *English*, but do very much contribute towards it.'[140] As an experienced schoolmaster, he knew that knowledge accumulates and accelerates further learning: 'To be able to read one Language does not increase the Difficulty of learning another, but always renders it easier.'[141] His well-founded view was surprisingly liberal, envisaging a broadening of minds, rather than cramping them in narrow fields of study. His pedagogy was, in principle, ambitious beyond a grudging minimum of instruction, though study of the Bible was an essential beginning. Jones stressed the impracticability of replacing Welsh by English. He presented anyone who should propose abolishing Welsh with dissuasive obstacles, likely to bring him to a nonplussed standstill. This made altering nothing seem the practical option:

> ADMITTING that no Conveniency attended the Discontinuing of the *Welsh Tongue*, and ... it may be desirable all the People spoke *English*; yet to bring this about is hardly practicable.[142]

Thus, by an exhaustive list of defences to Welsh, Griffith Jones insisted that Providence had preserved, until his own time, a language which must be allowed to remain till the end of the age:

> Let it suffice, that so great a part of her dominions have been usurped from her; but let no Violence be offered to *her Life:* Let Her stay the appointed Time, to expire a peaceful and natural Death, which we trust will not be till the Consummation of all Things.[143]

Griffith Jones used an argument persuasive for those feeling England to be under siege from hostile philosophies: an absence of corrupting literature in Welsh. Contemporary moralists were worried about the effect upon people's reading novels. The post-1660 flow of literature included attacks upon the authority of the Bible and conventional Christian morality.[144] Jones held that the use of Welsh protected its speakers from books in English which were likely to corrupt. He called Welsh literature 'the *chastest* in all *Europe*', asserting that it was 'free from the Infection and deadly Venom of *Atheism, Deism, Infidelity, Arianism, Popery, lewd Plays, immodest Romances, and Love Intrigues*'. Much of the latter was being propagated in books published in English.[145] His disapproval accorded with the alarm felt by many churchmen about the general airing in print of defiance of the authorities which informed 'good manners'.[146] The foundations were being worryingly disturbed. Jones believed that using Welsh guarded 'our common people' against the dangerous trends amongst English speakers. He pointed out the religious value of the language's having: 'a better Translation than common of the *Holy Bible*, and the *Publick Worship* of God therein ... We have also several sound *Authors* in *Divinity*, and *Tracts* of *Divine Poems*'.[147] Jones's statement may have been true, to an extent, that the peasantry were: 'less prejudiced, and better disposed to receive Divine Instructions'. Great numbers were humbly sitting under his and others' preaching in 1740, but there was no certainty that the Welsh would remain immune to unsound teaching.[148] Once legions of ordinary Welshmen had become literate, it would not always be books approved by the godly that captured minds. The Enlightenment, with its spirit of opposition to imposed authority, fostered radicalism in Wales too. Iolo Morganwg (1747–1826), for instance, would be a loud defender of the American and French revolutions, and an agitator who took the subversive Thomas Paine for a hero.[149] Griffith Jones affirmed, somewhat implausibly, that differences between languages: 'produced more intelligible Explications and forcible Proofs of many Doctrines than we could well have expected'.[150] He added: 'It has also kept up a Religious Emulation in the moral Life amongst the contending Parties, who otherwise would very probably have grown more remiss.'[151] He omitted to say, however, who exactly were the 'contending parties' that he meant. There had long been some hostility in England towards the Welsh, which had the possibility of worsening. Welsh oddities often induced more bantering mockery than hostile violence, though Geraint Jenkins notes of Iolo Morganwg when in London, even in the 1790s: 'Canfu fod gwrth-Gymreictod yn dal yn fyw ac yn iach ar strydoedd y brifddinas' (He found that anti-Welsh feeling was still alive and well on the streets of the capital).[152] Emrys Jones wrote: 'there was, however, no serious bad blood'.[153] Welsh integration into the whole kingdom was a promising sign of a flourishing 'unity in diversity'. Only the later rise of Romantic nationalism was to induce a concept of Wales as deserving the rights of a separate nation-state, animated by divisive complaints against English influence.[154]

Griffith Jones's unusual set of talents and idiosyncrasies produced long-lasting effects.[155] Despite his oddities, Jones kept surprisingly good relations with other people – though not without occasional failures.[156] His gift for sympathetic communication contributed to his success in preaching, sometimes when addressing people of importance.[157] Having joined the gentry by marrying into the Philipps family, but never losing sight of his reforming goals, Griffith Jones escaped the hindering preoccupations of social climbing.[158] As with his brother-in-law, Sir John, in his devotion to public service, Jones's contacts with the rich did not deflect him from his round of ministerial tasks.[159] Rather, he exploited his gentry contacts particularly in the interest of his poor countrymen. Jones's excessive, fawning obsequiousness towards his later patron, Mrs Bevan, in his many letters to her, alone seems to go against his usual better judgement.[160] He continued, with apparent contentment, to follow his established round of study, preaching, visitation of Llanddowror parishioners – including medical help – and making the complicated arrangements for the growing number of Circulating Schools.[161] Griffith Jones never lost the 'common touch', remaining sympathetic with the poor, mostly illiterate, Welsh-speaking peasantry. Crowds were moved by his fluent and deft use of the Welsh language.[162] Many of these developed a thirst to learn to read the Bible, and own a copy.[163] This primarily religious motive began a stupendous transformation of the Welsh into an unusually literate people, leading, in the next century, to a marked renaissance of their literature.[164] Though this was not Jones's ostensible aim, it did reveal a respect for his native culture.[165] Bibles came to be much in demand among Jones's learners.[166] His determination to forward popular literacy persisted, moreover, when others would have lost heart.[167] Lukewarmness arising in some colleagues, the lack of resources and of suitable schoolmasters, or accusations of Methodism continually tested his resolve.[168] But, so strong was the newly implanted taste for religious study that it frequently happened that, when the circulating school in a parish was discontinued, the pupils assembled in church for a 'Sunday school'.[169] Their principal textbooks were the Bible and the Book of Common Prayer. David Ceri Jones wrote:

> In Wales it was educational provision that captured the imagination of nonconformist leaders as Thomas Charles's Sunday Schools picked up on the earlier achievements of Griffith Jones's circulating schools, teaching pupils of all ages the basic skills of literacy and numeracy. It was to be a level of literacy that was soon to fuel the growth of an impressive print culture[170]

In light of this, it seems a sad irony that though, in the present century, government policy has elevated Welsh to official status, and the language has growing prestige as the core of a regional culture, there is no monument to Griffith Jones.[171]

NOTES

1 The parts of the 1535/6 Act concerning language were only repealed by the Welsh Language Act 1993.

2 *An Act for the Translating of the Bible and the Divine Service into the WELSH Tongue.*

3 'An Homily wherein is Declared that Common Prayer and Sacraments ought to be Ministered in Tongue that is Understanded of the Hearers'; *The Two Books of Homilies, Appointed to be Read in Churches* (Oxford, 1859), p. 357.

4 Produced by Christopher Barker, the Queen's printer, and displaying her royal arms on the top of the title page. Cf. Eryn M. White. *The Welsh Bible* (Cardiff, 2007), p. 35.

5 *Salmau Cân* bound together with the Welsh Book of Common Prayer, with the title *Llyfr y Psalmau, wedi eu cyfieithu a'i cyfansoddi ar fesur cerdd yn Gymraeg.*

6 F. A. Cavenagh, *The Life and Work of Griffith Jones of Llanddowror* (Cardiff, 1930), p. 10.

7 R. Jenkins, *Griffith Jones of Llanddowror* (Cardiff, 1930), p. 53.

8 John Davies, *Hanes Cymru* (London, 1990), p. 302.

9 The French-speaking Channel Islands and, until 1558 the Pale of Calais, had been adjuncts to the kingdom, but less closely knit to it.

10 Sir John Philipps was uncle to Catherine Shorter, wife of Robert Walpole, and great-grandson of Philip Stanhope, first earl of Chesterfield. His father's first wife was Lady Cecily Finch, daughter of Thomas, earl of Winchilsea.

11 Howell A. Lloyd, *The Gentry of South-West Wales 1540–1640* (Cardiff, 1968), p. 144.

12 Geraint H. Jenkins, *Literature, Religion and Society in Wales 1660–1730* (Cardiff, 1978), pp. 260–1.

13 G. Jones, *The Welsh Piety* (London, 1740), p. 44.

14 M. G. Jones, *The Charity School Movement: A Study of Eighteenth Century Puritanism in Action* (Cambridge, 1938), p. 302; W. Moses Williams, 'The Friends of Griffith Jones', *Y Cymmrodor*, XLVI (1939), 27.

15 James Stephen Taylor, 'Thomas Coram (*c.*1668–1751) Philanthropist', *ODNB.*

16 Governors included eighty-nine peers, thirty-five country gentlemen, sixty-six merchants and seventy-two MPs, to direct a grandiose foundation modelled on a joint-stock company.

17 His charity was switched to other causes; and there seems more than a hint that he lacked Jones's concern for the Welsh language.

18 Bridget Bevan, née Vaughan, became related to Griffith Jones when her cousin Richard Vaughan of Derllys (1653–1724) married Arabella Philipps, sister of Jones's wife Margaret Philipps.

19 Sir John may have been lukewarm to the language element, and this may account for the publication of the *Welch Piety* after his death in 1737.

20 Mary Clement, *The SPCK and Wales 1699–1740* (London, 1954), p. 111.

21 Jones, *The Charity School Movement*, p. 290.

22 Bridget Bevan's husband, Arthur Bevan (1689–1742/3) was also a supporter of the SPCK until his death. He was recorder of Carmarthen boroughs 1722–41, judge of equity in north and south Wales from 1735, and Whig MP for Carmarthen 1721–41. Cf. Peter D. G. Thomas, 'Carmarthen 1715–1754', *History of Parliament*,

http://www.historyofparliamentonline.org/volume/1715-1754/member/philipps-sir-john-1666-1737 (accessed 12 June 2019).

23 Jones, *The Charity School Movement*, p. 313.

24 Eryn M. White, 'Bevan [*née* Vaughan], Bridget', *ODNB*.

25 C. Morgan-Richardson, *History of the Institution once called 'The Welsh Piety', but now known as Mrs. Bevan's Charity* (Cardigan, 1890), p. 4.

26 Clement, *The SPCK and Wales*, p. 13.

27 E.g. Lady Dorothy Jeffreys in Flintshire, and Mrs Edward Vaughan in Montgomeryshire; also Lady Charlotte Edwin of Llanfihangel, Glamorgan. Cf. Clement, *The SPCK and Wales*.

28 D. Densil Morgan, *Theologia Cambrensis*, vol. 1 (Cardiff, 2018), p. 283.

29 Eryn M. White, 'Bevan, Bridget', *ODNB*; 'Bevan, Arthur' (1697–1743).

30 Clement, *The SPCK and Wales*, p. 139.

31 G. Jones, *Welch Piety: or a Succinct Account of the Rise and Progress of the Circulating Welch Charity Schools* (London, 1761), p. 19.

32 G. Jenkins, 'An Old and Much Honoured'; 'Griffith Jones, Llanddowror', *Welsh History Review*, II (1983), 451.

33 Jones, *The Charity School Movement*, p. 309.

34 Cf. the school for girls set up by Ziegenbalg's Tranquebar mission.

35 Cavenagh, *The Life and Work*, p. 46.

36 Clement, *The SPCK and Wales*, pp. 23–4.

37 Jones, *Welch Piety*; figures are corrected by Thomas Kelly.

38 Thomas Kelly mentioned numbers of adults at about 150,000, and successful learners to read at 100,000. Thomas Kelly, *Griffith Jones. Llanddowror, Pioneer in Adult Education* (Cardiff, 1950), pp. 45–7.

39 Clement, *The SPCK and Wales*, p. 17.

40 Jones, *The Charity School Movement*, pp. 285, 290–1.

41 Jenkins, 'An Old and Much Honoured', 459.

42 Jones, *The Charity School Movement*, p. 296.

43 Derec Llwyd Morgan, *Y Diwygiad Mawr* (Llandysul, 1999), p. 36.

44 Toby Barnard, 'Maule, Henry', *ODNB*.

45 Jones, *The Charity School Movement*, p. 312.

46 Williams, 'The Friends of Griffith Jones', 52–6.

47 The name of the report followed the example of the pietist works of Halle Lutherans. Cf. Jones, *The Charity School Movement*, pp. 37–8. In the 1740 edition, Griffith Jones uses the spelling 'Welsh', but 'Welch' later.

48 Kelly, *Griffith Jones Llanddowror*, p. 44.

49 Williams, 'The Friends', 33–5.

50 Williams, 'The Friends', 44–6.

51 Williams, 'The Friends', 37–44.

52 Williams, 'The Friends', 61.

53 Kelly, *Griffith Jones Llanddowror*, p. 43.

54 Partner of Gosling's Bank, 19 Fleet Street.

55 He had become rich as an agent for his family's plantations in Antigua, sending great quantities of English woollens to the Guinea coast, and purchasing Black people for the

British plantations; Brooke, *History of Parliament, http://www.historyofparliamentonline.org/volume/1754-1790/member/bethell-slingsby-1695-1758* (accessed 12 June 2019).

56   Founded 1674. Richard L. Greaves, 'Gouge, Thomas', *ODNB*.

57   Kelly, *Griffith Jones Llanddowror*, p. 44.

58   Kelly, *Griffith Jones Llanddowror*, p. 45.

59   Kelly, *Griffith Jones Llanddowror*, p. 45.

60   Jones, *The Charity School Movement*, p. 274; Clement, *The SPCK and Wales*, p. xvii.

61   David Jones, *Life and Times of Griffith Jones of Llanddowror* (London, 1902), pp. 168–9.

62   John Dryden (1631–1700) voiced a common high opinion of English, referring to 'speaking so noble a language as we do', quotes Simeon Potter, *Our Language* (Harmondsworth, 1950), p. 120.

63   G. Jones, *The Welsh Piety* (London, 1740), p. 30.

64   Robert Lowth was bishop of Oxford; *A Short Introduction to English Grammar with Critical Notes* (Oxford, 1762), pp. iii–iv.

65   William Gambold, *A Welsh Grammar* (1727), quoted in Jenkins, *Literature, Religion*, p. 10.

66   UCNWL Penrhos (1), MS. 604, quoted in Jenkins, *Literature, Religion*.

67   Jones, *The Welsh Piety*, p. 30.

68   John Evans, *Some Account of the Welch Charity-Schools, and the Rise and Progress of Methodism in Wales* (London, 1752), title page.

69   Jones, *The Welsh Piety*, pp. 44–5.

70   Jones, *The Welsh Piety*, p. 45.

71   William Jacob, 'The Restoration Church', in Glanmor Williams et al. (eds), *The Welsh Church from Reformation to Disestablishment 1603–1920* (Cardiff, 2007), p. 81.

72   Jones, *The Welsh Piety*, p. 45.

73   David Bebbington, *Evangelicalism in Modern Britain* (London, 1989), p. 12.

74   W. O. B. Allen and Edmund McClure, *History of the Society for Promoting Christian Knowledge 1698–1898* (London, 1898), pp. 260–1.

75   Bebbington, *Evangelicalism*, p. 40.

76   Jones, *The Welsh Piety*, pp. 51–3.

77   Jones, *The Welsh Piety*, p. 52.

78   Jones, *The Welsh Piety*, p. 30.

79   Jones, *The Welsh Piety*, p. 30.

80   Jones, *The Welsh Piety*, p. 51.

81   William Jacob, 'The State of the Parishes', in Williams et al. (eds), *The Welsh Church*, p. 158.

82   Bebbington, *Evangelicalism*, p. 12.

83   Jones, *The Welsh Piety*, pp. 31–3.

84   Jones, *The Welsh Piety*, p. 39.

85   Cf. 'Theron' representing Deists in James Hervey, *Theron and Aspasio* (London, 1755), p. 13; Julian Hoppitt, *A Land of Liberty? England 1689–1727* (Oxford, 2000), pp. 227–30.

86   Jones, *The Welsh Piety*, p. 37.

87 Cf. Thomas Cranmer (ed.), *First Book of Homilies* (London, 1547); pub. in *The Two Books of Homilies*, pp. 105–6.

88 Jones, *The Welsh Piety*, p. 33.

89 *Genesis* 11:1–9.

90 Jones, *The Welsh Piety*, p. 34.

91 Cf. frequent reference to 'divine providence', viz. Jones, *The Welsh Piety*, p. 34.

92 As opposed to Deistic dependence on impersonal and predictable 'laws of nature'.

93 George Bull, *The English Theological Works of George Bull D.D.* (Oxford, 1844), p. 349.

94 Cf. Joseph's view of his brothers' murderous intentions working out for good. *Genesis* 45:5.

95 Alexander Nowell, *A Catechism* (London, 1570; repub. Cambridge, 1853), p. 31. Ruerent enim universa, atque ad nihilum reciderent, nisi eius virtute, et quasi manu sustinerentur. A Deo etiam totum naturae ordinem, et rerum mutationes, quae fortunae vicissitudines falso putantur, pendere.
('For all things would run to ruin, and fall to nothing, unless by his virtue, and, as it were, by his hand they were upholden. We also assuredly believe, that the whole order of nature and changes of things, which are falsely reputed the alterations of fortune, do hang all upon God.') (p. 147).

96 S. N. Williams, 'Deism', in Sinclair B. Ferguson and David F. Wright (eds), *New Dictionary of Theology* (Leicester, 1988), p. 190.

97 'Of Faith in the Holy Trinity', I, *Articles of Religion*.

98 *BCP*, Prayer for the Day of Ascension.

99 NLW, 0210PICTLE, Notebook 936.

100 Jones, *The Welsh Piety*, p. 41.

101 Hoppitt, *A Land of Liberty?*, p. 232.

102 Jones, *The Welsh Piety*, p. 41.

103 Jones, *The Welsh Piety*, p. 43.

104 Erasmus D. D. Saunders, *A View of the State of Religion in the Diocese of St David's About the Beginning of the 18th Century* (London, 1721), pp. 33–4.

105 Saunders, *A View*, pp. 35–6.

106 Translated by Stephen Hughes, 1688. Cf. Jenkins, *Literature, Religion*, pp. 50–1.

107 Jones, *The Welsh Piety*, pp. 42–3.

108 Paul Langford, *A Polite and Commercial People: England 1727–1783* (Oxford, 1989), p. 65.

109 Jones, *The Welsh Piety*, p. 43.

110 Hoppitt, *A Land of Liberty?*, pp. 375–6.

111 A. S. Turberville, *English Men and Manners in the Eighteenth Century* (Oxford, 1926), p. 124.

112 Roy Porter, *English Society in the Eighteenth Century*, rev. edn (London, 1981), pp. 49, 91.

113 Jones, *The Welsh Piety*, p. 38.

114 Jeremy Gregory and John Stevenson, *Britain in the Eighteenth Century 1688–1820* (London, 2000), p. 216.

115 Langford, *A Polite and Commercial*, p. 179.

116 Leonard W. Cowie, *Henry Newman, An American in London 1708–43* (London, 1956), p. 103.

117 Jones, *The Welsh Piety*, p. 54.

118 Jones, *The Welsh Piety*, pp. 53–4.

119 Paul Hernon, *Sir Watkin's Tours. Excursions to France, Italy and North Wales 1768–71* (Wrexham, 2013), p. 20.

120 Jones, *The Welsh Piety*, p. 55.

121 Jones, *The Welsh Piety*, p. 55.

122 Jones, *The Welsh Piety*, p. 58.

123 John Brewer, *The Pleasures of the Imagination, English Culture in the Eighteenth Century* (London, 1997), pp. 471–2.

124 'Lhuyd Edward', in Meic Stephens (ed.), *The Oxford Companion to the Literature of Wales* (Oxford, 1990), pp. 348–9.

125 'Romanticism', in Stephens (ed.), *The Oxford Companion*, p. 534.

126 Jones, *The Welsh Piety*, p. 48.

127 Jones, *The Welsh Piety*, pp. 48–9.

128 Stephen Taylor, 'Gibson, Edmund (bap. 1669–1748)', *ODNB*.

129 William Camden (1551–1623). His very popular *Britannia*, first edition, in Latin 1586.

130 Jones, *The Welsh Piety*, p. 49.

131 Jones, *The Welsh Piety*, pp. 49–50.

132 Jones, *The Welsh Piety*. The similarities would have been evident perhaps to some of the Hebraists amongst his educated supporters, particularly clergymen. Cf. John Rhys, who speaks of 'convincing evidence of the presence of some element other than Celtic ... We allude to an important group of Irish names formed much in the same way as Hebrew names are represented in the Old Testament'; John Rhys and David Brynmor-Jones, *The Welsh People* (London, 1906), p. 66.

133 Although some writers, like Isaac Watts, wished to see tokens of ecclesiastical control in language removed. Cf. John Hoyles, *The Waning of the Renaissance 1640–1740* (The Hague, 1971), p. 161.

134 Thomas Hall, *Vindiciae Literarum, the Schools Guarded* (London, 1645), p. 3.

135 Jones, *The Welsh Piety*, p. 48.

136 The correspondence of Welsh parts of grammar, and even vocabulary, is with Semitic languages in general, not just biblical Hebrew.

137 Jones, *The Welsh Piety*, p. 64.

138 Jones, *The Welsh Piety*, p. 50.

139 Jones, *The Welsh Piety*, p. 51.

140 Jones, *The Welsh Piety*, p. 53.

141 Jones, *The Welsh Piety*, p. 45.

142 Jones, *The Welsh Piety*, p. 40.

143 Jones, *The Welsh Piety*, p. 51.

144 Marvin Perry, *Western Civilization. Ideas, Politics and Society* (Boston, 2004), pp. 432–8.

145 Jones, *The Welsh Piety*, p. 38.

146 Hoppitt, *A Land of Liberty?*, p. 237.

147 Jones, *The Welsh Piety*, p. 50.

148 Jones, *The Welsh Piety*, p. 39.

149 G. H. Jenkins, *Y Digymar Iolo Morganwg* (Talybont, 2018), pp. 79–80.

150 Jones, *The Welsh Piety*, p. 35.

151 Jones, *The Welsh Piety*, p. 41.

152 Jenkins, *Y Digymar Iolo*, p. 78.

153 Emrys Jones (ed.), *The Welsh in London 1500–2000* (Cardiff, 2001), p. 52.

154 Davies, *Hanes Cymru*, pp. 400–3.

155 Jenkins, 'An Old and Much Honoured', 466–7.

156 His scornful remarks about neglectful clergy, and intrusion in others' parishes brought him before the bishop's court. Cf. Cavenagh, *The Life and Work*, p. 12.

157 Jones, *Life and Times*, pp. 151–3.

158 Langford, *A Polite and Commercial*, pp. 69–70.

159 Jones, *Life and Times*, pp. 142–3.

160 G. Jones, 'Letter LXXIX, Preparation for Trying Times', in *Letters of the Rev. Griffith Jones to Mrs Bevan*, ed. Edward Morgan (London, 1832), p. 268.

161 Clement, *The SPCK and Wales*, p. 21.

162 Morgan, *Theologia*, p. 281.

163 New editions of 1718 and 1727 were distributed by the SPCK.

164 Cf. the influence of the Sunday schools and Nonconformity in continuing the stimulation of publishing in Welsh. 'Nonconformity', in Stephens (ed.), *The Oxford Companion*, pp. 430–1.

165 Reports of his amazing success in popular basic education reached Catherine the Great of Russia, who ordered an official report on his work in 1764. His schools were recognized as a model by UNESCO in 1955. Cf. Davies, *Hanes Cymru*, p. 295.

166 CUL, SPCK, *Committee Minutes* (Abs. 3656, 3900, 4936), SPCK MS A33/1.

167 E.g. with Sir John Philipps and John Vaughan of Derllys; Clement, *The SPCK and Wales*, p. 15.

168 Jones, *The Charity School Movement*, p. 302.

169 Jones, *The Charity School Movement*, pp. 154, 314–15.

170 Richard C. Allen (ed.), *The Religious History of Wales* (Cardiff, 2014), p. 189.

171 A primary school at St Clears bears his name.

Chapter 9

GRIFFITH JONES'S LEGACY TO THE CHURCH OF ENGLAND IN WALES

A VALUABLE BUT CONTRADICTORY LEGACY

Griffith Jones's lifelong pursuit of his Christian convictions was filled with achievements, but with ambiguities of principle of which he was perhaps – in part at least – unaware. He seems to have grown in tact, learning from early collisions with authority over failures to respect parish boundaries.[1] Jones probably also learnt to moderate his denunciations, from counterproductive youthful remarks that he had made about the lack of devotion to duty in some other clergy.[2] He learnt patience by long experience, but without his zeal's ever cooling into apathy. He gained no preferment in the Church's clergy, but, whilst admired and lionized by many as an evangelist, was viewed with deep resentment and distrust in high places. He contrived to exploit many opportunities to preach and teach, often with blunt frankness, whilst yet also with a deft alertness for knowing when it was wise to remain silent, even on matters of principle – sometimes simply avoiding or changing the subject. He was reproved by some as deviating from Church of England doctrine and practice, as one guilty of fomenting methodistical enthusiasm, though, in fact he remained a loyal High Church Anglican to the end, arguably with far more consistency than John Wesley.[3] Griffith Jones's ministry remained within the established Church. But as other, younger men were drawn into the circle of evangelistic preaching, he grew as their respected example and adviser – derided as the 'Methodist Pope', but whose recommendations for caution they did not always heed. The eloquent, but sometimes indiscriminating George Whitefield had an influence by his unsettling example of individualistic evangelism outside ecclesiastical discipline and order. Jones's own contrasting conformist parochial work itself became ambiguously interwoven with what was, at length, coalescing into a separate ecclesiastical connexion. Despite this tendency, the intense new 'Methodism' was not a deliberate flight from the Church of England and its faith. Like Griffith Jones, the younger preachers were influenced by the Welsh Bible and Prayer Book. Ordinary life provided the incidental, unplanned connections that shaped their careers. Howel Harris of Trefecca showed a simple initial pursuit of Anglican piety. His family's intention was that he should become a clergyman. He studied at Llwyn Llwyd Independent Grammar School near his home.[4] Thereafter, he was a schoolmaster from 1732 to 1735.[5] On Palm Sunday 1735, the preaching of Pryce Davies, vicar of Talgarth, reminded the congregation of their need to be rightly prepared for the Sacrament on the next Sunday. This pricked his already disturbed conscience. Geraint Tudur wrote:

> long before the conversion experience of 1735 the Anglican spirituality which had been part of Harris's upbringing had made him aware of his own sinfulness and anxious about his condition, a pattern visible in many similar conversion accounts.[6]

After gaining no peace of mind from reading *The Whole Duty of Man*, and Bryan Duppa's *Holy Rules and Helps to Devotion*, he found Lewis Bayly's *The Practice of Piety* a help to clarify his mind about forgiveness through faith.[7] Without prompting, Harris soon began to evangelize: in Eifion Evans's words, 'With spontaneous fervour he also began to talk to others about salvation.'[8] Conversation led to exhortation, and soon to a perambulating teaching and the extemporal gathering of converts into religious societies, uncalculatingly independent of any Church authority. Shortly afterwards, he visited the veteran Griffith Jones at Llanddowror, whose advice was, perceptively, that he should be more moderate. In 1737, Harris met Howel Davies (*c*.1716–70), who was working as a schoolmaster nearby, at Talgarth. He was struck by Harris's preaching of forgiveness in Christ. So arresting was Davies's conversion that he soon felt a call to the ministry, and was recommended by Harris to Griffith Jones. By this time, the enterprising Jones had added ministerial training at Llanddowror to his other educational projects, and accepted Davies into preparation for ordination. After a year, in 1739, Howel Davies was ordained deacon, and then priest in 1740. Such was Jones's confidence in him that he employed Davies as curate.[9] In 1741, Davies moved to be curate at Llys-y-frân, Pembrokeshire.[10] Leaving off the restraints of parish ministry, he linked with the growing Methodist movement, attending association meetings and making preaching tours throughout Wales. He was later able to become, more conventionally, settled in ministering to large congregations in Pembrokeshire until his death.[11]

Daniel Rowland was another example of those drawn into the budding strain of evangelism in the Church of England. He was born of Anglican parents. He studied for the ministry, privately and at Hereford Grammar School, and was ordained deacon in 1734, and priest in 1735.[12] He became curate to his brother John, who had become incumbent of his father's former charges. In 1735 or shortly afterwards, Rowland went to hear Griffith Jones preach at Llanddewibrefi, where he was shaken out of his clerical self-assurance, and began to understand and preach the faith in a new way.[13] The period was one of rapid changes of viewpoint. Soon Rowland's preaching began to turn from denunciation to offering encouragement to faith. The wide effect on his people at Llangeitho soon led to invitations to preach elsewhere, coming, in August 1737, from the curate of Defynnog, a supporter of the Circulating Schools.[14] Howel Harris, who did not know Rowland, was in the congregation that day. Quickly a collaboration in societies and preaching began, though Harris lacked Rowland's firm, conventional adherence to the Church. Harris's unstable temperament led to doctrinal vagaries and disagreement with the more strictly orthodox Rowland, which came to a head in a ten-year division in 1752. Rowland's monthly Communion Sundays at Llangeitho had an effect on the wider Church, attracting huge crowds from afar. In contrast to Rowland, William Williams was not brought up in the Church of England.[15] Like Howel Harris, he was sent to Llwyn Llwyd School in preparation for becoming a physician.[16] When there, he heard the unordained Howel Harris preaching arrestingly in Talgarth churchyard and was converted. Williams conformed to the Church, and was ordained deacon in 1740, becoming curate to Theophilus Evans (1693–1767).[17] In 1743, Evans refused to recommend him to Bishop Edward Willes for ordination as priest, thus shutting a door to him into the Church of England ministry. Though remaining on friendly terms with Griffith Jones, Williams turned willingly to minister within the diverging fellowship of the societies, preaching throughout Wales, and contributing famously to the developing ethos of Welsh Methodism by the intense subjective piety of his hymns, and other writings. Increasing rejection by leading churchmen strengthened cohesion among the young evangelists, of whom Peter Williams was one.[18] He studied at Carmarthen Grammar School, and while there, as a 20-year-old student, heard George Whitefield preach, and was converted. After a short while as schoolmaster, he was ordained deacon in 1745 and became a curate at Eglwys Gymyn, the parish of the absentee John Evans, Griffith Jones's great opponent. After ejection from that post for the trespass of 'Methodism', other curacies followed; but he too was refused ordination as priest. This rejection was followed by an opening to service by preaching among the Methodist societies from 1747. The appetite for theological knowledge among his hearers in turn stimulated Williams's literary gifts, as with others of the evangelists, besides his qualities of leadership. He wrote and published hymns, and a number of books, including very popular editions of the Bible with attached commentary. His useful career issued sadly in an accusation of Sabellianism; and in 1791, he was ejected from the association.

GRIFFITH JONES AND DIFFERENCES OVER DOCTRINE

Griffith Jones found the influence of Deism in the Church alarming.[19] In part, Deists were refashioning the Christian doctrine of Providence, in line with a rationalistic development of natural philosophy.[20] Deists were willing to grant an original divine creation, but with the presumption of rationally ascertainable, mechanistic 'laws' as a self-sufficient cause of physical events.[21] Hence, the doctrine of God's active immanence, everywhere and always, seemed increasingly an obsolete absurdity. For Deists, ordinary events, especially the most trivial, were not to be deemed the actions of God.[22] So for them, to profess a personal experience of the workings of Providence could only be enthusiasm. John Evans could deride as enthusiastic Griffith Jones's own assertion of a personal calling from God to minister:

> acquainting him ... that it was one of the everlasting Decrees of the Almighty, whereby he had disposed of every thing, from the Foundation of the World, that Mr. *Griffith Jones* was to be a *chosen Vessel to bear his Name*, a *peculiar Instrument*[23]

Jones may not have had a closely worked-out doctrine of Providence; for him it was an everyday psychological support, both for 'waiting upon God', and persisting in his enterprises against difficulties, with a sense of divine calling and provision.[24] His concept of divine, present, providential help sustained him in his ministry to a people regarded as in urgent need of moral and religious renewal. Griffith Jones's conviction of divine help gave him confidence leading to the establishment of the Circulating Schools. He achieved unusual success as a preacher and an educationist, under a persisting sense of God's guidance and provision of opportunities. But he could not be expected to foresee fully some of the unsought results of his ventures. His work constrained developments leading unavoidably away from his High Church ideal of a renewal to be achieved within the one intact national Church. It may not be unfair to Jones's sincere Anglicanism to say, moreover, that what became his particular concentration on conversion constrained, of necessity, a narrowing of his theological conspectus. Through his powerful expository preaching, which concentrated on evoking new, individual repentance and faith, he helped to set an engrossing precedent for younger preachers, and newcomers, to see 'conversionism' as a prime function of true

Christianity – even *the* prime function.[25] His followers' sense of having received a 'reviving' conversion under Jones's ministry tended to make such irruptive experience a necessary standard and preoccupation of all further endeavour. A converted minority met in part separately, in religious societies, and congregated, especially at Communion times, at Llanddowror and other centres. But the custom could not but impel a diverging movement which he strove, not without difficulty, somewhat to restrain.[26]

The presence of a distinct converted element in the Church naturally caused puzzlement and resentment, often with accusations, from the unsympathetic, of their being enthusiastic and schismatic conventicles.[27] Griffith Jones had initiated a movement, in conformity with the 'reforming' ideals of the SPCK, which was not one of deliberate schism. However, the new wine of sometimes obstreperous, evangelizing zeal could only have been expected eventually to result in a bursting of the bottle.[28] The agitating effect of the evangelistic ideal was compounded by a somewhat confused theological dissension among the preachers.[29] In light of the fact that salvation is to be offered to all hearers, John Wesley, amongst others, felt it necessary to deny the idea of divine predestinating election.[30] This he did uncompromisingly, with an overconfident, blundering magisterialism. The Anglican doctrine of the originating divine choice of individuals for salvation was conceived by Wesley as necessarily blunting the biblical message of promise which was having such notable effect in his own preaching. A controversy broke out amongst the evangelists, over what was loosely called 'Calvinism'.[31] The doctrine seemed – and still seems to many – harsh and rebarbative, incompatible with a declaration of God's willingness to receive anyone who has faith.[32] The division of opinion was to lead later, in Wales, to the formation of the 'Calvinistic Methodist' connexion, a body resistant to inclusion in Wesleyanism.[33] Jones was probably aware of the controversy, at the same time, in Scotland over the anonymous *Marrow of Modern Divinity* of 1645.[34] This was a selection of quotations from various theologians on the core doctrines of Reformed theology.[35] A Welsh translation was made in 1651, and remained a popular standard work.[36] *The Marrow* had been republished in 1710 by Thomas Boston (1676–1732), and avidly received by an active evangelizing party in the Church of Scotland, analogous with that in the Church of England. This grouping had a notable exponent in Ebenezer Erskine (1680–1754). These Scots had the conviction that the book provided a defence of their preaching indiscriminately the offer of salvation, whilst remaining loyal to Reformed theology as defined in the Westminster Confession. Their theory held that the Gospel might be offered immediately, without the demand for some kind of qualifying moral improvement in the hearers; and that preachers could make the offer without offending the doctrine of election and predestination. In 1720, after much controversy, the book was banned by the General Assembly for being antinomian.[37] The similarity to the debate in England and Wales on the subject of a 'free offer' of salvation is obvious. Some thoughtful men worried over the question: if a finite number of men are elect, and others are not, how can a preacher make a genuine offer of salvation to all comers?

Griffith Jones wisely kept clear of distracting controversies. He avoided preaching in depth on divine election and its implications, despite being reputedly well read in Reformation literature.[38] However, by the 1740s, controversy had arisen amongst the evangelists over Article XVII.[39] Griffith Jones seems to have become alarmed about the risk among some preachers of a weakening in the offer of salvation. Late in his career, at the age of sixty-one, he published, in 1744, an attempt to resolve the assumed discord between an indiscriminate preaching of salvation by the Gospel, and the doctrine of election. More particularly, he dealt with a corollary to election: reprobation. Jones wished to refute the idea of reprobation's consisting of an equally fixed purpose, a 'decree', of God. His *Platform of Christianity* was published under the authorship of an anonymous 'country clergyman'.[40] Its stated aim was to solve the quandary, and help 'Sincere Christians of different Persuasions' not to strive 'for Conquest or Mastery'.[41] The way that he handled this extremely abstruse subject is revealing. One is forced to acknowledge that he plunged into the controversy with a naive overconfidence:

> It is hoped, Readers ... may now perceive the Doctrine of the absolute Salvation of the Elect, and the conditional Offer of Salvation unto all

> Men, to be perfectly consistent; which may be a happy Mean to end the
> Controversy bandied to and fro concerning it for so many Ages[42]

He failed to recognize that this profound mystery, like that of the origin of evil, had defied astute theological minds 'for so many ages'. As we have seen (in chapter 7) Griffith Jones gave no sign of adhering fully to a covenantal (federal) theology, in the classic Reformed sense of a co-ordination of all the 'decrees' in the divine will. The 'Calvinism' of many others of his time was likewise non-covenantal. But his theology was consistent with the Articles; he could not justly be accused of flouting Article XVII, which mentions only 'predestination to life'. Jones was happy to express full acceptance of divine election and grace as the first cause in salvation. The thought of an eternal divine purpose of salvation for believers was part of the Church's faith. He asserted:

> the Election of some to sure Attainment of eternal Life, as it is taught in
> the Gospel and the Articles of our Church, must be owned to be a most
> gracious Decree, and sweet Savour of Life unto many[43]

Naturally Jones, like the Reformers, was prone to see the teaching of election as an additional reassurance, especially in preaching to new converts: 'unspeakable comfort to godly persons'.[44] His thinking was therefore, in this, also compatible with the Bible's presentation of election as an encouragement.[45] But Jones baulked at an inescapable implication, with surprising self-assurance. His rejection of an equally definite, converse non-election – or 'reprobation' – of others was vehement. He used the rhetorical ploy of a stark *ad hominem* expostulation against:

> the Scandal of asserting an eternal, or absolute irreversible Decree in God,
> whereby the far greatest Part of Mankind ... are doomed to eternal Misery,
> and excluded from all Possibility of Salvation for ever.[46]

Griffith Jones was understandably anxious to scotch this doctrinal corollary, which was being aired amongst some preachers. It might serve to obscure the bright, general message of salvation – and there seems, in any case, little occasion for anyone's actually preaching on the doctrine. His intention was to assert the doctrine of a foreordained salvation for an 'elect' number, but to keep open the avenue of hope for others. Whilst not fully denying the converse of election, Jones contrived to solve his difficulty by designating the non-inclusion among the elect as 'conditional reprobation'.[47]

Griffith Jones viewed conversion from the viewpoint of the convert's faith, as fulfilling a covenant engagement.[48] He saw the eternal purpose of God, therefore, predominantly as a decree confirming acceptance of the 'chosen' believer. This seems closely to align his thinking with the thrust of the evangelism of the time, whose mounting success encouraged an expectation of further limitless conversions. Although the doctrine of election envisaged a finite number of mankind, Jones refused to doubt the possibility of others coming to faith. But here his reasoning faltered. 'Election' denotes a divine secret: no one can tell in advance who will accept or refuse the call to faith. Therefore, any offer of salvation, in accordance with the Bible, is always 'conditional', being on condition of faith and repentance in the hearer. As such, it is a genuine offer to any hearer. Presumably it was a confusion over the Gospel's conditional promise that lay behind Griffith Jones's affirmation: 'This conditional Reprobation, by God's most just and awful Decree, is what the Scripture teacheth, and no other.'[49] Jones wished no doubts to be in the minds of his hearers about what was offered in the name of God. But his confusion over what was conditional led him into an astonishing further piece of muddled theology:

> neither God's Foreknowledge nor his Decree of Predestination in favour of some, do prejudice the State of others, nor in any degree render their Condition worse than if there had been no such Decree at all[50]

Attempting to assert – correctly – the wide preaching of the offer of salvation, Jones exposed an embarrassing exegetical incompetence, emptying of any force the theological locus of election: 'no such Sentence of God's Predestination as excludes any by an eternal, absolute, and irreversible Decree, from the Possibility of Salvation through Jesus

Christ'.[51] Apparently oblivious of the implications of his denial, Griffith Jones, ever the forceful evangelist, and ever the educator, showed his usual fervency going on to recommend the teaching of his version of the doctrine in schools:

> to submit it to Consideration, whether the Articles of Religion should not take place in the Education of our Youth; and whether they, as well as Candidates for holy Orders, should not be well instructed therein[52]

Jones's avoiding the actual force of the doctrine of election in the interest of conversionism set something of a precedent in the ethos of Welsh Calvinistic Methodism, and what became distinct Evangelicalism.

Though Griffith Jones strongly opposed separation from the national Church, his theological viewpoint did have an influence in that direction. Amongst younger preachers influenced by Jones, the theological priority of conversion quickly outweighed any precise theory of election, together with the attendant doctrine of the Atonement, as being connected in a covenantal scheme. The individual's own persuasion came to be viewed as supremely decisive. The concept of election was contingently weakened in favour of that of a broad divine will for men's salvation. This latter view entailed the tendency to think of Christ's Atonement – his making peace between man and God – also as 'unlimited': intended by God for every person. The dogmatic abandonment of 'limited Atonement' naturally became a distinguishing feature of the 'moderate Calvinism' of Welsh Methodists which continued into the nineteenth century. William Williams Pantycelyn (1717–91) was, from the first, opposed to limited Atonement. D. Ben Rees wrote:

> Nid oedd Williams yn arddel y rhan yna o Galfiniaeth, a gwnaeth gymwynas yn hyn o beth i Galfiniaeth Gymraeg trwy ein dysgu i ddeall y cysyniad o Iawn Penodol. A bod yn deg â John Elias o Fôn a Christmas Evans, fe fabwysiadodd y ddau safbwynt Pantycelyn yn hytrach na'r Iawn Cyfyngedig. Gwelent hwy bechodau'r etholedigion yn un pen i'r glorian ac Iawn Calfaria ar y pen arall, a'r ddau ben yn gydwastad â'i gilydd.[53]

[Williams did not espouse that part of Calvinism, and he did a favour in this matter for Welsh-speaking Calvinism through teaching us to understand the concept of Particular Atonement. To be fair to John Elias of Anglesea and Christmas Evans, they both adopted Pantycelyn's view rather than Limited Atonement. They saw the sins of the elect on one end of the scales and the Atonement of Calvary on the other end, and the two ends balancing one another.]

This reordering of cause and effect in theology, though not starkly at variance with the Prayer Book and Articles, added characteristic components to developing Welsh Evangelicalism, and so helped to lead towards its categorical break with classic Reformed theology.

THE CHURCH AND INDIVIDUALISM

During the time of Griffith Jones's ministry, authority was already coming to be placed in the self-validating individual experience of conversion.[54] Conversion was also sometimes linked to emotionalism, which could occur as a by-product of forceful evangelism amongst large gatherings, though unbridled, disruptive emotion was deplored by Griffith Jones.[55] Some preachers, like Daniel Rowland, found recurring noisy outbursts hard to rein in.[56] The later development of revivalism would in places, however, turn heightened excitability into something even to be cultivated as a means of inducing conversions.[57] Despite all his conservative caution, Griffith Jones's preaching of conversion naturally leant support to the growing emphasis on individuals and their sensibilities. The gradual, overall effect of the trend was to diminish the apprehension of the established Church of England as a divinely ordained, 'elect' body, the exclusive national pivot and focus of faith and worship. For some under the impressions of the rising evangelism, the springs of vibrant spiritual life came to seem principally outside the constituted Church, whose staid formalities consequently commanded less respect. The overmastering pursuit of individual conversions eroded any willingness to avoid breaches in the Church's cohesion. The ideal of the formally established, inclusive 'visible' Church could not but be weakened before euphoriant, 'gathered' companies of converts. In Griffith Jones's circle of hearers with their complementing religious societies, the exercise of Christian fellowship in separated groups, though composed of Church people, had, in effect, the nature of conventicles. In any case, many of the unconverted masses in the land, though claimed in theory for the national Church, were acknowledged, in practice, as beyond its reach.[58] These masses, were all the more outside the 'gathered' fellowships of converts (*seiadau*), who came also to see the unconverted members within Church congregations as being, no less, in the same abandonment. In the preoccupations of the narrowed sphere of societies and roving evangelism, a sense of obligation to parish-church life was inevitably weakened – though not in Griffith Jones's mind. But the growing number of his schools also tended to bolster the work of religious societies. His instructions to his schoolmasters and mistresses – who were all required to be members of the Church of England – were explicitly: 'to revive the now much impaired Christian religion amongst us.'[59] Jones attempted to improve understanding and conduct by them: 'The masters are likewise to catechise and inculcate the principles and duties of religion, and admonish them against the reigning vices of the times, twice every day.'[60] All these aims were consistently Anglican, and received gratefully by some clergy. But, by this very work, they unavoidably appropriated to themselves some Church functions, putting them, along with the societies, at a certain distance from the ministrations of her ordained clergy. This activity helped to habituate people to parallel bodies which were distrusted by some clerics as being enthusiastical and schismatic. Under the uniting title of 'Methodist', some societies would eventually feel their own predominating common bond, and come to claim ordination for their own ministers and the administration of the sacraments for themselves.[61] Griffith Jones strove to dissuade his friends from any steps away from the formal Church, forbidding his schoolmasters to preach, unordained, in religious societies.[62] Nevertheless, the rhetoric of leaders in these voluntary gatherings could not be muzzled, but continued, merely camouflaged as 'exhorting'. All such relabelling could not halt the trend towards the societies' assuming, at length, the functions of distinct congregations: gatherings with a strong bond of mutual agreement and interaction. Jones strove to keep all his efforts within the Church, but his work was bound to draw the understandable accusation of 'schism' and heterodox enthusiasm from some quarters. The evangelistic religious societies, by nature, stood apart from the Church established by law, which they could not alter, and of which they were not legally part. As gatherings of converted believers and seekers, they approximated to the ideal of the 'gathered churches' of much modern Evangelicalism.[63] Conformably, the pervasive influence of Continental Pietism, as exemplified at Herrnhut, promised an idealized – yet in fact, unobtainable – separation from the sinful outside 'world'.[64] Pietism stressed godliness in stripping away the pleasures and occupations of polluted culture. Some marks of this same unbiblical asceticism appeared clearly in Griffith Jones's fretful rejection as 'vanities' such things as dancing, song, or even guileless banter.[65] It left its mark on Welsh Nonconformity, and foreshadowed a tradition in Evangelicalism which has asserted a mutual exclusivity between, at least, some aesthetic pleasures and the pursuit of holiness.[66] Griffith Jones died half a century before Welsh Calvinistic Methodism's final separation from the Church of England, in 1811.[67] His Circulating Schools' magnificent legacy to Wales is the survival of Welsh as a vibrant and fruitful minority language: an outstanding cultural phenomenon in the present age of corrosive global uniformity, and a monument to his priceless efforts. But ironically, in Wales, his religious work is remembered little more than within Evangelical circles, where he receives some honour as a faintly remembered forerunner. But he was a forerunner of a fragmented movement that came to embody a form of church, worship and lifestyle quite contrary to his own strong convictions, in a Welsh nation that has resolutely rejected almost all of what he spent his labours to promote, and whose Nonconformist Christian identity has now, sadly, almost completely withered.

NOTES

1   D. Densil Morgan, *Thelogia Cambrensis*, vol. 1 (Cardiff, 2018), pp. 268–9.

2   Morgan, *Theologia*, p. 269.

3   R. Jenkins, *Griffith Jones of Llanddowror* (Cardiff, 1930), p. 55.

The Theology of Griffith Jones and Religious Thought

4   The school was in Llanigon, 8 miles north of his hmome in Trefecca, under David Price (*fl*. 1700–42) who was ordained minister of Maesyronnen Independent church, Radnorshire about 1700.

5   At Llan-gors and Llangasty Breconshire, 3 miles from Trefecca.

6   Geraint Tudur, *Howell Harris, from Conversion to Separation 1735–1750* (Cardiff, 2000), p. 15.

7   Tudur, *Howell Harris*, pp. 16, 17.

8   Eifion Evans, *Daniel Rowland and the Great Awakening in Wales* (Edinburgh, 1985), p. 53.

9   In Jones's other parish of Llandeilo Abercywyn.

10   In 1744, like Jones and other evangelists, he 'married up': to Catherine Poyer, a wealthy heiress, of Parke, Henllan Amgoed near Whitland, Carmarthenshire, 10 miles from Llanddowror.

11   Gomer Morgan Roberts, 'Davies, Howel (*c.*1716–1770) Methodist Cleric', *Dictionary of Welsh Biography* (London, 1959).

12   His father was vicar of Llangeitho and Nantcwnlle. Llangeitho, Cardiganshire, is 45 miles north-east of Llanddowror.

13   Llanddewibrefi, 5 miles south-east from Llangeitho.

14   Defynnog, Breckonshire, 18 miles west of Trefecca, and 48 miles south-east of Llangeitho, Cardiganshire.

15   His parents were members of Cefnarthen Independent church, his father an elder.

16   His home was in Llanfair-ar-y-Bryn, Llandovery, 30 miles west of Trefecca.

17   At Llanwrtyd, Llanfihangel and Llanddewi Abergwesyn.

18   His home was in Llansadyrnin, Carmarthenshire, 6 miles south of Llanddowror.

19   G. Jones, 'Letter V, 'The religion of the age lamented', in *Letters of the Rev. Griffith Jones to Mrs Bevan*, ed. Edward Morgan (London, 1832), pp. 23–4.

20   S. N. Williams, 'Deism', in Sinclair B. Ferguson and David F. Wright (eds), *New Dictionary of Theology* (Leicester, 1988), p. 190.

21   Gerald Robertson Cragg, *From Puritanism to the Age of Reason* (Cambridge, 1950), pp. 98–103.

22   John Toland, *Christianity Not Mysterious* (London, 1696), p. 63.

23   John Evans, *Some Account of the Welch Charity-Schools, and the Rise and Progress of Methodism in Wales* (London, 1752), p. 6.

24   David Jones, *Life and Times of Griffith Jones of Llanddowror* (London, 1902), p. 141.

25   David Bebbington, *Evangelicalism in Modern Britain* (London, 1989), pp. 5–7.

26   Morgan, *Theologia*, p. 386.

27   Evans, *Some Account*.

28   Cf. Edmund Gibson's visitation charge of 1747; Norman Sykes, *Edmund Gibson* (Oxford, 1926), p. 319.

29   Morgan, *Theologia*, p. 371.

30   Frank Baker, *John Wesley and the Church of England* (London, 1970), p. 18.

31   'Calvinism' taken to mean almost exclusively election and predestination, not the complete Reformed system of doctrine.

32   Cf. *BCP*, 'Morning/Evening Prayer' Absolution.

33 John Walsh, 'Origins of the Evangelical Revival', in G. V. Bennett and J. D. Walsh (eds), *Essays in Modern Church History* (London, 1966), pp. 134–5.

34 Anonymous (Edward Fisher?), *The Marrow of Modern Divinity*, in two parts (London, 1645, 1649).

35 J. D. Douglas, 'Marrow Controversy, The', in J. D. Douglas (ed.), *The New International Dictionary of the Christian Church* (Grand Rapids, 1974), p. 635.

36 John Edwards (1606?–*c*.1660) translated it as *Madruddyn y Difinyddiaeth Diweddaraf*.

37 The General Assembly is the highest gathering for oversight in the Church of Scotland, being composed of delegated ministers and elders from all the district presbyteries.

38 Anonymous (Henry Phillips?), *A Sketch of the Life and Character of the Reverend and Pious Mr Griffith Jones, late Rector of Llanddowror in Carmarthenshire* (London, 1762), p. 5.

39 'Of Predestination and Election', XVII, *Articles of Religion*.

40 Griffith Jones, *The Platform of Christianity, being the General Head of the Protestant Religion, as Professed by the Church of England* (London, 1744).

41 Jones, *The Platform of Christianity*, p. lxviii.

42 Jones, *The Platform of Christianity*.

43 Jones, *The Platform of Christianity*, p. xliii.

44 *Articles of Religion*, XVII, second para.

45 Cf. *Epistle to the Romans*, 8:28–30.

46 Jones, *The Platform of Christianity*, p. xxx.

47 Jones, *The Platform of Christianity*, p. xlvii.

48 Cf. chapter 7, on 'baptismal covenant'.

49 Jones, *The Platform of Christianity*, p. xlvii.

50 Jones, *The Platform of Christianity*, p. lvi.

51 Jones, *The Platform of Christianity*, p. lviii.

52 Jones, *The Platform of Christianity*, p. lxxii.

53 D. Ben Rees, 'Pantycelyn ar y Blaen', *Y Traethodydd*, CLXXIV/733 (April 2020), 79.

54 W. R. Ward, *The Protestant Evangelical Awakening* (Cambridge, 1992), pp. 136–9.

55 Jenkins, 'An Old and Much Honoured', 452.

56 Evans, *Daniel Rowland*, p. 74.

57 Elliott-Binns baldly makes it part of Evangelicalism from the start. L. E. Elliott-Binns, *The Early Evangelicals, a Religious and Social Study* (London, 1953), pp. 13, 56.

58 Cf. New Churches in London and Westminster Act 1710 (9 Anne cap. 17).

59 G. Jones, *The Welsh Piety* (London, 1740), p. 30.

60 Jones, *The Welsh Piety*, p. 35.

61 D. D. Morgan, 'Continuity, novelty and evangelicalism in Wales, c. 1640–1850', in Michael A. G. Haykin and Kenneth J. Stewart (eds), *The Emergence of Evangelicalism* (Nottingham, 2008), pp. 100–1.

62 William Jacob, 'Methodism in Wales', in Glanmor Williams et al. (eds), *The Welsh Church from Reformation to Disestablishment 1603–1920* (Cardiff, 2007), pp. 170–3.

63 The trend in Evangelicalism would come to take Baptism by immersion as a seal the converts' right, as 'born again' believers, to exclusive membership in many later independent gathered churches.

64 Douglas H. Shantz, *An Introduction to German Pietism* (Baltimore, 2013), p. 257.

65 F. A. Cavenagh, *The Life and Work of Griffith Jones of Llanddowror* (Cardiff, 1930), p. 8.
66 E. J. Tinsley, 'Asceticism', in Alan Richardson (ed.), *Dictionary of Christian Theology* (London, 1969), p. 17.
67 Morgan, *Theologia*, p. 394.

BIBLIOGRAPHY

PRIMARY SOURCES

MANUSCRIPTS

Cambridge University Library, SPCK, *Committee Minutes*, SPCK MS A33/1.

Cardiff Central Library, MS 2.162, MS 2.1103: *Trysor o Ddifinyddiaeth*, Griffith Jones, Transcripts of Sermons.

National Library of Wales, MS 24057B, MS 4495A, CMA 8326, *Trysor o Ddifinyddiaeth*, Griffith Jones, Transcripts of Sermons.

National Library of Wales, *Ottley Papers*.

National Library of Wales, Philipps of Picton Castle archives, MS GB 0210PICTLE, Notebook of Sir John Philipps.

PRINTED PRIMARY SOURCES

Anonymous, *A letter to the Reverend Mr. George Whitefield, occasioned by his remarks upon a pamphlet, entitled, The enthusiasm of Methodists and Papists compared* (London,1750).

Anonymous (Henry Phillips?), *A Sketch of the Life and Character of the Reverend and Pious Mr Griffith Jones, late Rector of Llanddowror in Carmarthenshire* (London, 1762).

[On Griffith Jones's birthplace and ancestry] *Archaeologia Cambrensis*, 269–78 (1923).

Beveridge, William, *The Theological Works of William Beveridge D.D.* (Oxford, 1846).

Bray, Thomas, *Catechetical Lectures on the Preliminary Questions and Answers of the Church-Catechism* (London, 1703).

Bull, George, *A Companion for the Candidates of Holy Orders, or the Great Importance and Principal Duties of the Priestly Office* [sermon] (London, 1714).

——, *The English Theological Works of George Bull D.D.* (Oxford, 1844).

Calvin, John, *Commentary upon the Book of Genesis* (Geneva, in Latin 1554; English trans., 1578; London, 1965).

Clement, Mary, *Correspondence and Minutes of the SPCK relating to Wales 1699–1740* (Cardiff, 1952).

Cranmer, Thomas (ed.), *First Book of Homilies* (London, 1547). Published in *The Two Books of Homilies, Appointed to be Read in Churches* (Oxford, 1859).

——, *A Defence of the True and Catholick Doctrine of the Sacrament of the Body and Blood of Our Saviour Christ* (London, 1551).

Deffray, John, *The Christian's Daily Manual of Prayer and Praises* (London, 1701).

Edwards, Jonathan, *A Narrative of Surprising Conversions* [1736], in *Select Works of Jonathan Edwards* (London, 1965).

Evans, E. D., 'A Providential Rescue. Griffith Jones and the Malabar Mission', *Journal of Welsh Religious History*, 8 (2000), 35–42.

Evans, John, *Some Account of the Welch Charity-Schools, and the Rise and Progress of Methodism in Wales* (London, 1752).

Finney, Charles G., *Form of Prayers and Ministration of the Sacraments &. of English Congregation at Geneva: and approved by the famous and godly learned man, John Calvin* (Geneva, 1555; Edinburgh, 1577).

——, *Sermons on Various Subjects* (New York, 1834).

Gillies, John, *Historical Collections Relating to Remarkable Periods of the Success of the Gospel* (1754; Kelso, 1845).

Griffiths, G. Milwyn (ed.), 'A Visitation of the Archdeaconry of Carmarthen, 1710', *National Library of Wales journal*, XVIII/3 (summer, 1974); XIX/3 (summer, 1976).

Guy, John R., 'Riding against the Clock. The Visitations of Edward Tenison in Carmarthen and Ossory in the Early Eighteenth Century', in John R. Guy and W. G. Neeley (eds), *Contrasts and Comparisons. Studies in Irish and Welsh Church History* (Llandysul, 1998).

Hardman, Keith J., *Charles Grandison Finney* (Darlington, 1987).

Harrison, William, *Description of England etc.* (London, 1577).

Hervey, James, *Theron and Aspasio* (London, 1755).

——, *Mr Wesley's Principles detected: or a Defence* (Edinburgh, 1765).

Hooker, Richard, *Of the Laws of Ecclesiastical Polity* (London, 1594).

Jones, Griffith, *The Welsh Piety* (London, 1740).

Bibliography

——, *The Platform of Christianity, being the General Head of the Protestant Religion, as Professed by the Church of England* (London, 1744).

——, *The Christian Covenant, or the Baptismal Vow, as stated in our Church Catechism* (London, 1761).

——, *Welch Piety: or a Succinct Account of the Rise and Progress of the Circulating Welch Charity Schools* (London, 1761).

——, *Letters of the Rev. Griffith Jones to Mrs Bevan*, ed. Edward Morgan (London, 1832).

Jones, Robert Rhos-Lan, *Drych yr Amseroedd*, ed. G. M. Ashton (Cardiff, 1958).

Law, William, *A Serious Call to a Devout and Holy Life* (London, 1728).

Lewis, John, *The Church Catechism Explain'd* (London, 1700).

Lowth, Robert, *A Short Introduction to English Grammar with Critical Notes* (London, 1762).

Nelson, Robert, *The Life of Dr George Bull, Late Lord Bishop of St. David's* (London, 1713).

Nowell, Alexander, *A Catechism* (London, 1570; Cambridge, 1853).

Owen, John, *Works of John Owen* (London, 1967).

Ray, John, *The Wisdom of God Manifested in the Works of Creation* (London, 1691).

Robe, James, *Narratives of the Extraordinary Work of the Spirit of God at Cambuslang, Kilsyth, & Begun 1742* (Glasgow, 1790).

Romaine, William, *An Essay on Psalmody* (London, 1755).

Saunders, Erasmus, *A View of the State of Religion in the Diocese of St. David's* (London, 1721; reproduced in facsimile, Cardiff, 1949).

Taylor, Jeremy, *Of the Sacred Order and Offices of episcopacy by Divine Institution, Apostolical Tradition and Catholic Practice* (London, 1647).

Tenison, Edward, 'Visitation 1710', ed. G. Milwyn Griffiths, *National Library of Wales Journal*, XVIII/3 (summer 1974); XIX/3 (summer 1976).

Toland, John, *Christianity Not Mysterious* (London, 1696).

Vincent, William, *Considerations on Parochial Music* (London, 1787).

Wesley, John, *The Journal of the Rev. John Wesley A.M.*, ed. N. Curnock (London, 1911).

Wesley, Samuel, *Westminster Confession of Faith* (London, 1646).

——, *Westminster Shorter Catechism* (London, 1648).

——, *The Pious Communicant Rightly Prepar'd; or a Discourse Concerning the Blessed Sacrament* (London, 1700).

——, *An Account of the Religious Society begun in Epworth, in the Isle of Axholm Lincolnshire, Feb. 1, An. Dom. 1701–2* (London, 1701).

Whitefield, George, *Journals*, pub. separately 1738–41, unabridged edn (London, 1960).

Woodward, Josiah, *Account of the Rise and Progress of the Religious Societies in the City of London, &c. and of their Endeavours for Reformation of Manners* (London, 1698).

Wynne, Ellis, *Gweledigaetheu y Bardd Cwsc*, ed. A. Lewis (London, 1703; facsimile Cardiff, 1976).

SECONDARY TEXTS

Aaron, John, *Torf Ardderchog, Teithiau Cristnogol Trwy Gymru*, vol. 1 (Bridgend, 1992).

Ackroyd, Peter, *The Life of Thomas More* (London, 1998).

Allen, Richard C. (ed.), *The Religious History of Wales* (Cardiff, 2014).

Allen, W. O. B. and McClure, Edmund, *History of the Society for Promoting Christian Knowledge 1698–1898* (London, 1898).

Baker, Frank, *John Wesley and the Church of England* (London, 1970).

Baker-Jones, Leslie, *Princelings Privilege and Power, the Tivyside Gentry in their Community* (Llandysul, 1999).

——, *Jeremy Taylor (1613–1667)* (Llandysul, 2016).

Balleine, G. R., *A History of the Evangelical Party in the Church of England* (London, 1908).

Bannerman, James, *The Church of Christ*, 2 vols (London, 1960).

Barker, Felix, and Jackson, Peter, *London, 2000 Years of a City and its People* (London, 1974).

Bavinck, Herman, *The Doctrine of God*, trans. William Hendriksen (Edinburgh, 1977).

Bebbington, David, *Evangelicalism in Modern Britain* (London, 1989).

Bennett, G. V. and Walsh J. D. (eds), *Essays in Modern Church History* (London, 1966).

Berkhof, Louis, *Systematic Theology* (London, 1958).

Black, J. B., *The Oxford History of England 1558–1603* (Oxford, 1959).

Bolam, C. G. (ed.), *The English Presbyterians* (London, 1968).

Brewer, John, *The Pleasures of the Imagination, English Culture in the Eighteenth Century* (London, 1997).

Briggs, Robin, *Early Modern France 1560–1715* (Oxford, 1998).

Bibliography

Bromham, Ivor J., 'Welsh Revivalists of the Eighteenth Century', *The Churchman*, 72/1 (1958).

Brown, Roger Lee, *The Welsh Evangelicals* (Cardiff, 1986).

——, *A Social History of the Welsh Clergy circa 1662–1939* (Welshpool, 2017).

Buchanan, James, *The Doctrine of Justification* (Edinburgh, 1867).

Burleigh, J. H. S., *A Church History of Scotland* (London, 1960).

Cameron, Euan (ed.), *Early Modern Europe* (Oxford, 2001).

Cavenagh, F. A., *The Life and Work of Griffith Jones of Llanddowror* (Cardiff, 1930).

Clark, George, *Oxford History of England: The Later Stuarts 1660–1714* (Oxford, 1956).

Clement, Mary, *The SPCK and Wales 1699–1740* (London, 1954).

Collinson, Patrick, *The Elizabethan Puritan Movement* (London, 1967).

——, *Archbishop Grindal, 1519–1583, The Struggle for a Reformed Church* (London, 1979).

Coontz, Stephanie, *Marriage, a History* (New York, 2005).

Cornwall, Robert D. and W. Gibson (eds), *Religion, Politics and Dissent 1660–1832* (Farnham, 2010).

Coss, Peter, *The Lady in Medieval England 1000–1500* (Stroud, 1998).

Coward, Barry, *Stuart Age England 1603–1714*, third edn (Harlow, 2003).

Cowie, Leonard W., *Henry Newman, An American in London 1708–43* (London, 1956).

Cragg, Gerald Robertson, *From Puritanism to the Age of Reason* (Cambridge, 1950).

Cruickshanks, Eveline (ed.), *Ideology and Conspiracy: Aspects of Jacobitism, 1689–1759* (Edinburgh, 1982).

Dallimore, Arnold, *George Whitefield* (London, 1970).

——, *Spurgeon, a New Biography* (Edinburgh, 1985).

Davies, Godfrey, *The Oxford History of England (1603–1660)* (Oxford, 1945).

Davies, Gwyn, *Griffith Jones, Llanddowror: Athro Cenedl* (Bridgend, 1984).

——, *Golau Gwlad, Cristnogaeth yng Nghymru 200–2000* (Bridgend, 2000).

Davies, J. G., *A Dictionary of Liturgy and Worship* (London, 1972).

Davies, John, *Hanes Cymru* (London, 1990).

—— et al. (eds), *Gwyddoniadur Cymru* (Cardiff, 2008).

Davis, A. P., *Isaac Watts, his Life and Works* (London, 1948).

Dearmer, Percy, *Everyman's History of the Prayer Book* (London, 1912).

Dickens, A. G., *The English Reformation* (London, 1964).

Douglas, J. D. (ed.), *The New International Dictionary of the Christian Church* (Grand Rapids, 1974).

Ella, George M., *James Hervey: Preacher of Righteousness* (Eggleston, Co. Durham, 1997).

Elliott-Binns, L. E., *The Early Evangelicals, a Religious and Social Study* (London, 1953).

Elton, G. R., *The English* (Oxford, 1992).

—— (ed.), *The Tudor Constitution* (Cambridge, 1960).

Evans, Eifion, *Daniel Rowland and the Great Awakening in Wales* (Edinburgh, 1985).

Evans, Martin, *An Early History of Queen Elizabeth Grammar School Carmarthen 1576–1800* (Carmarthen, 1978).

Fairchild, Hoxie Neale, *Religious Trends in English Poetry*, 5 vols (New York, 1939–62).

Fawcett, Arthur, *The Cambuslang Revival* (London, 1971).

Ferguson, Sinclair B. and David F. Wright (eds), *New Dictionary of Theology* (Leicester, 1988).

Francis, Keith A. with William Gibson (eds), *The Oxford Handbook of the British Sermon 1689–1901* (Oxford 2012).

Gibbard, Noel, *'Elusen i'r Enaid'* (Bridgend, 1979).

Gibson, William, *The Church of England 1688–1832* (London, 2001).

——, *Enlightenment Prelate* (Cambridge, 2004).

Green, V. H. H., *The Young Mr Wesley* (London, 1961).

Greengates, Mark, *The French Reformation* (Oxford, 1987).

Gregory, Jeremy and John Stevenson, *Britain in the Eighteenth Century 1688–1820* (London, 2000).

Gruffydd W. J., art. in *Y Llenor*, II/3 (autumn 1923).

Guy, John, *Tudor England* (Oxford, 1988).

Hampton, Stephen, *Anti-Arminians. The Anglican Reformed Tradition from Charles II to George I* (Oxford, 2008).

Hardman, Keith J., *Charles Grandison Finney 1792–1875* (Syracuse, NY, 1987).

Harris, Kenneth, *Attlee* (London, 1982).

Harrison, D. E. W., *The Book of Common Prayer, the Anglican Heritage of Public Worship* (London, 1959).

Hart, A. Tindal, *William Lloyd 1627–1717 Bishop, Politician, Author and Prophet* (London, 1952).

Haykin, Michael A. G. and Kenneth J. Stewart (eds), *The Emergence of*

Evangelicalism (Nottingham, 2008).

Hazlett, W. Ian P., *The Reformation in Britain and Ireland* (London, 2003).

Hernon, Paul, *Sir Watkin's Tours. Excursions to France, Italy and North Wales 1768–71* (Wrexham, 2013).

Hindmarsh, D. Bruce, *The Evangelical Conversion Narrative: Spiritual Autobiography in Early Modern England* (Oxford, 2005).

Hodge, Charles, *Systematic Theology* (London, 1960).

Honderich, Ted, *The Oxford Companion to Philosophy* (Oxford, 1995).

Hoppitt, Julian, *A Land of Liberty? England 1689–1727* (Oxford, 2000).

Hoyles, John, *The Waning of the Renaissance 1640–1740* (The Hague, 1971).

Hughes, J., *Welsh Reformers* (London, 1861).

Hylson-Smith, Kenneth, *High Churchmanship in the Church of England: From the Sixteenth Century to the Late Twentieth Century* (Edinburgh, 1993).

James, William, *The Varieties of Religious Experience* (London, 1902).

Jarman, A. O. H. and Gwilym Rees Hughes (eds), *A Guide to Welsh Literature*, 2 vols (Llandybïe, 1984).

Jenkins, Geraint H., *Literature, Religion and Society in Wales 1660–1730* (Cardiff, 1978).

——, '"An Old and Much Honoured Soldier": Griffith Jones, Llanddowror', *Welsh History Review*, II (1983).

——, 'The Established Church and Dissent in Eighteenth-century Cardiganshire', in Geraint H. Jenkins and Ieuan Gwynedd Jones (eds), *Cardiganshire County History: Volume 3* (Cardiff, 1998).

——, *Y Digymar Iolo Morganwg* (Talybont, 2018).

Jenkins, R. T., *Griffith Jones of Llanddowror* (Cardiff, 1930).

——, *Hanes Cymru yn y Ddeunawfed Ganrif* (Cardiff, 1931).

——, *Yng Nghysgod Trefeca* (Caernarvon, 1968).

Jones, Colin, *Cambridge Illustrated History: France* (Cambridge, 1994).

Jones, D. Ambrose, *Griffith Jones Llanddowror* (Wrexham, 1923).

Jones, D. J. Odwyn, *Daniel Rowland Llangeitho* (Llandysul, 1938).

Jones, David, *Life and Times of Griffith Jones, sometime rector of Llanddowror* (London, 1902).

Jones, David Ceri, *The Fire Divine* (Nottingham, 2015).

Jones, Emrys (ed.), *The Welsh in London 1500–2000* (Cardiff, 2001).

Jones, J. Morgan and William Morgan, *Y Tadau Methodistaidd*, 2 vols (Swansea, 1895).

Jones, M. G., *The Charity School Movement: A Study of Eighteenth Century Puritanism in Action* (Cambridge, 1938).

Jones, M. H., 'Bibliography of the Works of Griffith Jones', *The Carmarthen Antiquary*, xvi (1980).

Jones, Maldwyn A., *The Limits of Liberty, American History 1607–1992* (Oxford, 1995).

Kearney, Hugh, *Scholars and Gentlemen, Universities and Society in Pre-Industrial Britain 1500–1700* (London, 1970).

Kelly, Thomas, *Griffith Jones. Llanddowror, Pioneer in Adult Education* (Cardiff, 1950).

Kidder, Richard, *Life of the Reverend Anthony Horneck D.D. Late Preacher at the Savoy* (London, 1698).

Laborie, Lionel, *Enlightening Enthusiasm* (Manchester, 2015).

Langford, Paul, *A Polite and Commercial People: England 1727–1783* (Oxford, 1989).

Laslett, Peter, *The World We Have Lost further explored*, third edn (London, 1983).

Legg, J. Wickham, *English Church Life 1660–1833* (London, 1914).

Lloyd, Howell A., *The Gentry of South-West Wales 1540–1640* (Cardiff, 1968).

Lowther, Clarke W. K., *Eighteenth Century Piety* (London, 1944).

MacCulloch, Diarmaid, *Reformation, Europe's House Divided 1490–1700* (London, 2003).

Macfarlane, A., *The Origins of English Individualism* (Oxford, 1978).

McGrath, Alister E., 'The Emergence of the Anglican Tradition on Justification 1600–1700', *The Churchman*, 98/1 (1984).

Mack, Phyllis, *Heart Religion in the British Enlightenment* (Cambridge, 2008).

Mackenzie, Alexander and Elizabeth Sutherland, *The Prophecies of the Brahan Seer* (London, 1977).

MacLeod, John, *Scottish Theology* (Edinburgh, 1974).

Maitland, F. W., *The Constitutional History of England* (Cambridge, 1920).

Manning, Bernard Lord, *The Hymns of Wesley and Watts* (London, 1942).

Marcel, Pierre Ch., *The Biblical Doctrine of Infant Baptism, Sacrament of the Covenant of Grace* (London, 1953).

Marsden, George M., *Fundamentalism and American Culture* (Oxford, 2006).

Meyer, Carl S., *Cranmer's Selected Writings* (London, 1961).

Miles, David, *The Tribes of Britain* (London, 2005).

Miller, John, *The Glorious Revolution* (London, 1983).

Mitchell, R. J. and M. D. R. Leys, *A History of the English People* (London, 1967).

Mooney, Annabelle and Betsy Evans, *Language, Society and Power, an Introduction*, fourth edn (London, 2015).

Moorman, John R. H. (ed.), *The Cure of Souls* (London, 1958).

Morgan, D. Densil, *Theologia Cambrensis*, vol. 1 (Cardiff, 2018).

Morgan, Derec Llwyd, *Y Beibl a Llenyddiaeth Gymraeg* (Llandysul, 1998).

——, *Y Diwygiad Mawr* (Llandysul, 1999).

Morgan, Edward, *John Elias, Life and Letters* (Edinburgh, 1973).

Morgan-Richardson, C., *History of the Institution once called 'The Welsh Piety', but now known as Mrs. Bevan's Charity* (Cardigan, 1890).

Murray, Iain H., *The Reformation of the Church* (London, 1965).

——, *Revival and Revivalism, the Making and Marring of American Evangelicalism 1750–1858* (Edinburgh, 1994).

Murray, John, *Christian Baptism* (Nutley NJ, 1952).

Neill, Stephen, *Anglicanism* (Harmondsworth, 1960).

Nockles, Peter, *The Oxford Movement in Context, Anglican High Churchmanship, 1760–1957* (Cambridge, 1994).

Noll, Mark A., David W. Bebbington and George A. Rawlyk (eds), *Evangelicalism* (Oxford, 1994).

O'Day, Rosemary, *The Debate on the English Reformation* (London, 1986).

Owen, John, *Memoir of Daniel Rowlands* (London, 1848).

Owen, Thomas, *The Atonement Controversy in Welsh Theological Literature and Debate, 1707–1841*, trans. John Aaron (Edinburgh, 2002).

Parker, T. H. L., *John Calvin: a Biography* (London, 1975).

Patrick, Millar, *Four Centuries of Scottish Psalmody* (London, 1949).

Patterson, W. B., *King James VI and I and the Reunion of Christendom* (Cambridge, 1997).

Penn-Lewis, Jessie, *The Awakening in Wales and some of the Hidden Springs*, with introduction by J. Jones (Cynddylan) (London, 1905).

Perry, Marvin, *Western Civilization. Ideas, Politics and Society* (Boston, 2004).

Phillips, Bethan, *Peterwell, The History of a Mansion and its Infamous Squire* (Llandysul, 1983).

Picard, Liza, *Dr Johnson's London* (London, 2000).

Porter, Roy, *English Society in the Eighteenth Century* (London, 1981).

——, *Enlightenment, Britain and the Creation of the Modern World* (London, 2000).

Potter, Simeon, *Our Language* (Harmondsworth, 1950).

Powell, Ken and Chris Cook, *English Historical Facts 1485–1603* (London, 1977).

Powicke, F. M. and E. B. Fryde (eds), *Handbook of British Chronology* (London, 1961).

Richardson, Alan (ed.), *Dictionary of Christian Theology* (London, 1969).

Roberts, Gomer Morgan, *Bywyd a Gwaith Peter Williams* (Caerdydd, 1943).

—— (ed.), *Hanes Methodistiaeth Galfinaidd Cymru*, vol. 1 (Caernarfon, 1973).

Ryle, John Charles, *Christian Leaders of the Eighteenth Century* (London, 1885).

Schlenther, Boyd Stanley, *Queen of the Methodists: The Countess of Huntingdon and the Eighteenth-Century Crisis of Faith and Society* (Bishop Auckland, 1997).

Shankland, Thomas, 'Sir John Philipps; the Society for Promoting Christian Knowledge;and the Charity-School Movement in Wales 1699–1737', *Transactions of the Honourable Society of Cymmrodorion* (1906).

Shantz, Douglas H., *An Introduction to German Pietism* (Baltimore, 2013).

Sheppard, Francis, *London: A History* (London, 1998).

Smith, David L., *A History of the Modern British Isles 1608–1707* (Oxford, 1998).

Spurr, John, *The Restoration Church of England, 1646–1689* (New Haven, CT, 1991).

——, *The Post-Reformation. Religion, Politics and Society in Britain 1603–1714* (Harlow, 2006).

Steinmetz, D. C., *Reformers in the wings: from Geiler von Kaysersberg to Theodore Beza* (Oxford, 1971).

Stephens, Meic (ed.), *The Oxford Companion to the Literature of Wales* (Oxford, 1990).

Stone, Lawrence, *The Crisis of the Aristocracy 1554–1641*, abridged edn (Oxford, 1967).

Sydney, W. R., *England and the English in the Eighteenth Century*, 2 vols (London, 1892).

Sykes, Norman, *Edmund Gibson* (Oxford, 1926).

——, *Old Priest and New Presbyter* (Cambridge, 1957).

Tanner, J. R., English *Constitutional Conflicts of the Seventeenth Century 1603–1689* (Cambridge, 1960).

Thomas, Isaac, *Y Testament Newydd Cymraeg 1551–1620* (Cardiff, 1976).

Thomas, Peter D. G., 'Jacobitism in Wales', *Welsh History Review*, 1/3 (1962).

——, *Politics in Eighteenth-Century Wales* (Cardiff, 1998).

Thompson, Andrew C. (ed.), *The Oxford History of Protestant Dissenting Traditions*, vol. II (Oxford, 2018).

Thompson, H. P., *Thomas Bray* (London, 1954).

Toon, Peter, *The Emergence of Hyper-Calvinism in English Nonconformity 1689–1765* (Weston Rhyn, 2003).

Treasure, G. R. R., *Cardinal Richelieu and the Development of Absolutism* (London, 1971).

Trevelyan, G. M., *English Social History* (London, 1944).

Trevor-Roper, H. R., *Catholics, Anglicans and Puritans* (London, 1987).

Tudur, Geraint, *Howell Harris, from Conversion to Separation 1735–1750* (Cardiff, 2000).

Turberville, A. S., *English Men and Manners in the Eighteenth Century* (Oxford, 1926).

Tyerman, L., *The Oxford Methodists* (London, 1873).

Vaughan, Herbert M., *The South Wales Squires* (London, 1926).

Walker, David M., *The Oxford Companion to Law* (Oxford, 1980).

Waller, Maureen, *1700 Scenes from London Life* (London, 2000).

Ward, W. R., *The Protestant Evangelical Awakening* (Cambridge, 1992).

Watson, J. R., *The English Hymn* (Oxford, 1997).

Wesley, John, *Journals*, in ed. N. Curnock, 8 vols (London, 1938).

Wesley, Samuel, *The pious communicant rightly prepar'd, or, A discourse concerning the Blessed Sacrament* (London, 1700).

White, Eryn M., *The Welsh Bible* (Cardiff, 2007).

Willey, Basil, *The Eighteenth Century Background* (London, 1946).

Williams, A. H., *John Wesley in Wales 1739–1790* (Cardiff, 1971).

Williams, Basil, *The Whig Supremacy 1714–1760*, Oxford History of England (Oxford, 1960).

Williams, E. N., *The Ancien Régime in Europe* (London, 1970).

Williams, Glanmor, W. Jacob, N. Yates and F. Knight, *The Welsh Church from Reformation to Disestablishment 1603–1920* (Cardiff, 2007).

Williams, Gruffydd Aled, 'William Salesbury: Yr Ysgolhaig Prin', *Y Traethodydd*, CLXXIII/725 (2018).

Williams, W. Moses (ed.), *Selections from the Welch Piety* (Cardiff, 1938).

——, 'The Friends of Griffith Jones', *Y Cymmrodor*, XLVI (1939).

INDEX

Abergavenny 156
Abermarlais 13, 81
Aberystwyth 5, 26
Abjuration Oath, Act of (1701) 42
Absentee clergy, non-Residence 17, 19, 228
Absolution 93, 100, 193, 238
  see also Penitence
Act against cursing and swearing 41, 42
Act of New Churches in London and Westminster (1711) 45
Act of Settlement 28
Act for translation of the Book of Common Prayer and Bible into Welsh (1563) 197
'Acts of Union' (1536, 1542) 17, 197
Adiaphora, non-essential practices 143
Advowsons 43
Amyraldus, Moses (Moïse Amyraut), Amyraldianism 177–8
Anabaptists 46
Ancient Britons, the Most Honourable and Loyal Society of 27
Andrewes, Bp Lancelot 72, 137, 23
Anglicanism *see* Church of England
Anglicization 26, 29, 198
Anglo-Saxon language 212
Anne, Queen (1702–14) 18, 28, 198
Antinomianism 46, 155–7, 162, 165
Antiquarianism 27, 211
ap Gruffydd, John, Griffith Jones's father 10

Apostolic Succession 11, 18, 121, 136
Arianism 215
Arminianism 154, 158, 177
  see also Remonstrants
Articles, 39 of Religion 11, 15, 99, 152–6, 162, 178, 186, 190, 198, 208, 232, 234–5
  Article XVII 231–2
Assurance, reassurance of salvation 93–4, 97, 107, 111, 129, 134, 155, 161, 165, 232
Atheism 215
Atonement 106, 122, 161–2
Asceticism 48, 120, 123–4, 237
Awakening 16, 20, 49, 90, 104, 146, 181, 186

Babel, tower 208, 213
Bangor 17, 183, 204
Baptism 18, 65, 74, 96, 119, 183–8
  Baptismal vow, covenantal vow 183–8
Barlow, Thomas Bp 158–9
Basel 177
Bath 12, 26–7, 80, 203, 210
Bayly, Bp Lewis 179, 226
Bethell, Slingsby 203
Benefactors, English 12
Bevan, Arthur 200
Bevan, Bridget (*née* Vaughan) 6, 11, 15, 19, 64, 199–200
Beveridge, Bp William 180
Beverley 80

Beza, Theodore (Théodore de Bèze)
154, 188
Bible 5, 11, 15, 19, 22–3, 40, 44, 45–6,
53, 55, 72, 74, 77, 83, 91, 93, 98,
105–6, 128, 136–7, 143, 153, 159,
175–6, 178, 180, 181, 197–8,
201–2, 207–8, 214–5, 217, 226,
228, 232–3
Biblicism 128
Bibliomancy 47
New Testament, whole Bible, in
Welsh 19, 55–6, 71, 98, 128, 176,
178, 181, 198, 201
Bishops 5, 17–20, 22, 27, 43–7, 63–9,
70–5, 79–81, 96, 103–4, 106,
110–11, 121, 126, 151, 153,
155–9, 162, 175, 180, 208, 212,
228
Blockley 19, 22
Boehm, Anthony William 53–4, 69–70
Book of Common Prayer 43, 71, 79,
83, 92, 95–6, 123, 154, 176, 180,
197, 217
Liturgy 71, 98, 103, 111, 120–1, 163,
179
Theological consistency 99–100,
190, 22
Bossuet, Bp Jacques Bénigne 65
Boston, the Revd Thomas 230
Bowen, Arnold 99
Bowen family of Llwyngwair 43
Boyle lectures 45
Bray, the Revd Dr Thomas 54, 82,
175–6
Brief Exposition of Church-Catechism
180
Bristol 26
Britannia 212
Brownists and Barrowists 96
Bull, Bp George 5, 12–14, 17, 39, 43,
63–76, 78–83, 104, 110–11, 151,
153–2, 166, 180, 208

Defensio fidei Nicenae 65
Harmonia Apostolica 70, 153–4, 158
Burnet, Bp Gilbert 65, 103
Butler, William 203

Calvin, John (Jean) 136, 187
Institutes of the Christian Religion 187
Calvinism 99, 158, 162, 183, 188–90,
230, 232, 234–5
Calvinistic Methodism 166, 178, 230,
234–5, 237
Cambridge 12, 13, 20
Cambuslang 168
Camden, William 212, 214
Britannia 212
Cannwyll y Cymry (1699) 179
Carmarthen 12, 20, 23, 28, 40, 64, 81
Grammar School 12–14, 66
Carmarthenshire 10, 26, 49, 67, 159,
199, 200
Caroline Divines 94, 153
Caste system 53
Catechism 11, 14–15, 41, 80, 99, 108–
9, 175–80, 182–3, 185–190, 208
Catechetical method in preaching
108
Catechizing 3, 19, 41, 63, 97, 99,
107, 109, 176, 178–82, 188, 201
Published *Expositions* of the church
Catechism 177, 179–80, 186–7
*The Church Catechism Explain'd by
Way of Question and Answer* 185
Catholicity 11
Celtic Christianity 20
Celtic languages 206
Chamberlayne, John 54
Charity-Schools 5–6, 15, 24, 26, 30,
40–1, 80, 82, 95, 175, 179, 183,
199–205, 210, 214
*The Christian Covenant, or the
Baptismal Vow, as stated in our Church
Catechism* 183, 185–6

254

Index

Christianity 2, 6, 20, 49, 55, 92, 168, 182, 186, 230–1

Christocentrism 106

Christomonism 135

Church, established, of England 11, 17, 25, 28, 67, 99, 111, 198, 205, 226, 235, 237

Gathered churches 95–6, 236–7

'Visible' Church 82, 95, 97, 111, 236

Church of England 1, 3–5, 9–11, 14–22, 24–5, 29, 39, 42–4, 47, 53–4, 67, 70, 72, 90, 120

Anglicanism 4, 11, 15, 16, 20, 23, 25, 50, 67, 72, 84, 90, 96, 98, 102–3, 106, 109, 111, 120, 124, 136, 152–9, 166, 169, 181–2, 184, 190, 197, 202, 204, 224, 226, 229–30, 236

Cilrhedyn, Pembrokeshire 10

Circle of the White Rose 29, 211

Circulating Schools *see* Education

Clagett, the Revd Nicholas (1654–1727) of Little Thurlow 46

Clagett, Bp Nicholas of St Davids 106

Classical Learning 12, 18, 66, 204, 211–14

Clergy Ministry 11, 14, 15, 16, 17–23, 43–4, 49–50, 63, 65, 67, 69–73, 78–9, 82, 99–101, 104, 109, 111–12, 121, 123, 126–7, 144, 156, 158, 159, 162, 163, 165, 167, 169, 180, 186, 189, 204, 205, 225, 236

Curates 5, 12–15, 18, 24, 40–1, 49, 76, 80, 98, 108, 123, 180, 200, 203, 227–8

Cockburn, the Revd Patrick 54

Collects 100, 104, 106, 111

Commonwealth 71, 153, 190

Communion service (Lord's Supper), Holy Communion 49, 74, 90, 97, 99, 123, 153, 182, 226

'Sacrament Sundays' 74–5, 99, 123, 182, 226

Confession 93, 100

Confirmation 18, 70, 109, 188–9, 121, 132

Conformist attitude 22, 103, 158, 198, 204, 226

Congregations at services 69, 75, 93, 95, 165, 227, 236

Consensus Helveticus 177

Continental tour 29

Controversies 23, 30, 98, 102, 143, 151, 151, 159, 183, 230–2

Conversionism 95, 106, 113, 155, 166, 229, 234

see also Revivalism

Coram, Capt. Thomas 199

Cornwall, Cornish language 17, 212

Covenant, Covenantalism, Federal theology 101, 109–10, 112, 137, 153–5, 166, 177, 183–8, 232, 234

see also Divinity, Theology

Creeds 11, 65, 90, 103, 177

Curacies 5, 12–15, 18, 24, 40–1, 43, 49, 76, 80, 98, 108, 123, 180, 200, 203, 227–8

Cymmrodorion, the Honourable Society of 27

Dalton, John of Clog-y-Frân, St Clears 73

Dancing 237

Danish mission to India 50, 53, 206

Darcy, Catherine 23

Davies, the Revd Howel 227

Davies, the Revd Pryce 226

Decline of piety alleged 64, 92, 98, 178, 24, 201

Defensio fidei Nicenae see Bull, George

Defynnog 227

Deism 15, 102, 215, 228

Denbighshire 180, 204

Devotio Moderna 18
Dissent *see* Nonconformity
Divinity *see* Theology
Dordt, Synod of 158
Duppa, Bp Bryan 226
Duty of faith and religion 11, 25, 72, 78, 97, 122, 134, 208, 211

Ecclesia Anglicana 119
Ecclesiolae in Ecclesia 128
Edict of Nantes 47
Education
    Charity-Schools 5, 15, 24, 26, 41, 80, 82, 95, 175, 179, 183, 199–200, 202, 204, 214
    Circulating Schools 3, 6, 9–10, 12, 18, 21–3, 30, 50, 54, 82, 181–3, 199–202, 217, 227, 229, 237
    Grammar-Schools 12, 14, 82, 227
    Liberal, of a gentleman 198, 213–14
Edwards, the Revd Andrew 204
Edwards, the Revd Jonathan 164
Elias, John 79, 234–5
Elite *see* Gentry
Elizabeth I, Queen 17, 23
Ellis, the Revd Thomas 204
Enlightenment, Rationalism 15, 95, 189, 216
Enthusiasm, Fanaticism 43, 48, 72, 78, 97, 105–7, 144, 204, 225, 229, 237
Epidemics 10, 102, 131–2
    see also Famines
Episcopacy 11
    see also Bishops
Erskine, the Revd Ebenezer 231
European Protestants, Continental *see* Protestants
'Evangelical Law' 155, 160–1
Evangelicalism 166, 235
Evangelism 4, 6, 26, 45–6, 53–6, 72, 78, 97–8, 103, 106–8, 111, 121, 123, 128–9, 137, 139, 143–4, 146,

159, 161, 164, 169, 206–7, 230–1, 233, 235–6
Evans, the Revd John, Eglwys Gymyn 12, 70, 75, 77, 127, 163, 189, 228–9
Evans, the Revd Theophilus 12, 228
Exhorters 106

Faith *see* Piety
Famines, Malnutrition 102
Family worship *see* Piety
Fell, Bp John 65
Ferrar, Robert 20
Fetter Lane Society 120
Finch, Cicely 23
Flintshire 180
Forgiveness, Pardon 5, 89, 94, 97, 100–1, 107, 128, 132–3, 152, 155–6, 160, 162, 165, 226–7
Form of Prayers of English Congregation in Geneva 96
Fort St George 177
Foundling Hospital *see* Coram
France 47, 177, 210, 212
Francke, August Hermann 54
French Church, Huguenots 47
French 'Prophets' 48
Fundamentalism 163, 168

Gaelic languages 206
Gataker, the Revd Charles 158
Gathered churches, Voluntarism 95–6, 236–7
    see also Individualism, Independency
Geneva 96, 154, 177
Gentry, Welsh and Elite local magnates, landowners 6, 9, 12, 15, 19, 22–3, 25–6, 29–30, 39–40, 42–3, 45, 63–4, 76, 79, 80, 82–3, 107, 198, 203–4, 206, 210, 216–17
    Anglicized in language, education and

Index

culture 12, 198
  English marriages 216
George, King I 28, 42
George, King II 20, 28
George, King III 17
German Protestants 47, 53–5
  Lutheran Chapel at St James's Palace 54
Gibson, Bp Edmund 82, 90–1, 109, 165, 212–13
  Family-devotion: or, An exhortation to morning and evening prayer in families 82
Godliness 14, 92, 97, 122, 139, 145, 237
Gonville and Caius College, Cambridge 12
Gosling, Sir Francis 203
Gospel *see* Preaching
Gouge, the Revd Thomas 203
Greek language 13, 213
Griffiths, the Revd David 43
Griffiths, Mrs Sidney 78
Grimshaw, the Revd William 121
Gwynne, Marmaduke 45

Hales, the Revd Dr Stephen 203
Halle 47–8, 53–5, 105, 175
Hammond, the Revd Henry 65
Hanoverian rule 22–3, 27–9, 94, 202
Harmonia Apostolica see Bull, George
Harries, the Revd James 179
Harris, Howel 6, 11, 19, 45, 47, 78, 107, 226–8
Hastings, Lady Margaret 26
Hastings, Selina, countess of Huntingdon 26
Hastings, Theophilus, earl of Huntingdon 26
Haworth 123
Heart religion 68–70, 78, 97, 106–7, 110, 122, 124
  see also Piety

Heaven, doctrine of 109, 120–3, 126, 134, 139, 160, 185, 207
Hebrew language 13, 213
Hell, doctrine of 121, 131
Henry, King VIII 17
Herbert, the Revd George 74, 136, 176
Hereford Grammar School 227
Herefordshire 17, 123, 227
Hervey, the Revd James 142, 151, 155, 166, 203
Herrnhut *see* Moravians
High Church 1–5, 9–11, 16–18, 29, 42–4, 47, 49, 66–7, 70–1, 76, 94–5, 98, 102, 106, 112, 119, 121, 124–6, 152–4, 161, 169, 176, 186, 188, 198, 225, 229
'High Fliers' 99
Hoare, Benjamin 54
Hoggeston 158
Holy Club 15, 49
Holy Rules and Helps to Devotion 226
Book of Homilies 29, 72–3, 106, 121, 154
Hooker, the Revd Richard 65, 95, 119
Hope, with Faith 97, 101, 106, 112, 138, 160, 162, 187, 191, 207, 233
Humphreys, Bp Humphrey 17
Huntingdon, Selina Countess of 26
Hutton, Archbp Matthew 121
Hymns 128, 228

Illiteracy 201, 217
Impropriations 42–3, 52
Independency *see* Gathered Churches
India 15, 19, 22, 46, 48–56, 69, 112, 177, 206
  Caste system 53
Individualism 3, 95, 235
Ingham, the Revd Benjamin 26, 105
Iolo Morganwg *see* Williams, Edward
Ireland 179, 202, 206

257

Jacobitism 28–9, 210–11
James, King I and VI 153
Jesus College *see* Oxford
Johnson, Samuel 161, 210
Jones, Griffith 1–6, 9–15, 19–30, 39,
    41–56, 63–4, 66–80, 82–3,
    89–113, 119–46, 151–69,
    176–91, 197–217, 225–37
    As a conforming Anglican 22, 29, 49,
        103, 119, 121, 166, 198, 204,
        225–6
    Madras mission 19, 22, 46, 48–9,
        50–2, 53–6, 112, 177, 206
    Notebook 1, 5, 89, 91, 98, 107, 109
    Preaching 89–121, 123, 130, 137
    As Schoolmaster 12–13, 15, 24, 50,
        53, 67, 80, 98–9, 200, 214
    As Theologian 2, 10, 98, 231–4
    Welsh, his use of, advocacy for 11, 73,
        121, 137, 182, 212–15
Jones, Elinor *née* John, Griffith's mother
    10
Jones, the Revd Dr John, dean of Bangor
    183
Jones, the Revd John, rector of
    Llanddowror 42
Jones, Robert 22
Justification through Faith 3, 119,
    151–7, 159–62, 164–6, 190
    see also Neonomianism

Ken, Bp Thomas 177
Kerrick, the Revd John, vicar of
    Llangernyw, Denbyshire 204

Lacy, John 48
Latin language 13, 153, 206, 213
Latitudinarianism 10
Laudian churchmanship 20, 158
Laugharne 13–15, 24, 49, 51–2, 55, 64,
    67, 69, 75, 80
Laugharne, the Revd Arthur 80

Laugharne, John 40
Law, English 29, 42, 104, 237
Lee, Ann 48
Lewis, George 50, 54
Lewis, the Revd George, chap. in
    Madras 82
Lewis, the Revd John 177
    Exposition of the Church Catechism
        179, 185
Lhuyd, Edward
Libraries, Home libraries 80–3, 175
Literacy, Literature 2–4, 16, 19, 30,
    50, 53–6, 83–4, 113, 159, 176,
    178, 215–7, 231
Literate clergy 66
Liturgy *see* Book of Common Prayer
Llandawk 40, 41
Llanddowror 2, 15, 25, 26, 39–42, 45,
    55, 56, 73, 75, 82, 123, 124, 181
Llandeilo Abercywyn 15, 49, 52, 67, 69,
    98, 124
Llangadock 79
Llanllwch 109
Lloyd, David 15
Lloyd, Herbert 45
Lloyd, Bp William 17
Llwyn Llwyd School 226, 228
Llys-y-frân, Pembrokeshire 227
London 12, 24, 26, 27, 44, 45, 48,
    52–4, 80, 199, 203, 210–12, 216
    Lutheran Chapel 54
Lowth, Bp Robert 204
Loyalty *see* Hanoverian regime
Lupton, the Revd Dr William 44
Luther, Martin 161
Lutherans 47, 54, 134, 206

Maddocks, John 12, 14, 66, 73
Madras *see* India
Malabar *see* India
Manners, Societies for Reformation of
    79, 92, 152

Index

Marrow of Modern Divinity 230
Martyrdom, Protestant 20
Maryland 175
Masses, 'unchurched' 56, 236
Mazel, Abraham 48
'Means of Grace' 72, 98, 101, 104, 139, 164, 175, 187, 235
Membership of Church 17, 25, 28, 47, 95–7, 111, 189
Methodism 2, 12, 15, 18, 22–4, 102, 107, 113, 120, 135, 156, 178–9, 183, 186, 217, 226, 228, 234, 237
Middle-class Evangelicals 79
Millennialism 16, 39, 45–8, 56, 106
  Restoration of the Jews 45
    see also 'Prophecies' in Scripture
Ministers *see* Clergy
Ministry *see* Clergy
Miracles 16, 135
  of Apostles 142–3
Missions, Missionaries 5, 15, 19, 39–41, 45, 47–56, 206
Montagu, Lady Mary Wortley 26
Montgomeryshire 180
Moralism, Anti-solifidianism, 'Works–Righteousness' 10, 92, 124, 129, 151, 155, 158
    see also Justification
Moravians 26, 47, 55, 105, 120, 237
Morley, Bp George 153
Morris, the Revd D. 204
Morris, the Revd Humphrey 204
Muggletonians 46
Munro, George, *Just Methods of the Pious Institution of Youth* 41
Music 90, 120
Mysticism 77, 105

Nationalism, National feeling 17, 29–30, 47, 210–11, 216
Nelson, Robert 71–2, 74, 78, 80, 180

Neonomianism 158
Netherlands 177
'New Birth', Regeneration 112, 130, 145, 151, 155, 163–8, 189
Newman, Henry 210
Newton, the Revd John 190
Nicene *see* Creeds
Noble, Mark 64
Nonconformity 2, 15, 47, 90, 94, 97–8, 102, 158, 166, 177, 180, 190, 217, 237
Non-residence 17, 19, 228
Norse 212
Notebook, Memorandum *see* Sir John Philipps
Nowell, the Revd Alexander 208

Old Testament *see* Bible
Ordination 5, 13, 66, 70, 73, 76, 130, 227–8, 236
Ostervald, Jean-Frédéric 48, 177–8
  his Catechism 178
Ottley, Bp Adam 27, 46, 176
Owen, the Revd John 137
Oxford 13, 15, 20, 26, 49, 65, 80, 151, 158–9
  Jesus College 12
  St Edmund Hall 151
  University 15, 49, 66

'Palatines' *see* European Protestants
Pant-yr-Efel 10
Papacy *see* Roman Catholicism
Parliament, MPs 24–5, 42, 152, 197–8
Patronage, Patrons 6, 11, 17, 19, 22, 24–6, 30, 39–43, 49, 64, 67, 79–80, 157, 199–200, 213, 217
Peasantry *see* Welsh people
Pelagianism 157
Pembrokeshire 10, 13, 23–4, 26–7, 40, 42, 48, 99, 227
Penboyr 13

Penbryn, Cardiganshire 13–14
Pendine 40–1
Penitence *see* Repentance
Penrhydd, Pembrokeshire 13–14
Pepys, Samuel 90
Philanthropy 24, 28, 39, 48, 53
Philipps, Elizabeth Shorter 23
Philipps, Sir Erasmus 23
Philipps, John, of Carmarthen 23, 40
Philipps, Sir John 6, 9, 11, 15, 19,
    23–30, 45–52, 54, 56, 64, 75,
    80–1, 83, 92, 94, 97, 105, 108,
    124, 152, 157, 179, 183, 185–6,
    198–9, 202–3, 208, 216
  Notebooks 25, 39, 43–6, 48
Philipps, Sir John, 6th Baronet Philipps
  28
Philipps, Margaret 26
Philipps, the Revd Thomas 13
Picton Castle 23, 43–4, 48, 51
Pietas Hallensis 54
Pietism 3, 43, 48, 53–5, 105, 23
Piety, Anglican
  Religious societies 4, 21, 24–5, 26,
    39–40, 44, 47 54, 66–8, 74, 79,
    80, 91, 97–8, 101, 105–6, 111,
    120, 123, 125, 135, 141, 143,
    152, 158, 163, 180, 184, 186,
    201–2, 204, 226, 228
    see also Heart Religion
The Pilgrims's Progress
The Platform of Christianity
Pluralism 17, 19
Popery *see* Roman Catholicism
Portuguese language 48, 53
Poverty 10, 15, 17, 19–21, 41, 64–5,
    70, 80, 82, 102, 131, 142, 179–80,
    202, 210, 217
  Poor clergy 17, 19–20
Powell, the Revd Robert 54
The Practice of Piety 179
  i.e. *Yr Ymarfer o Dduwioldeb* 179

Prayer, special purpose 49, 66, 178
Prayer Book, Book of Common Prayer
  3, 5, 11, 15–17, 21, 25, 29, 40–1,
  43, 52, 71, 83, 89–90, 92–3,
  95–103, 105–6, 111, 119–20,
  123, 151, 154, 161, 163, 176–7,
  179–80, 186–88, 197–8, 208,
  217, 226 , 235
  Welsh Prayer Book 71, 83, 93, 197–
    8, 226, 235
Preaching 2–5, 11, 13–14, 16, 19,
  21–3, 24–5, 44–5, 49, 55–6,
  67–8, 72–5, 76, 78–9, 89–92,
  94–5, 99–100, 102–6, 108–12,
  119, 121–25, 128–30, 133, 136–7,
  144–5, 152, 156–7, 161–5, 167,
  181–2, 184, 186, 189–90, 198,
  200, 206–7, 216–17, 226–33,
  235
  'Experimental' 190
  Gospel 24, 44, 70, 94, 101, 105–6,
    109, 125, 129, 133, 139–42,
    144,152, 156, 160, 162, 165–6,
    203, 205, 231–3
  Impromptu 163
  Lectures 45, 90, 163, 180
  in the Open Air 75, 156, 165
  Popularity 2, 72–3, 90, 99, 121, 129,
    163–4
  Pre-industrial Society 77, 131
    see also Jones, Griffith
  in Welsh 137, 217
Pretenders *see* Jacobitism
Prichard, the Revd Rhys (Rees) 119,
  179
A Priest to the Temple, or the Country
  Parson see Herbert, George
Priesthood *see* Clergy
Presbyterianism 158
Printing 53, 83, 102, 179
Proclamation against vice and
  profaneness 41

Index

'Prophecy' in Scripture, 'accomplished' 16, 39, 45–48
   see also Millennialism
A proposal for the Conversion of the Popish Natives of Ireland to the Protestant Religion... 179
Protestantism 20, 29, 39, 95, 113, 206
   Protestant Theory of Worship 11, 16, 44, 78–9, 83, 90–1, 95–8, 102, 111, 119, 124, 143, 152, 197–8, 215, 235, 237
Providence, doctrine of 50–2, 68–70, 77, 125, 188, 207–10, 211–12, 215, 228–9
Prys, the Revd Edmund 198
Puritanism 2, 4, 9, 24, 75, 79, 94, 98, 121, 129, 135, 137, 152–3, 156, 158, 169, 189, 191
   anti-puritan polemics 156

Rank, Social Station 13, 23, 25–6, 30, 39, 48, 79, 209–10
Ranters 156
Rationalism 15
Reform, desire for in the Church of England 5, 11, 24, 40, 68, 79, 82, 92, 95, 98, 152, 167, 176
Reformation 11, 20–1, 71, 79, 95–6, 100, 152, 161, 163, 206, 231
   in Wales 20, 22, 79, 209
Reformed churches, theology 11, 20, 47, 96, 98, 130, 153–5, 157–8, 161–2, 164, 166, 177, 186–9, 230–2, 235
Regeneration 119, 151, 165–8
   Conversion assumed to be 130, 145, 163–4
Religious Societies 4, 16, 24, 92, 95, 98, 104, 109, 124–5, 128, 179–80, 188, 207, 226–7, 230, 236–7
   Ecclesiolae in ecclesia 128
Religiosity 19, 21, 97

   see also Pietism, Enthusiasm
Remonstrants *see* Dutch Arminians
Repentance 5, 16, 46, 73, 92–4, 100, 110–11, 124–5, 132, 140, 156, 160, 164, 185–7, 229, 233
Reprobation 231–3
Resurrection 134
Revival 2, 16, 23, 78–9, 94–5, 106
   Spiritual Renewal 16, 24, 75, 98, 100, 104, 106, 132, 152, 164, 167–8, 176, 189, 229
Revivalism 16, 129, 163, 166–9, 201, 235
Richardson, the Revd John (1668–1747) 179
Roman Catholicism 20, 21, 22, 28–9, 39, 47, 179, 206, 215
Rowland, the Revd Daniel 6, 11, 15, 19, 123, 227–8, 235
Royal Society 45
Ryle, Bp John Charles 168

Sabellianism 228
Sacraments 10–11, 18, 74–5, 99, 121, 182, 187–8, 226, 236
Sacramentalism, view of 'Apostolic' tradition 188
St Davids diocese 13, 17, 20, 42, 44, 63–4, 81
   commissioners 63
Salters' Hall conference 190
Salzburgers relief 181
Saunders, the Revd Erasmus 19– 23, 42, 68, 209
Schools 12, 234,
   Charity Schools 11, 14–5, 24, 26, 30, 40–1, 50, 79–80, 82, 95, 109, 119, 175, 179–80, 200, 210
   Circulating Schools 3, 6, 9–10,11–12, 18, 21–23, 30, 50, 54, 56, 66, 82, 169, 181–3, 199–204, 210–11, 214, 227, 229, 236–7

'College' 3, 201
Grammar Schools 12–14, 82, 198, 226–7
In Halle 54, 175
In India 53, 177
'Seminary' training 3, 41, 53, 82, 227
Sunday-Schools 217
Welsh-speaking pupils in English-language schools 198
Schoolmasters and Schoolmistresses 3, 24, 82, 180, 182, 199, 201, 217, 236
Scotland, Church of Scotland 79, 121, 168, 230–1
Sea-Serjeants 27–8
Self-Examination 94, 97, 135
    see also Piety and Repentance
Semi-Pelagianism see Arminianism
Sermons see Preaching
Sheldon, Archbp Gilbert 158
Shorter, Catherine, Walpole 23
Shorter, John 23
Shropshire 17
Sickness see Epidemics
Siddington, Gloucestershire 65, 75, 80
Sin, theology of see Jones, Griffith
Sketch of the Life and Character of the Reverend and Pious Mr Griffith Jones 12–13, 69, 159
Smalbroke, Richard Bp of St Davids 44
Social Station see Rank
Societies and Clubs 27, 45, 49, 120
Socinianism 65, 158
Solifidianism see Justification through Faith
Soteriology 22, 154, 157–8, 161
Sovereignty of God 77, 155, 188, 190, 208, 229
Spanish language 48
Sparrow, the Revd James 203
SPCK (Society for Promoting Christian Knowledge) 6, 13, 47–52, 54, 64,

80–1, 83, 99, 175–6, 178–9, 183, 186
SPG (Society for the Propagation of the Gospel in Foreign Parts) 203
Spiritual seeking and concern 16, 70, 89, 105, 112
Stebbing, Henry 102
Stonhouse, the Revd James (or Stonehouse) Bart 203
Stuart, Charles Edward see Jacobitism
Succession see Apostolic
Swift, Jonathan 13
Swiss Triumvirate 177
Switzerland 177

Tabernacle, Whitefield's, Tottenham Court Road 165
Tamil language 53
Taylor, Bp Jeremy 65, 153
Teachers see Schoolmasters, Schoolmistresses
Tenby 26
Theology, Divinity 1–3, 5, 14, 46, 65, 81, 99, 102, 109, 129–30, 132, 141, 152–3, 155, 158–9, 163, 166, 177, 180, 182, 188–9, 215, 230–3, 235
Theron and Aspasio 155
Thomas, the Revd George 40–1
Thomas, Timothy 166
Thorold, Sir John, Bart 203
Tillotson, Archbp John 63, 75, 97, 103
Tractarianism 11
Tranquebar see India
Truth Defended, and Boldness in Error Rebuk'd see Clagett, the Revd Nicholas
Trysor o Ddifinyddiaeth ('A Treasure of Divinity') 1, 5, 14, 73, 89, 109
Tully, the Revd Thomas 158
Turretini, Jean Alphonse 177, 188

Index

Universities 12–13, 15, 49, 66

Vaughan, John, of Derllys 23, 40, 64, 80–1, 200
Vaughan, Rowland 179
View of the State of Religion 19–20
Visible Church *see* Church
Visitations 18–19, 40, 42, 52, 70, 90, 104, 182, 217
Voluntarism *see* Gathered Churches

Wales, Principality 1, 10, 12, 16–17, 19–20, 22–9, 46, 49, 51–3, 55–6, 63–4, 69, 73, 75, 79–80, 82–4, 92, 98–9, 119, 125, 158, 163, 168–9, 176, 178–80, 183, 189, 197–8, 200–7, 209–14, 216–17, 227–8, 230, 237
Walpole, Sir Robert 23, 28
Watson, the Revd Thomas 137
Watson, Bp Thomas 63–5
Welsh, 'British language' 2, 4, 9–10, 17–18, 22–3, 29–31, 55–6, 83, 91, 121, 179–83, 197–9, 201–2, 204–17
   Non Welsh-speaking clergy 56, 20
   Welsh-speaking population 83, 198, 198, 217
   Welsh-speaking bishops, clergy 17, 22, 198
   Welsh-speaking gentry 29–30
   Welsh-language schools 56, 183, 198, 205
      see also Bible, Book of Common Prayer, Books
Welsh literature 2, 83
The Welch Piety 30, 54, 83, 184, 203–4
The Welsh Trust 16, 203
Werenfels, Samuel 177

Wesley, the Revd Charles 45
Wesley, the Revd John 15, 21, 47, 105, 124, 127, 151, 155, 225, 230
Wesley, the Revd Samuel 50, 152, 176
Wesley, Susanna 50
Wesleyans 166, 230
Westminster 29, 45, 70, 203
Westminster Confession of Faith 231
Whigs 18, 23, 29
Whiston, the Revd William 39, 45–6, 48
Whitefield, the Revd George 49, 78, 123, 137, 163, 226, 228
Whole Duty of Man 74
Willes, Bp Edward 17, 228
Williams, Edward (Iolo Morganwg) 216
Williams, Archbp John 17
Williams, Bp John 180
Williams, the Revd Moses 12
Williams, the Revd Peter 6, 228
Williams, the Revd Robert 204
Williams, William (Pantycelyn) 6, 11, 101, 128, 228, 234–5
Williams-Wynn, Sir Watkin 27, 29
Y Wisg Wen Ddisglair (1759) 166
Women 6, 200
Woodward, the Revd Josiah 98, 125
Worship *see* Book of Common Prayer, Hymns, Liturgy
Wrexham 99
Wynn, Edward
Wynne, the Revd W. 204
Wynnstay 29

Yr Ymarfer o Dduwioldeb 179
York 80, 121

Ziegenbalg, Batholomaüs 53

263